Small Arms
for Urban Combat

Small Arms for Urban Combat

*A Review of Modern Handguns,
Submachine Guns, Personal Defense Weapons,
Carbines, Assault Rifles, Sniper Rifles,
Anti-Materiel Rifles, Machine Guns,
Combat Shotguns, Grenade Launchers
and Other Weapons Systems*

Russell C. Tilstra

McFarland & Company, Inc., Publishers
Jefferson, North Carolina, and London

LIBRARY OF CONGRESS CATALOGUING-IN-PUBLICATION DATA

Tilstra, Russell C., 1968–
Small arms for urban combat : a review of modern handguns, submachine guns, personal defense weapons, carbines, assault rifles, sniper rifles, anti-materiel rifles, machine guns, combat shotguns, grenade launchers and other weapons systems / Russell C. Tilstra.
p. cm.
Includes bibliographical references and index.

ISBN 978-0-7864-6523-1
softcover : acid free paper ∞

1. Firearms. 2. Urban warfare — Equipment and supplies. I. Title.
UD380.T55 2012   623.4'4 — dc23   2011046889

BRITISH LIBRARY CATALOGUING DATA ARE AVAILABLE

© 2012 Russell C. Tilstra. All rights reserved

No part of this book may be reproduced or transmitted in any form or by any means, electronic or mechanical, including photocopying or recording, or by any information storage and retrieval system, without permission in writing from the publisher.

Front cover design by David K. Landis (Shake It Loose Graphics)

Manufactured in the United States of America

*McFarland & Company, Inc., Publishers
Box 611, Jefferson, North Carolina 28640
www.mcfarlandpub.com*

To my wife and children
for their love and support.
Thanks for putting up with me.

Table of Contents

Acronyms and Abbreviations viii
Preface 1
Introduction 3

1. Handguns 9
2. Submachine Guns 33
3. Personal Defense Weapons 50
4. Carbines/Rifle Caliber Submachine Guns 54
5. Assault Rifles 69
6. Sniper Rifles/Precision Tactical Rifles 101
7. Anti-Materiel Rifles 116
8. Machine Guns 122
9. Combat Shotguns 142
10. Grenade Launchers 154
11. Miscellaneous Weapon Systems 169

Notes 185
Bibliography 191
Index 193

Acronyms and Abbreviations

ACP — Automatic Caliber Pistol
ATGM — Anti-tank Guided Missile
AUG — Armee Universal Gewehr (rifle)
BAR — Browning Automatic Rifle
BDA — Browning double-action
BMG — Browning machine gun
CQB — close quarter battle
CQBR — close quarter battle receiver
CT — counter-terrorist
DA — double action
DAO — double action only
FAL — Fusil Automatique Léger (Light Automatic Rifle)
FN — Fabrique Nationale
FNC Fusil Nouveau type Carabine
fps — feet per second
GPMG — general purpose machine gun
HK — Heckler & Koch
IED — improvised explosive device
KAC — Knight's Armament Company
LAW — Light Anti-tank Weapon
LB — long barrel
LMG — light machine gun
LTL — less than lethal
MAG — Mitrailleuse d'Appui Generale

MANPADS — Man Portable Air Defense System
MOUT — Military Operations on Urban Terrain
PDW — personal defense weapon
PSP — Polizei Selbstlade Pistole
QCB — quick change barrel
RHA — rolled homogenous armor
rpm — rounds per minute
SA — single action
S&W — Smith and Wesson
SAR — shortened assault rifle
SAS — Special Air Service
SAW — squad automatic weapon
SMAW — Shoulder Launched Multipurpose Assault Weapon
SMG — submachine gun
SOCOM — Special Operations Command
SPW — special purpose weapon
SWAT — Special Weapons and Tactics (unit or team)
UAV — unmanned aerial vehicle
UMP — Universal Machine Pistol
UO — Urban Operations
U.S.M.C. — U.S. Marine Corps
USP — Universal Self-loading Pistol (series)
WMR — Winchester Magnum Rimfire

Preface

This work, serving a basic reference function, is meant to provide both professional soldiers and students of small arms study with a working knowledge of the most common and successful urban combat weapons in use today, as well as some in development that have potential as service weapons. There are far more complete reference books already in existence—*Jane's Infantry Weapons* is the first such work that comes to mind. I have used several excellent sources in the course of this work.

This book is intended, however, to be more than just a summary of the small arms systems in common use. It is also meant to provide the reader with a clear picture of how warfare has changed and why these changes have taken the small arms industry in the direction it has recently gone. My decision to write this book resulted from a desire to share my knowledge of small arms systems both in terms of design and purpose. I have spent years in this area of study and noticed that very little work had been done with respect to correlating the conditions of modern combat with the choice of weapons used for various tasks. While dimensional data are given for almost every model mentioned, these are only close estimates based on information from the manufacturers and from other reference works. I have tried to provide some insight into the designs with regard to application. Some are first rate performers, while others are mediocre designs that still see use due to reasons other than quality of design or manufacture. While personal opinion may creep in from time to time, I have attempted to maintain objectivity. Any generalized claims have been supported with documentation, and sources are listed in the chapter notes and bibliography.

One linguistic note: While anti-material and anti-materiel carry the same meaning, I have adopted the second spelling, as more commonly used.

More than anything, I would like to see this work closely studied by those currently serving in uniform, as they stand the most to gain from this information and they are most at risk, given the brutal combat environments in which they are forced to operate.

With the exception of photographs on pages 19, 20 and 22, military photographs are provided courtesy of defenseimagery.mil. Use of military imagery does not imply or constitute Department of Defense endorsement.

Introduction

The purpose of this book is to examine, in detail, the most successful small arms in use today, and how changes in modern warfare have affected how those weapons are employed. It will also examine how technology has drastically affected the small arms industry. While many of these weapon systems were designed for military applications, some are seeing increased use among the law enforcement community as well.

The book will cover these weapons by category: handguns, submachine guns, assault rifles, and others. Some of these categories are relatively new, and some of the weapons covered here are not often seen on the battlefield but are proving quite useful and, in some cases, indispensable.

Some Things Never Change

The various types of small arms popular today have not changed much. Those in the law enforcement community are still primarily using what they have been using for years, chiefly handguns and shotguns, although some departments have begun keeping carbines or rifles as extra firepower when needed. This was mostly a result of the North Hollywood shootout.[1] Many rural police departments have been using carbines for years. The long range weaponry is generally reserved for Special Weapons and Tactics (SWAT) units. In Europe, it is common to see officers carrying around submachine guns. Here such a practice may not be politically acceptable. This may explain why we are still seeing a largely limited selection of weapons within the law enforcement community.

City Streets Become the New Battleground

In the military, things are a bit different. There are several new categories of small arms in service. Some categories, like submachine guns, have become less popular, while others are seeing a significant increase in use. Handguns are a prime example of a resurgent weapon class. Several new categories are seeing service as well. Anti-material rifles, which

Armor and infantry are best kept in close proximity for urban operations. Weapon in foreground is a U.S. M4 carbine mounted with an ACOG scope, AN/PEQ-2 infrared aiming unit, and Knight's Armament RIS rail. This is probably the new U.S. Army standard shoulder arm (Spc. J. Crosby, U.S. Army).

The typical urban combat environment can provide a great deal of cover, but this also applies to the enemy (Spc. G.A. Alisan, U.S. Army).

Introduction

A wide street such as this can be a deadly route for troops or vehicles (Cpl. M.S. Richards, U.S. Marine Corps).

first saw use in the 1980s with the Barrett model 82,[2] have made a place for themselves in the modern military. Other classes have increased so much in capability that they have completely changed the category parameters. New sniper calibers like the .338 Lapua and the .416 Barrett have more than doubled, in some cases tripled, the range of sniper weapons from 20 years ago. Other categories have come along to turn small patrol units into a company in terms of firepower. Multi-shot grenade launchers, with ranges of up to 900 yards, are now in service, 1800 yards in the case of the new Chinese launchers. Patrol mortars weighing less than 15 pounds offer 2000 yard range, and soon, precision round placement, once guided mortar rounds become commonplace, which is a reasonable likelihood. The changes in warfare are being quickly met with new weapon systems that possess scary levels of efficiency.

Warfare has changed much throughout the years. The variables behind these changes are too numerous to be covered here, and that is not the purpose of this book. What is relevant to this study is the type of warfare that troops face today. The world is becoming more urbanized. This change has had a profound effect on warfare. For the first time in human history, the majority of the world's population lives in urban settings.[3] What this means is an increased likelihood that any outbreak of conflict will occur in an urban environment. Also, the urban areas now hold even more strategic value than they have in the past. This is true in terms of both population control and infrastructure value. This being the case, most fighting is likely to take place in or near cities and developed areas. In military terms, this used to be known as Military Operations on Urban Terrain or MOUT; it is currently most often called Urban Operations (UO). There are exceptions to this rule, like parts of Africa and Asia, where a great deal of fighting still takes place in rural areas. Exceptions aside, much of future warfare will take place in urban areas. Given that a new threat has also arisen in the form of terrorist attacks, this trend towards urban fighting is both troublesome to those in uniform as well as advantageous to terrorists.

Urban warfare makes it all too convenient for terrorist groups to hit a small unit or convoy, break contact, then blend into the crowd and quickly disappear. Weapons used in the attack can be stashed just about anywhere, as cities provide a multitude of locations for weapons caches. The ability of terrorists to blend in with the local population also makes it very difficult to determine with any certainty the identity of the attackers. U.S. forces operating in Iraq, and to a lesser extent Afghanistan, have been dealing with this very problem for some time now. It is this issue that has brought small arms to the forefront of modern warfare. When combatants are mixed in with a civilian population, they must be hunted down one by one. Carpet bombing cannot achieve this. Only small arms fire can bring that kind of precision firepower to bear.

This trend towards urbanization has not only altered warfare, but has also changed what is required by the tools of war. The small arms in use are called upon to fulfill tasks for which they were not originally designed. This has led to a realization that many designs fall short when performing some duties. No weapon system can fulfill every need. However, this has also spurred a great deal of new development within the field of small arms, in order to find a solution to changing needs.

New Weapons for a New Type of War

A prime example of this is the popularity of the Colt M4 and M4A1 carbines. These have become standard in both Iraq and Afghanistan.[4] Their compact size allows for a more convenient weapon when entering a building. The need for this stems from the constant house to house searches necessary in Iraq and Afghanistan. A full size M16A4 is simply too long to allow for maneuvering in such tight quarters. At the same time, the M4A1 loses some of its ballistic potential due to its abbreviated barrel length. Judging by the popularity of the smaller versions of the M16, this is a tradeoff many troops are willing to live with. At the same time, the excessive muzzle blast and powder flash created by the shortened barrel, has led Knight's Armament among others, to develop a new generation of weapons and cartridges that were designed for short barrel lengths. Knight's Armament, has developed a new round, the 6x35mm. This cartridge was engineered to consume its powder charge before the bullet leaves its 10 inch barrel.[5] The end result is roughly the same bullet weight and a muzzle velocity only a few hundred fps slower than the 5.56 NATO when fired from the M4A1's 14.5 inch barrel. However, there is no powder flash or excessive muzzle blast as with the M4A1. More will be covered on the M4 carbine in the chapter on assault rifles, but this is a good example of how small arms are being adapted to new roles in order to meet the changing needs of modern warfare.

Adapting existing small arms to fill new roles is often done out of necessity, but the end result is usually less than ideal. Unfortunately, to develop a perfect weapon system to fill every need is often quite costly. It can also be time consuming even with the help of modern computer aided design methods. It can still take up to several years to fully develop an effective new weapon system. Often, before the new design is finalized, the needs of the military or law enforcement community may have changed. This is often why it is easier to adapt an existing weapon to fill the immediate need.

Tougher, Lighter, More Accurate

Changes in technology have helped ease the cost of development and testing considerably in recent years. Gone are the days of slide rules, crunching numbers on paper, expensive prototype work, and initial tooling costs, all this just to see if the idea will work at all. Much of this can be done in minutes with the help of modern software. However, if the design idea shows merit, modern CNC machining equipment is capable of making nearly flawless products. Combined with much improved standards within the ammunition industry, the reliability of today's automatic weapons exceeds that of the manual repeaters of the turn of the last century.

Technology has also brought another major advancement to the small arms field in the form of modern composites used in the construction of new weapon systems. Forty years ago, plastics were used only on stocks and other parts not essential to the weapon's function. The old Remington Nylon 66 .22 rimfire rifle was a rare exception to this. At the time of its introduction, the Nylon 66 was revolutionary.[6] However, things are far different today. Beginning back in the 1970s, with weapons like the Heckler & Koch (HK) VP 70 pistol from Germany, and the more influential Austrian Steyr Armee Universal Gewehr (AUG) rifle, plastics became an integral part of the weapon's design. Early high tech designs like these proved the viability of "plastic" guns. It was the Glock 17 9mm pistol, however, that set the trend of heavy plastics use in gun design.[7] After the introduction of the Glock in 1983, many companies soon followed suit with their own plastic designs.

The liberal use of plastics in a gun's construction brings several advantages to modern weapons. Primarily, there is often a significant reduction in weight. Also, modern plastics are tougher than alloys, in that they don't dent as easily and offer more flex without damage. This is especially true in magazine construction. When compared to aluminum magazines, for example, plastics are far tougher and less prone to the kind of damage which can render a magazine useless. Polymers also offer superior corrosion resistance to alloys, something especially appreciated in maritime environments. The use of plastics usually represents a considerable reduction in production cost as well. They can also be molded to perfect ergonomic shapes, improving handling characteristics. There is no doubt that plastic guns are here to stay.

Introduction

Technology has brought several other major changes to the small arms industry. One of the most important needs of any small arm is accurate shot placement. This has become even more the case in modern urban warfare, with terrorists operating among large civilian populations. The consistency and precision offered by modern machining methods and computer aided design have brought an accuracy potential to small arm systems that has never existed before. When combined with new computerized sighting systems, targets anywhere inside of 4000 yards are now within the sniper's wrath.[8]

Despite recent technological advances, many older designs are still considered state of the art. It may just be the genius behind some of these designs that has kept them going strong. The designs of John Moses Browning come to mind more than any others as examples. Many of the most successful modern designs are nothing more than new twists on some of these classic models. The Colt M1911 .45 ACP pistol is a perfect example. Many of the most common handgun designs in use today have copied their recoil systems, either directly or indirectly, from this 100 year old design. In fact, the M1911 is more popular now than ever before. Several companies are offering copies. The U.S. military is still using it, as well as other makers' versions of the same gun. The demand for this large caliber pistol continues to rise, as the 9mm ball round in use by the U.S. military has proven to be an ineffective and unreliable stopper.

The following chapters will cover the various categories of small arms in detail. We will only be examining the most successful and common models in use, to better evaluate their mechanical design and tactical applications. Some of these systems are well proven and have seen a great deal of service, while others are relatively new but are proving quite useful on today's battlefields. These battlefields are, unfortunately, more and more becoming cities and streets. This is a type of warfare which has never held appeal, even among military strategists, but is nonetheless a sign of the times.

Chapter 1

Handguns

As early as World War II, handguns were thought to be obsolete by at least some military authorities. The U.S. M1 carbine was adopted to replace the handgun for many military personnel due to this idea. This belief could not have been more wrong. Handguns will always fill a very specific role in each and every conflict, and in many situations, they are an absolute necessity. This latter fact is especially true within the law enforcement community.

Old complaints against handguns still continue. It is true that handguns have many deficiencies. They suffer from severely limited range and lack long range accuracy. Stopping power is often questionable. The last factor primarily depends on caliber and ammunition selection. Most military units are restricted to using ball ammunition only, although the Hague accords have been called into question lately with regards to counter-terrorist warfare. As a rule, the use of expanding, hollow-point ammunition violates the Hague accords.[1] Also, handguns tend to require far greater training time in order for one to become proficient in their use.

Despite their many shortcomings, they fill many voids that no other class of small arm can. Many attempts have been made to find a suitable replacement for the handgun. None were overly successful. From the U.S. World War II era M1 carbine to today's Fabrique Nationale P90, no weapon has been able to replace the handgun with the exception of another handgun, usually one larger in caliber. In fact, this very solution is being proposed as this is written. Many U.S. troops serving in the Middle East would like to see the standard Beretta M9 9mm replaced by a new .45 caliber pistol, or bring back the Colt M1911A1.[2] This seems rather strange, given that we just did the reverse in 1985. Sometimes, progress and technological advancement just can't take the place of a proven design chambered in a lethal caliber. Although the Beretta has proven a durable and reliable design, the stopping ability of the 9 × 19mm ball round has never been superb.

In this chapter, we will examine the many handguns in common use today. Many models covered here have their advantages as well as their detractions. The designs of some nations will no doubt be excluded, but to evaluate everything out there would require a volume of books. So, we will try to stick with the most common and successful designs and those most likely to be encountered in modern warfare and law enforcement

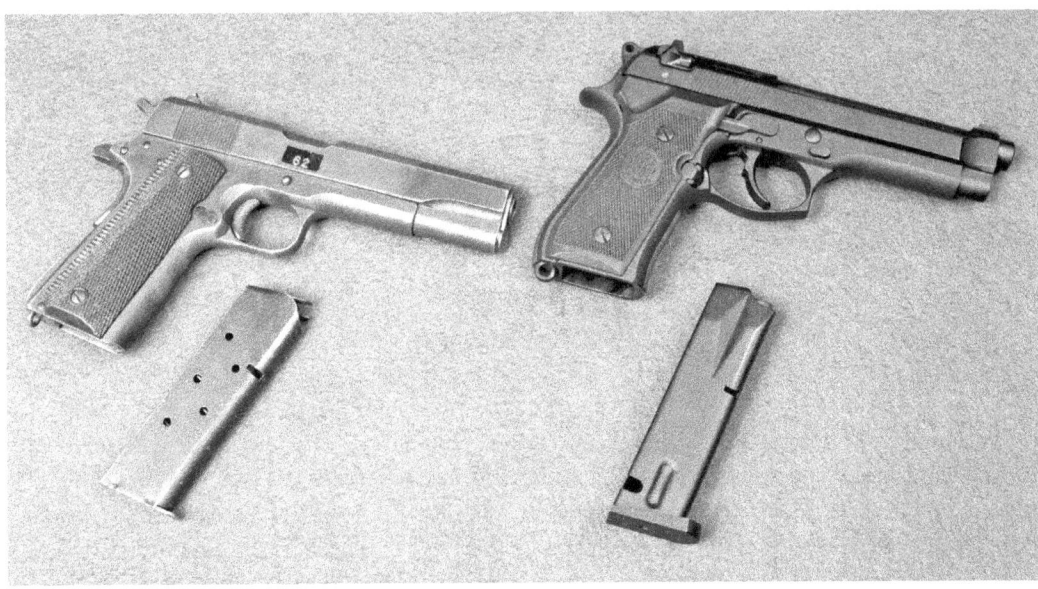

The beloved U.S. M1911A1 .45 Colt-Browning (left) next to its 9mm replacement, the Beretta M9 (R.D. Ward, Department of Defense).

use. Western pistols will be the main focus primarily because they have proven the most successful. The only former Soviet pistols to see widespread use worldwide are the Tokarev TT-33 and Makarov PM. These are only common because of the numbers manufactured over the years, and the former Soviet Union's liberal export policy during that time.

Browning's Big Bore

While there were successful models before the turn of the last century, such as the German model 1896 Mauser "broomhandle," none are still with us today. The honor of the first truly reliable semi-automatic pistol goes to the Colt M1911 Government model .45 Automatic Caliber Pistol (ACP). The brainchild of one of the most influential firearms designers in history, John Moses Browning, this pistol would set the standard for years to come. It was reliable, well designed, reasonably accurate, and most important, very hard hitting. The U.S. involvement in the Philippine insurrection after the Spanish American War led many military personnel to the conclusion that the .38 caliber revolvers in use at the time were not reliable man stoppers. Oddly enough, it was these double-action revolvers that replaced the .45 Colt 1873 Single Action Army revolver several years earlier. I can't explain the pattern of the military flip-flopping between the .45 and .38/9mm, but there's no doubt as to the effectiveness of the M1911 and later M1911A1.

Handguns like the Luger and 1896 Mauser are gone, but the Colt Government model is still with us to this very day, in fact, now more than ever. Several years ago, the Los

Angeles Police Department's SWAT unit adopted a Kimber made variation as its standard sidearm.[3] The U.S. military is still using the M1911A1 as well as other makers' versions. The Colt M1911/M1911A1 is regarded by many to be the ultimate combat handgun to this day. Given that the design is nearing 100 years old, this is quite an endorsement. I must admit to having a nostalgic support of this belief, but it is not necessarily true. The M1911 does have its flaws, although many of these are correctable, especially with the multitude of accessories available for this weapon. The M1911 aftermarket is one of the strongest in the firearms industry. However, it does have one fault that cannot be fixed, though there are many who would argue that it is not really a fault.

The M1911 is a single-action only semi-automatic. What this means, with regards to its use in modern warfare, is that the gun must be carried with the chamber loaded and the safety on, also known as "condition one" carry. The M1911 can be carried with the chamber empty, but this would be slow to put into use and would require both hands to manipulate the slide. It may also be carried with the hammer down or resting on the safety sear, but this method is not safe in practice. Most law enforcement agencies that authorize carry of the M1911 or its variants allow condition one carry only. The Government model does have a built in grip safety, but no firing pin block. Some later versions have added passive firing-pin blocks. Other variations have installed titanium firing-pins in order to reduce the mass of this part. This provides an added measure of safety, but may reduce the energy of primer strikes somewhat. The main problem with condition-one carry is that one must manipulate the thumb safety in order to fire the weapon.[4] This is somewhat slow to perform during combat, even to those who are well trained in the Government model's use, although it becomes second nature with practice.

Aside from its single-action only design, there isn't much bad to say about the Colt M1911. It was, and will probably continue to be, perhaps the best combat sidearm ever devised, especially when self-defense is the primary use of the weapon. Where hardball ammunition is concerned, the .45 ACP is without a doubt more effective than the 9 × 19mm.

As for its technical specifications, the M1911/M1911A1 is 8½ inches long, with the standard 5 inch barrel,[5] the same as for the current Beretta M9.[6] Its empty weight is approximately 40 ounces, a bit heavy, but this helps with managing the recoil of the .45 ACP. Standard magazine capacity in the past was seven rounds, but eight round magazines have been available for some time now.[7] Some users still have concern over the reliability of these newer ones, though the better brands have proven quite fieldworthy. With all it has going for it, the Government model .45 will be around for some time. This is especially true among law enforcement SWAT and counter-terrorist units, where its single-action design doesn't bother highly trained officers and troops who practice constantly with this weapon.

This book is not intended to be an historical work, so I will only briefly cover the history of the Colt M1911. After a thorough series of military tests in the early 20th century, the Colt-Browning design was selected as the M1911. It beat out the competing Luger and Savage designs, among others. Browning had been working with recoil systems for several years by this time, and the short-recoil, tilting barrel method he chose for the M1911 worked perfectly. It proved reliable under any conditions, and his design was relatively well sealed from dirt entering the pistol's mechanism.[8] This is especially noticeable when compared to wide open slide designs like the Walther P38 or Beretta 92. Also, the single column magazine design used in the Colt has, over the years, proven to be more dependable than many double-stack magazine designs. This is even more so when used in desert or sandy environments. The small grains of sand often lodge between rounds in the magazine at the taper point, causing magazine failure.

The Colt was designed with a passive grip safety, which blocked the sear from moving unless depressed during gripping. It was also designed with a manual thumb safety and internal disconnector which prevented the weapon from firing unless the slide was returned to battery. Newer versions often add a passive firing pin block, which prevents forward movement of the firing pin unless the trigger is depressed. This feature does tend to reduce the quality of the trigger pull, but is a nice safety feature to have. It is really a matter of personal preference, however as some users do not like this feature due to its interference with the trigger feel. There are also grip safety activated firing pin blocks as used on the Kimber. This was first tried in earlier M1911 models but was not widely adopted.

The M1911 had very few weak spots, but one of them is generally regarded to be its standard sights, which are sights in name only. This is usually one of the first things altered on the pistol when setting it up for modern counter-terrorist work.

Other features sometimes added to this pistol include an extended safety, extended magazine release and extended slide release, a flared or beveled magazine well, speed hammer, a lightweight replacement trigger, and often a lowered and flared ejection port. None of these are necessary to the reliable functioning of the weapon, however, and any stock M1911 will perform just as well to this very day. These are merely available to suit a user's preference.

The Commander model is quite popular with some users. It offers the same frame size, but with a 4¼ inch barrel instead of the standard 5 inch. This improves handling in many cases, but does change the balance and ballistics of the weapon somewhat.[9]

Many quality pistol manufacturers offer their own versions of the M1911. Quite a few have altered the design some, but the results are still recognizable as an M1911. Makers like Kimber, Les Baer, and Wilson Combat offer their own models; even SIG and Smith & Wesson have joined the club. These are not the only firms in the game, just some of the better ones. Perhaps the company offering the largest selection of copies is Springfield Armory. The days of Colt being the only place to go for an M1911 are over. Wilson Combat offers one of the best quality copies.[10] It is heavily modified but is still recognizable as an M1911. It is a favorite among many professional units employing the M1911. It is also quite pricey, but much care is put into semi-production pistols like these. This does not mean that other makers' versions are inferior. The end user should choose whatever suits them best.

The M1911 is an excellent tactical weapon. It is chambered in one of the most lethal service calibers ever and is a durable design which can easily handle the rigors of combat.

It does not offer the high magazine capacities of more modern pistols, but its single-column magazine is more reliable by design than double-stack magazines, and is less finicky in a sandy environment. The Government model is a well balanced and natural pointing pistol which lends itself to close quarter battle (CQB). As many in service revere the M1911, it is almost blasphemy to say that this pistol is not perfect in that its single-action only design is best kept on safe until ready to fire. This cannot be done silently. Standard procedure with most pistols of this type is to ready the weapon as it is drawn, so this is not really a problem. The primary problem is in carrying the pistol with the chamber loaded. A proper holster is a must. If the safety is inadvertently disengaged, it doesn't take much to pull the trigger. This is why double-action pistols have become the standard today.

When limited to the use of ball ammo only, the .45 ACP has proven to be a superior stopping round when compared to the 9mm. The round has significantly more momentum than the 9mm. Also, since the .45 tends to penetrate less, it tends to exit the target less often. When a bullet exits a target, much of its potential energy is wasted. Where handgun calibers are concerned, this difference can be a big deal, as they tend to have far less power to begin with when compared to rifle calibers. This tends to explain recent complaints among troops serving in Iraq and Afghanistan concerning the 9mm's ability to stop combatants reliably.

While the U.S. has yet to replace its current M9 and M11 9mm pistols, there has been interest in returning to the .45 ACP as the standard pistol caliber. The HK Mk23 Special Operations Command (SOCOM) pistol is proving popular among troops serving in the Middle East. The U.S. is also using the M1911A1 and its copies. Where reliable stopping power is required, it's hard to beat the .45 ACP for a service cartridge. It seems clear that the .45 Government model is not yet obsolete and will likely remain in service for some years.

The First of the Wondernines

Aside from the Colt Government model, perhaps the most common early to mid 20th century design in use today is the FN GP35, also known as the Browning High Power. Browning did not actually finish the design. That was left to Dieudonne Saive, a designer at Fabrique Nationale. FN had a long history making Browning designs. The design was finalized by 1935, but few had been produced by the time the Nazis occupied Belgium. The Germans continued production at FN, and Allied production took place in Canada at the John Inglis Company. This is common knowledge to many already, so let's look at the High Power's assets, as it is still often used today. It possesses many excellent qualities for a sidearm of modern warfare. It had good balance, accuracy, reliability, and what, at the time of its introduction, was unheard of, a 13 round magazine capacity. Many German soldiers were quite fond of the design. J.M. Browning seldom disappointed with any of his ideas. It is somewhat shorter and lighter than the M1911. It is 7¾ inches long and weighs roughly 2 pounds empty. It did have a single-action only limitation, and the magazine disconnect was not widely popular. This feature is easily deactivated and often was. Doing this had an added advantage of improving the trigger pull. The current MKIII is the standard production model today. This is mainly improved in production standards, but did incorporate some design changes like the addition of an ambidextrous safety and epoxy surface finish. A firing pin block is also used. When combined with high performance ammunition, this makes a very effective sidearm capable of competing with even the most modern designs. This is not bad for a pistol first seen 75 years ago.

The Browning (FN) HP is by far the most widely used service pistol in the world. The only pistol that even comes close in terms of the number of nations using a given model is the SIG-Sauer P226. Over a dozen nations call the HP their standard pistol, or at least one of several standard issue pistols. The United Kingdom and Canada have made use of the pistol for years. Belgium still prefers it, as do many other European nations.

Browning began his work on the design but died in 1926 before he was finished. He wanted a high capacity pistol, hence the double-stack magazine. He also chose to do away with the M1911's grip safety. The original hammer was the keyhole, rounded pattern, which tended to reduce catching when being drawn. The High Power was an instant classic. Its performance during World War II no doubt helped. The only major change to the design through the years was the relocation of the extractor to an exterior position via a slot cut into the slide's right side. An M1911 style hammer is also usually seen on most American imported models. Some still prefer the original style hammer, and for a time, Browning even brought back the tangent rear sight that was seen on some early models. These were usually fitted with a slotted grip to allow for mounting a detachable stock, which also doubled as a holster when not in use. For whatever reason, this model was popular in China for many years.

The High Power has proven reliable under all conditions, and aside from its single-action design, has very few flaws, leaving the end user with one of the best pistol designs ever put forth. One of its best features is its beautiful balance and grip design, making for one of the most comfortable pistols out there. This also gave the pistol a natural pointing and shooting hold. The High Power has seen service as the FBI's hostage rescue pistol. This is also a standard for the British Special Air Service and was seen being used by their personnel during the Iranian embassy incident in 1980, although the SAS has recently purchased the SIG in some numbers. The Browning has attained a reputation bested only by the Colt Government model.

The High Power is somewhat heavier than more modern alloy or plastic framed pistols, but its steel frame adds to both controllability and durability as with the Colt. This, combined with the quality of its design, has created a pistol that has yet to be beaten by any margin. Given that the design was first seen in 1935, it makes one wonder if the design will ever be pushed aside. Given that many units still using it are more than content, it is unlikely.

1. Handguns

Behind the Iron Curtain

During this time, there were successful ideas coming from behind the iron curtain as well. The Soviet Tokarev TT-30 and TT-33 7.62mm pistols borrowed their lock-up from the Colt-Browning short recoil system. However, they did have some original design merits of their own. The trigger group of the TT-33 could be removed as a single unit, which greatly eased repairs. Its 7.62 × 25mm caliber had a high velocity, and this design's mention here is due to its popularity with many Russian criminal groups. A great many were manufactured during World War II, and it is no doubt easier to obtain one of these than a comparable western pistol design. The primary difference between the two models was the locking lugs of the TT-33 being turned completely around the outside diameter of the barrel rather than just the top half, as in the M1911.[11] This was primarily done as a time saving measure. There were some other minor differences as well. The Tokarev had a reputation as a reliable semi-auto, and due to its caliber's high velocity, it has a reputation for punching through body armor. Many Russian police agencies are no doubt aware of this trait.[12] Its weight and overall length were similar to the GP35, although it had a straighter and more slender grip, as it used an in-line 8 round magazine.[13] The Tokarev had no manual safety but did have a safety notch on the hammer as do most pistols. This was merely to prevent a misfire should the hammer, accidentally be disengaged from the sear. This measure is not intended as a safety device in normal operation of the weapon.

A 9 × 18mm PM Makarov taken from suspected terrorists along with the rest of their kit (GSgt. K.A. Milks, U.S. Marine Corps).

The Tokarev served the Soviet Union well during the war and was one of the most mass produced pistols in history. The 7.62 × 25mm Tokarev caliber is really nothing more than the 7.63mm Mauser round first seen on the model 1896 "broomhandle." At the time, this was considered a powerful chambering for a handgun and is still a capable round today, even though the bullet is a bit light.

Probably the most likely pistol to be encountered in the former communist bloc is the PM or Makarov. It was not nearly as powerful as the earlier Tokarev, although it did offer a safer double-action design. It is quite similar in size to the Walther PP. It is actually quite similar to the PP in design. It operates on the straight blowback principle and takes down in much the same way as the Walther. Its 9 × 18mm caliber is between the .380 ACP and the 9 × 19mm in terms of power.[14] It is a simple, reliable, if somewhat low powered pistol with an eight round single column magazine. It is quite common worldwide, and is probably the most likely pistol to be encountered by U.S. forces operating in the Middle East, due to the numbers made by the former communist bloc over the years.[15] The 9 × 18mm is not considered a potent round,[16] which may explain why the Russians have moved toward the 9 × 19mm in more recent designs, though export potential may have something to do with this as well.

The Soviet Stechkin or APS is a 9 × 18mm selective-fire blowback operated pistol which was relatively complex and expensive to produce. It is not often encountered in today's military and counter-terrorist operations, due to its lack of control when fired automatically. It is occasionally used by some Russian special police and military units, but there are more modern designs available. It was often issued with a detachable stock like that of the Browning High Power due to its selective-fire capability.[17] It is nonetheless a deadly close range weapon in trained hands. It is 8.8 inches long, weighs approximately 2.3 pounds empty, and is equipped with a 20 round magazine.[18]

Russia's current standard pistol is the M443 "Grach," also known as the Yarygin PYa.[19] It has a 17 round magazine and can be carried in either double-action or single-action modes. It is not seen much in the West. It is a Browning style lock-up design, with conventional features popular on many modern designs. It was designed as a replacement for the Makarov PM as Russia's primary service pistol. The design is relatively new and has not seen widespread use. Time will tell if it has any staying power. It does appear to have everything necessary for a modern combat handgun. It appears to have a well designed grip shape and should point quite well. Accuracy is probably on par with most Russian weapons. Russian pistols have never been known for target grade accuracy like the SIG pistols but the same can be said of most pistols. Combat handguns are meant to be reliable first and accurate second.

Handguns on the Back Burner

Semi-auto pistol design seemed to take a slow road for much of the mid 20th century. Many of the designs seen today didn't begin to show up until the mid–1980s. There were a few exceptions, like the Smith and Wesson model 59 used by the U.S. Navy SEAL (Sea, Air and Land) teams during the Vietnam War as a suppressed pistol. It was designed to eliminate guard dogs and was known as the Mk 22 Mod 0 "hush puppy." It had a 14 round magazine capacity and was a double-action that did not see widespread military adoption, but it was a good example of designs that would follow.[20]

Aside from the S&W model 59, not a lot of designs came forth during the 1960s. The real focus at this time was on rifles. The M16 was busy competing with the AK-47 in Vietnam. Handgun design was not given the same priority as rifle design during this time. This would change much with the coming years.

New Generation of Pistols

The term "wondernine" came about during the 1980s. It was used to describe any modern high magazine capacity 9mm pistol, generally one with a conventional double-action/single-action trigger system. The Czech CZ75 was one of the first. The Czechs have a long history of quality gun manufacturing combined with good, solid designs; the CZ75 was no exception.[21] This pistol was difficult to come by in the west during the 1970s and 80s. Perhaps because of this, it had a reputation as being some kind of new "super pistol." It wasn't anything magical, just a good solid design. In fact, it wasn't all that original. It merely combined many desired features into one pistol. It borrowed its lock-up design work from the Browning system. It had a smooth, well designed double-action mechanism and a comfortable grip angle. The last feature was somewhat similar to the Browning High-Power. Later, the updated CZ85 was put into production. This had ambidextrous safety levers among other minor changes. The current CZ P-01 is a compact, alloy framed, modernized version that has been accepted as a NATO standard pistol and is considered by many to be one of the better pistols in use today. Dimensions for the original CZ75 were roughly 8.1 inches in length and 2.2 pounds in weight.[22] The newer P-01 is around 7.2 inches and weighs 1.8 pounds. empty. Slide rails running inside the frame aid accuracy and allow for a lower barrel axis, increasing control of the pistol. The Italian made Tanfoglio was a popular copy.[23] The Swiss company Sphinx also made a very nice, but expensive, version of this pistol known as the AT-2000. The CZ75 had one feature that was unique at the time. It could be carried with the hammer cocked and the safety on as well as in the hammer down, double-action mode. This option primarily appeals to those accustomed to the M1911 action.

The Government Model's Replacement

About a year after the CZ75 first appeared, another well known 9mm made its debut. The first Beretta model 92 came out around 1976. The earliest version differed quite a bit from today's standard model 92FS.[24] The safety was located on the frame and did not de-cock the hammer. The triggerguard was rounded, not squared off as in today's version. There have been other minor changes made in later models. The Beretta was and is one of the best looking pistols out there. I don't want to say this was the reason for its popularity, but I can't say it wasn't either. In use, the Beretta has proven to be an accurate and durable gun. It did have some problems during development and even after its adoption as the M9 for that matter. Many have heard of the shameful U.S. pistol trials of the 1980s. There were claims that some competing models were unfairly disqualified. The slide separation incidents were quite well known, and Beretta quickly altered the design to fix the issue. The current 92FS is one of the best modern pistols available. Its overall performance has been quite satisfactory, with the stopping power of the 9mm being the primary complaint coming from the troops in the Middle East.

Other than the relocation of the safety lever, the design alterations have been minor. The only true design flaw that had to be corrected was the slide separation issue. A catch was added to prevent the rear portion of the slide from flying back into the user's face. With this change, it became known as the model 92FS, The "S" denoting the added safety lug. After research, it was determined that the slide separations were caused by metallurgical issues. The slide catch probably wasn't necessary but Beretta left it just in case.[25]

One other minor flaw in the Beretta's design applies more to law enforcement. The Beretta's takedown lever is positioned and contoured in such a way that it is easy for a knowledgeable assailant to disable the pistol if he grabs the barrel. With one hand, he can depress and rotate the takedown lever quite quickly and effortlessly, leaving the officer holding only the frame of the pistol. Fortunately, this part is easily replaced with a flush fitting takedown lever, eliminating the issue entirely. If this is done, a small punch is used when taking the weapon apart for cleaning. Aside from these two minor issues, the Beretta has proven an outstanding service pistol, despite its early teething troubles. No pun intended, as some users did lose teeth during the slide separation incidents, as the back portion of the slide flew back to hit the user in the mouth. The Beretta is still considered state of the art and capable of competing with any top combat pistol. It is slightly longer than some others however, and Beretta no longer offers its compact 92FSC model. Beretta also offers the Cougar, a newer closed slide design that is available in .45 ACP. None of these newer models have gained the popularity of the model 92 though.

For combat use, the model 92 is a bit long when compared to the SIG or Glock, but it does offer slightly improved ballistics with the longer barrel. It has a fairly heavy and long double-action pull that tends to throw the aim off somewhat, but double-action fire is meant for close range, fast work anyway. The single-action pull is fairly good for a military pistol, though not as crisp as that usually found on the SIG P220 series. Many users prefer the Beretta over the SIG for its manual safety which also serves as the de-cocking lever. However, the user of the model 92 must remember to return the safety lever to the up position after dropping the hammer if the weapon is to be ready for instant use. The frame of the Beretta does not quite offer the same length of slide support as does the SIG, but this does not appear to affect the accuracy of the pistol in any tactical sense.

The tilting-block recoil system of the Beretta makes for a smooth operating pistol that shoots quite well in rapid fire, making for a top combat weapon.

Swiss + German = Quality

Perhaps the toughest competition at the time of the Beretta's adoption came from what many regard to be the cream of the crop, the SIG-Sauer P220 series. To give a brief history, the standard Swiss service pistol since 1949, the SIG P210 was perhaps the finest quality production handgun ever made. Unfortunately, it was also one of the most expensive. The Swiss army wanted a modern double-action that would equal the P210 in performance yet cost much less. What they got in 1975 was the SIG P220. They saw export potential, but due to Swiss export laws couldn't sell the design where they wanted.[26] SIG decided the solution was to set up production with the German firm of J.P. Sauer & Son. The SIG-Sauer P220 series included the original P220, the compact P225, the high-capacity P226, and finally the compact P228 high-capacity pistol.[27] The SIG models gained quite a reputation that lasts to this day. The model's design has changed very little since 1975. The current models are still big sellers. Even though the modern P220 series are far less expensive than the P210, they are far from cheap handguns. However, many

The choice of the British SAS and the U.S. Navy SEALS, the SIG-Sauer P-226 9mm.

The plastic framed pistol that changed the handgun industry, the Glock. This is the larger model 21 .45 ACP variation.

were willing to pay the extra cost to have top performance in a production pistol. SIGs have always been known for great out of the box accuracy. The reliability and ergonomics of these pistols have always been first rate.

The P220 may have been a little ahead of its time when first introduced. Oddly enough, when it first entered the U.S. market, it was not a big seller. Originally known as the BDA or Browning Double-Action, the P220 didn't quite catch on at first.[28] After several years, however, word of its performance began to spread. By the mid–1980s, it was generally regarded as one of the best of all current production handguns. Whether or not this is true is hard to say, but the P226 did tie for first place with the Beretta for the U.S. pistol trials of the 1980s. It was only rejected based on cost. This matter was also in dispute for several years, as it has been claimed that the SIG was actually less expensive when replacement part costs were factored in.[29] However, as a weapon of modern warfare, it would be hard to find anything to outperform the SIG. By the late 1980s, the SIG pistols had become one of the most popular choices for a standard pistol. The U.S. Navy adopted it for its SEAL teams, as did the SAS.[30] To this day the SIG is still one of the most respected service pistols.

The design of the SIG-Sauer was quite unique at the time of its introduction. It did not have a cast or machined slide. Instead, the slide's body came from a heavy steel stamping. The breech block was a separate part which was held in place by a proper fit and a simple roll pin. This helped reduce production cost. The current models now have a machined slide for some reason. The extractor has been relocated to a notch in the slide. This actually seems like a step backwards. There were some complaints that the original stamped slides tended to rust in certain areas if proper cleaning was not done, though this can be true of any weapon. Other than that, very few complaints ever applied to the P220 series. On rare occasions, the roll pin would work its way out, but this could easily be monitored and replaced with a tighter fitting pin if needed.

A tactical advantage the SIG has over the Beretta is the lack of any manual safety lever. This means that it cannot be inadvertently left on. SIGs are known for having great accuracy and a clean trigger pull, with less creep than that of the Beretta. Also, some preferred the closed off slide design, as it allowed for little dirt to enter the weapon's mechanism. There is little merit to this, as the Beretta's open slide design has never proven to be a reliability issue. The SIG is also a shorter pistol, especially the P225 and P228, both being only a little over 7 inches in length as opposed to the 8½ inch Beretta. The P220 and P226 are slightly longer at around 7¾ inches long.[31] This length seems to be pretty much standard for most modern service pistols, with the Glock being a bit shorter. These overall lengths are likely due to use of the Browning style recoil system, which sets limits as to the minimum length required. Barrel lengths on pistols utilizing this system generally range between 3 and 5 inches. The accuracy of SIG pistols is target grade most of the time. Reliability is unequalled by most weapons. The grip design creates a perfect holding pistol for most hands. With all it has going for it, the SIG is likely to remain a standard service pistol for years to come. After gaining this kind of reputation, it is hard to see why SIG recently altered the design of the pistol a bit. I have read of several complaints with the new machined slide with regard to balance issues. As to how this new slide affects reliability, time will tell. I suspect reasons for the change were economic more than anything.

Austrian Plastic Perfection

One pistol from the 1980s that was definitely to set new trends was the Glock 17. First introduced in 1983, the Glock brought many firsts to the field of handguns. It was the first truly successful plastic gun. Heckler & Koch made an attempt with the VP-70 in the 1970s, but this was never a great commercial success. The VP-70 may have been another handgun a little too ahead of its time, but the Glock showed up at just the right moment.

One of the major innovations of the Glock design was its safe-action trigger mechanism. With no manual safety, the striker fired cocking mechanism was easy to use. This gave shooters a consistent trigger pull for each shot. There was no more heavy double-action pull for the first shot with a far different single-action pull for all following shots. It had firepower unequaled at the time, with the exception of the HK VP-70 and the Austrian Steyr GB, a gas delayed blowback 9mm which showed promise but didn't last in production. Glock magazines were originally offered in 17 or 19 round capacities. There

This is one of a number of high quality M1911 derivatives, the very compact Kimber Ultra CDP II .45 ACP. Its relation to the M1911 is easily recognized.

was even a 33 round magazine available, which was originally designed for the Glock 18 machine pistol. Shortly after Glock came out with the model 17, they soon offered the model 19 compact, which had a 15 round magazine, although model 17 mags will also fit. Subcompact versions and different caliber offerings would follow.[32]

Machine pistols never really gained much of a following in either military or law enforcement circles. This was most likely do to controllability factors. This makes sense, because machine pistols would otherwise make an ideal weapon for house clearing and other aspects of urban warfare. Machine pistols such as the HK VP 70, the Beretta 93R, and Glock 18 have seen limited testing and use[33] but were never widely adopted by any large organization.

Getting back to the Glock 17, the pistol set durability records yet to be matched. There have been reports of some Glock 17s firing more than 300,000 rounds without failure.[34] This is unheard of for any service pistol. Some critics argue that Glocks are not as reliable as SIGs or Berettas. Others argue Glock handguns are the most reliable made. What is not in dispute is that Glocks have taken the law enforcement market by storm, and combined with SIG and Beretta, have traditionally seen the largest share of the world market for modern 9mm handguns, although HK has made headway as of late with their Universal Self-loading Pistol (USP) series.

The Glock is one of the simplest modern designs made. It has roughly 33 parts in all. A new 4th generation model, recently introduced, may add to this number a bit. This is due to its new recoil reduction system that was introduced to allow it to compete with the HK USP. The basic Glock design has seen several changes through the years. When a design change took place, the pistol was usually given a new generation number. One of the first changes made was a captive recoil spring. This occurred back in the 1990s. They also later added finger grooves and mounting rails on the frames. Other minor dimensional changes were made, as well as magazine improvements. The basic design has remained the same in spite of these changes. The Glock is based upon the familiar Browning short-recoil principle. The magazine release and slide lock lever are positioned similarly to those on the M1911. There is no manual safety, which further simplifies operation.

The only issue some users have a problem with is the unconventional trigger system. Today, striker fired pistols are much more common. It simplifies the safety issues often associated with conventional double action semi-autos. This is because the cocking of the mechanism is done by pulling the trigger. This is true of conventional double action pistols as well. However, there is no change in the trigger pull for follow up shots, as is the case with traditional DA/SA systems. Also, with the Glock, the safety is passively located on the trigger itself. Merely pulling on the trigger deactivates the safety. There is also a passive firing-pin block located within the slide. Despite all of the built in safety systems, it is recommended that Glocks be carried with an empty chamber. For obvious reasons, this can't be done with law enforcement weapons, so a well designed holster that protects and covers the triggerguard is a must. The new SERPA (designer's name) lock holsters are popular for this reason.[35] These holsters are safe yet allow fast, easy access. Thumb break holsters also offer fast access.

As a modern combat pistol, the Glock has few equals. It is simple, reliable, rugged to the extreme, and highly accurate. From the ones I have personally fired, they are the equal of any SIG or Beretta. They have a magazine capacity that is matched by few other pistols. The trigger isn't quite as conventional as that of the SIG and as a result, takes some getting used to. The Glock has a lower bore axis than many other pistols and recoil has a different feel than more conventional pistols. The lack of a manual safety means it can't be inadvertently left in the on position. This is one of the reasons for its popularity with the law enforcement community. The Glock wouldn't have the following that it has if its lack of a safety lever were its only quality. It is not the newest design on the market but is still considered one of the best and will likely remain so for some time.

Germany Goes into High Gear

Walther first entered into the "wondernine" field with the P88, but this didn't sell as well as hoped. They later tried the P99, with somewhat better luck the second time. The P88 had its share of troubles, but the P99 has proven a rugged and reliable design.[36] It came along a little late in the game, however, and has only seen adoption by Finland

and some police services in Germany along with a few small orders from others like Poland and Canada. The P99 is also a striker fired pistol with well placed controls and an ergonomic design. It offers backstraps which can be changed out to suit different sized hands to provide the best fit possible. This feature is being seen on several new designs, primarily those offered by HK.

The P99 possesses all the traits necessary for a modern combat pistol. It is available in DA/SA or double-action only (DAO). Its standard trigger has two distinct phases, an initial heavy first pull and a lighter release phase second.[37] It appears to be equal in performance to any other modern combat pistol being made. It is just a latecomer and there are only so many positions available in the service pistol industry. At the time of its introduction, many nations had just switched to new models and were not looking for another.

HK has perhaps had the best luck competing with Glock, SIG, and Beretta. They first introduced the USP in 1993. The USP was not the first HK to see service. The Polizei Selbstlade Pistole (PSP), known later in slightly modified form as the P7, was to become a standard German State Police pistol. The P7 was an original design. It used a gas retarded blowback system which used gases tapped at the breech to lock the slide until the bullet had left the barrel. It was a compact 9mm which was also unique in that it had a squeeze cocking lever which kept the pistol in safe condition until the user was ready to fire. This could prove a potential problem in that it was loud in readying the weapon unless the user was practiced in squeezing and firing at the same time, which is not conducive to accurate shooting. With the addition of a heat shield just above the trigger and a relocation of the magazine release, it became known as the P7M8 with an 8 round magazine, and the P7M13 with a 13 round option. The P7M13 was one of the competing pistols during the U.S. pistol trials that ultimately led to the adoption of the Beretta 92FS.[38] Perhaps its squeeze cocking device was too unusual for conservative attitudes.

HK also produced the P9S, a double action that utilized the HK roller locking system as found in its popular service rifles and submachine guns. This saw some use by the U.S. Navy SEAL teams as a suppressed pistol during the 1980s, as it was easily modified for that purpose.[39] None of these saw big commercial sales, so HK decided to take a new approach in the USP.

The HK USP was closely related to the U.S. SOCOM's Mk 23 Mod 0 suppressed pistol and HK decided to offer it commercially. This was a wise move, as the Mk 23 proved a rugged and reliable design, with traditional looks. The Mk 23 was designed to fulfill a request by the U.S. special operations community for a new suppressed pistol to meet the needs of elite units.[40] The request was for a .45 pistol that had all modern features and could withstand the rigors of modern combat without any drop in performance. HK soon realized that the pistol they designed for the job would make an excellent pistol for the commercial market as well. The USP has become one of the contenders for much of the U.S. law enforcement market, its primary competition coming from Glock, although Beretta and SIG have provided stiff competition within law enforcement as well.

However, the USP offers what the other guns do not. One of the unique patents in the pistol's design is its recoil reduction system. This is basically two recoil springs instead of one. The primary recoil spring does what any recoil spring does. It returns the slide to battery. However, the second spring is there to absorb much of the recoil force of the slide's rearward movement. In essence, it prevents the slide from battering the frame as it approaches the slide stop pin. The secondary spring is a small but very heavy spring which quickly stops the slide's movement. This feature has become so desired that aftermarket companies have offered similar options for other pistols. It is said to reduce the recoil force by almost one third. It has an added benefit of increasing the life of an already very tough weapon.

Combined with a tough nitride coating on the pistol's exterior, this makes for one of the most durable handguns out there. It is also preferred over the Glock by some, who claim that it has a more ergonomic grip design and a more conventional trigger system with a manual safety lever. This last feature is something the Glock pistol's lack. It is likely that the USP will be around for some time. Its only deficit is its high price tag. Some users also complain about the mag release pinching fingers when performing a change. This is really a matter of how one holds the weapon during a magazine change. There is a USP compact model that has a different recoil system that does not have the secondary spring. Consequently, the recoil is slightly different than that of the standard model.

The USP and its derivatives have become quite popular. It is available in 9 × 19mm and .40 S&W as well as a slightly larger .45 ACP version. As a service pistol it has proven quite rugged. It has recently been adopted by its country of origin with a modified safety lever. The USP has a reputation for excellent accuracy and reliability and has proven as rugged as the Glock. It does require more training time due to its safety/de-cocking lever, although DAO models are available.

HK has also offered the newer P2000, a similar weapon with improvements in trigger options and, on the P2000, interchangeable backstraps to fit different hand sizes. The P30 is also offered, which has even more ergonomic options, with different grip side options, as well as the same trigger options. These are manufactured with the recoil system of the USP compact model.

The HK USP is available with a variety of trigger options, as are other HK pistols. It can be carried cocked and locked, hammer down in DA mode, and is available in DA only. The USP and USP Tactical differ from the Mk 23 pistol in that they combine the safety and de-cocking lever into one part. The Mk 23 has separate levers for each. While the USP Tactical is quite similar to the Mk 23, it is a bit smaller. The Mk 23 is a big pistol at 9½ inches in length, the Tactical model is only 8½ inches, and the standard USP is just over 7⅝ inches long. There is even a compact Tactical model as well.

Like the Mk 23, the Tactical model is issued with a barrel that is already threaded for suppressor use, but has different threads than that found on the Mk 23. The threads are reversed so the two suppressors cannot be interchanged, as using the wrong model suppressor would lead to malfunctioning on either pistol if they had identical threads. Both the Mk 23 and the USP Tactical models have the Colt-Browning recoil system and as such they require special suppressors that can function under this type of movement.

Suppressors made for this system usually have some type of counterweight system in place to help with reliable functioning, though there are some conventional designs that function with this type of recoil system. Externally, the standard suppressors for both HK pistols are alike, hence the different threads.

As mentioned, some users do not care for the Glock's striker fired trigger system, and prefer a conventional DA/SA trigger, as well as a manual safety option. For such users, the HK is often the first choice when these features are desired. In most other areas, the two pistols offer similar qualities. Both the HK and Glock offer rugged plastic frames, great accuracy, and absolute reliability. Some users claim that the Glock has an inferior feel to the HK, that the Glock is block shaped and too flat on the grip sides. This really depends on the user's hands. To be fair, Glocks can be altered with grip sleeves to give them a more ergonomic feel. These are often known as "Glock socks."[41] In either case, both pistols are a first rate pick as a standard service pistol.

There are other quality pistols being made today, but none have gained the popularity of the models covered so far. Ruger has provided the synthetic frame P95 to the U.S. military on at least one occasion and received favorable reports on performance. The Springfield XD has gained a good reputation as well. This is a Croatian design that is also known as the HS2000. It is offered in several configurations from full size to subcompact. The FN Five-seveN is a new idea that uses the 5.7 × 28mm PDW caliber, and has an original delayed blowback method of operation. This caliber is not well proven as a stopping round however, especially from a handgun length barrel.

For the present, many of the models discussed will most likely continue to serve units worldwide. It is odd, but other than in materials and construction methods, many of the most popular models in use today differ very little from the tilting barrel recoil method pioneered by Browning many years earlier.

New Tactical Applications Applied

Handguns, while often low powered in comparison to rifles, offer today's law enforcement and counter-terrorist units what no other weapons can. A handgun is far smaller than any other type of small arm and lends itself well to room-to-room fighting and clearing a building of hostiles. They also serve well as a backup weapon. For these reasons alone, they will no doubt continue to serve for many years to come. No other small arm is as easy to manipulate in confined spaces or as easy to conceal.[42] A grenade may be an exception to this, but a grenade can only be used once, and detonating a grenade indoors can be just a dangerous to the user when thin interior walls are the only cover available. Grenades also tend to be less picky in choosing their targets, not a good trait to have when a building is filled with both hostiles and friendlies.

Rather than handguns being phased out, use has increased in recent years. This is apparent in the massive growth of the number of accessories available for handguns. As recently as 1980, most of these add-ons were unheard of. No handguns had built in mounting rails until recently. After World War II, handgun use seemed to be in decline except among law enforcement. In fact, the U.S. military hadn't accepted a large order of Colt Government models since 1945. Though the U.S. military had often looked for a suitable replacement for the sidearm, none ever appeared.

With the trend toward highly specialized military and law enforcement operations being conducted against terrorist organizations, and with organized crime groups becoming increasingly well equipped and well funded, there's a realized need for sidearms as standard weapons of choice in such operations.

As for action type, the semi-automatic pistol has pretty much become standard, with revolvers seeing very little use today. A revolver just cannot compete with any pistol capable of delivering up to 20 rounds on target without a magazine change. Also, the old argument of revolvers being more reliable isn't as relevant today, with ammunition production standards being so high. A "dud" in a batch of factory ammunition is very rare today.[43]

The need for law enforcement to remain on equal footing with criminal groups is always a must. Criminal organizations, as mentioned, are well funded and equipped. They also have access to the latest training techniques used by law enforcement and paramilitary organizations. The latter problem is compounded by the fact that many of the most well trained personnel, formerly in military or law enforcement units, have begun working for such criminal organizations. The pay is far greater than that offered serving the public. With many people, the financial issue is often the deciding factor in choosing which job to take. For years, this was primarily an overseas problem, but with an increasing number of veterans returning to the U.S., which at this writing is suffering a bleak economic outlook, this could prove a problem in the future here as well.

Personally, I like to think of veterans as being above mercenary behavior of this type. Seeing this in Mexico is disturbing, however, as many of these personnel have advanced training in urban warfare operations. These days, the best trained personnel are often working directly for the drug cartels in Mexico. Many of these are former Mexican military or law enforcement personnel who have chosen to take this work for the security and the money. One wouldn't have thought of such a job as secure until recently. Mexico's government seems to be the underdog as of late. Ciudad Juarez alone has been seeing over 2000 murders a year lately due to the drug war. Even some U.S. law enforcement personnel have been killed as a result.[44]

Terrorist groups are likewise often well trained and funded, especially when the children of wealthy Saudi Arabian construction moguls are footing the bill. There is an added disadvantage in fighting terrorist groups, in that they often fight with a firm religious fervor that the profit motivated cartels lack.

Being forced to operate against such groups, it is clear why our officers and troops need only the best equipment available. This is an absolute must with regards to the small arms they use. Only the most reliable and proven systems should even be considered for operational use.

The handguns covered in this chapter represent the best examples of what side arms should be. They should be reliable, rugged, and accurate, with good handling characteristics, and they should possess sufficient firepower for the job. Those with a simple manual of arms are best for troops or officers that are not budgeted for constant training. This would apply to smaller police departments and troops that are not directly involved with tactical operations.

The operational use of the handgun has undergone a rather drastic change from previous years. For much of the handgun's military history, it was seen as a weapon of last resort. It was used as a backup to something more powerful, or its use had been relegated to those who did not require the use of a weapon as part of their normal duties. This often included radio operators, tank crews, air crew, and so on. During much of the 19th and early 20th century, officers often carried a handgun rather than an issue rifle. In earlier times, the officers were required to buy their own handguns. By World War II, many officers had chosen not to carry a handgun, as it often identified them to enemy snipers. A handgun has long been recognized as a symbol of authority or command, and over the years, this trait tended to draw a great deal of enemy fire. Killing a high value target often created the most confusion and destabilized the command structure quite handily. Following the massive casualty counts of World War I, the officers often chose to remain as anonymous as possible on the battlefield.

Following World War II, rifle development pushed handgun research aside for the most part. Beginning with the M16, lightweight rifles have become the standard. A new class of small arms have entered the fray recently. The Personal Defense Weapon (PDW), exemplified by the FN P90 and the HK MP7A1, has seen recent use in modern warfare. With such lightweight, portable small arms readily available, one would think the sidearm was on the way out. This has not been the case. Some handguns are now even considered offensive weapons by certain units in the military.

The HK Mk23 Mod 0 was designed to be an offensive handgun from the start. As large as the Mk23 is, it is still far more compact than any PDW. It may not offer the rate of fire or effective range of a PDW, but a PDW does not offer the quiet hitting power of a suppressed pistol in .45 ACP. In fact, there's been a great deal of debate as to the viability of PDW calibers in general. They do offer extended range and ability to penetrate body armor, but they do not offer the stopping ability of much heavier bullets. Law enforcement in particular has been a skeptical group with regard to the PDW. The performance of such weapons is more akin to the .22 Winchester Magnum Rimfire (WMR) with regards to energy and bullet weight.[45]

In urban warfare settings, handguns lend themselves well to offensive use as suppressed weapons used for room clearing. Among the law enforcement community, the handgun is often the only weapon available for going into a building. This is because officers often have no other choice when responding to a call. Many times, a pump shotgun is the only other weapon available for law enforcement patrol units. Traditionally, only SWAT units had access to submachine guns and rifles. This changed somewhat after the North Hollywood shootout in the late 1990s. By and large however, the handgun still dominates American law enforcement as the primary weapon for duty. This will most likely continue to be the case, unless drastic changes take place in American civil organization models. Many Americans may have a problem with seeing police carrying automatic weapons and I must admit to being among those who would have a problem with this.

Among counter-terrorist units, the handgun will continue to see offensive use under many circumstances. As a suppressed weapon, it is still far more compact and maneuverable than any other small arm available. It has sufficient stopping power, if the right caliber and ammunition are selected. Close range accuracy is more than adequate, especially in well trained hands. Where concealment is concerned, the handgun has no equal. Even the diminutive HK MP7A1 can't beat the Mk23 for size, and the Mk23 is a fairly large pistol. The military has also made use of the M9 as a suppressed handgun for some time now. To be a truly suppressed weapon, the use of specialized subsonic ammunition is required for the 9mm, as the standard 9mm ball round is supersonic. The standard .45 ACP ball round is already subsonic, so this isn't an issue with the Mk23. The advantages of suppressors on handguns when used for room clearing are many. A suppressor acts as a very efficient flash hider, a factor if operating in an indoor area filled with flammable stores. It also eliminates the ringing in one's ears common when firing without the use of subsonic ammunition and sound suppressors. This latter factor is especially important for unit communications, since ear plugs are a detractor to the unit's efficiency, and can quickly ruin the user's hearing.

Custom Features Become Standard

Many modern handgun design features have become standard by most manufacturers. The reasons for these features often become clear when tactical uses are considered. High visibility sights are a feature seen on many tactical handguns in use today. These are usually in the form of a white dot front sight, with a rear sight that has either two white dots, a vertical white bar, or a u-shaped white outline. The three dot system can be a problem at times, as the dots can be incorrectly aligned, creating major issues with regard to bullet placement. Radioactive night sights are often fitted as an option. Sight rails have recently become quite common. This allows for the attachment of any number of accessories. These often include laser aiming devices, small high intensity flashlights, and red-dot sights. Many pistols now have beveled or flared magazine wells to facilitate faster changes. HK even offers threaded barrels on some USP variants, allowing for easy attachment of sound suppressors. None of these features were common 30 years ago. Most were not even heard of at that time.

This signifies the changing view of the handgun as a purely defensive, last ditch weapon, to one definitely intended for offensive use, or even as a primary weapon for certain jobs. Once again so much for the handgun being an obsolete weapon. Quite the contrary, the tactical needs of modern warfare have given the military sidearm a new lease on life.

The most common handguns in use today seem to be limited to a fairly small selection. That is because after much testing and use, these models have proven the most worthy. The M1911, the Browning HP, Beretta 92, SIG-Sauer, CZ, Glock, HK USP, and to a lesser extent, the Ruger P-series and S&W autos are among the most common in the U.S. The Jericho, a CZ75 clone which is an Israeli made pistol, has seen use in that nation. Seldom seen due to its price tag, the Sphinx AT-2000 was a CZ clone of superior quality. The Springfield XD series is also gaining in popularity, especially among U.S. law enforcement. Experiences in the Middle East have brought about a request for a new .45 caliber service pistol. The HK Mk 23 and Springfield M1911 copies are serving alongside the original M1911s and Beretta M9s, as mentioned earlier.

Wherever ball ammunition is used, the .45 will always prove the more reliable stopping round when compared to the 9mm. My guess is the current economic situation here has been the main reason for no replacement pistol being adopted as of yet. Time will tell if we're to see the return of the .45 caliber U.S. Service pistol.

The issue here is that the 9mm in ball configuration often over penetrates, wasting a good deal of the energy possessed by the round. The difference becomes more apparent when top quality expanding bullets are used in the 9mm. Its reliability as a stopping round is increased dramatically. One of the top 9mm rounds available is the 115 grain + P + JHP. This round, which leaves the muzzle of most pistols between 1300 and 1350 feet per second, is quite reliable as a man stopper, almost equal to the best .45 loads in use. Since The Hague agreement does not allow for the use of expanding bullets, the military often has no choice but to use ball rounds. The issue of whether or not terrorists are viewed as enemy combatants or criminals has become hotly debated. This is likely due, in part, to the desire to use high performance rounds in 9mm service pistols. The mere fact that this issue has even come up is proof that there has been no decrease in the importance of the pistol in modern warfare. Another indicator of the resurgence in military handgun use is the development of modern tactics in handgun training. This has never stopped within the U.S. law enforcement community, where the handgun remains the primary duty weapon. However, in military circles, there has been a realization of the need to take full advantage of the handgun's qualities over other types of small arms. Many of these modern combat pistol tactics were developed by the Israelis. These tactics have become standard among many units worldwide. It is unlikely that an obsolete weapon would receive such widespread focus with regards to training.

What Lies Ahead

For the future, it is reasonable to assume that handguns will maintain a place of importance in modern warfare, especially in counter-terrorist areas of operation. Due to the cost of restocking an entire army with a new caliber of ammunition, it is likely that the 9mm and .45 will continue to be the most common calibers in use in the West, with the 9 × 18mm serving in Russia and Eastern Europe to a lesser extent. The popularity of this last round has been waning since the collapse of communism. Here in the U.S., the .40 S&W round is proving quite popular among the law enforcement community.

As for design, the revolver has already fallen by the wayside. Even the best revolvers can't compete in terms of rapid reloading and firepower. The highest capacity for any centerfire revolver on the market is 8 rounds. This would be considered average by semi-auto standards. The revolver's longtime advantage in terms of reliability has been minimized due to the quality and consistency of modern factory ammunition. In military ammunition, the points most vulnerable to solvent contamination are often sealed with varnish, or crimped, specifically the case mouth and primer face. This helps reduce the chances of excess cleaning solvents or oils collecting on the chambered round and causing a misfire or "dud." It was often this issue that kept the revolver popular. All that was necessary in the event of a misfire was to pull the trigger again. With a pistol, two hands and too much time are necessary to clear the misfire. This issue tends to take a back seat when compared to the advantages offered by pistols in terms of speed and firepower. Making sure to keep excess solvent or oil out of the breech after cleaning helps to minimize this issue.

As for the tactical advantages held by the handgun over other small arms, there are several. The pistol is easily suppressed. Usually, only an extended and threaded barrel is required. The Colt-Browning system does present some problems here, as the barrel tilts in order to facilitate un-locking. Adding the extra weight of a suppressor can lead to functioning issues. Several firms have solved this either through recoil adaptors or use of lightweight materials. With straight recoil systems or fixed barrel, blowback systems, this is not an issue. The Beretta 92 even has a small portion of barrel extending out enough to facilitate threading.[46] The HK Mk 23 and USP Tactical have similar barrels that are factory threaded. With many other models, a special extended barrel must be fitted to the pistol.

The use of suppressors is a great benefit for many indoor operations as well as for standard military jobs. Some suppressors are so effective that the shot cannot be made out beyond a range of 50 yards. This is primarily dependent on terrain. Desert or open areas allow sound to travel much more clearly.

As mentioned earlier, the ability to operate without earplugs is a must for house clearing. Repeated, unsuppressed firing indoors, or for that matter outdoors, will cause permanent hearing damage in short order. The ability of the suppressor to act as an effective flash hider is also appreciated with regards to preserving night vision for all personnel in the immediate area.

For any operation where concealment of weapons is required, the handgun is really the only viable option. Here there may not be room for a suppressor unless it is carried separately and attached after the pistol is drawn. There are no submachine guns or PDWs that can provide this level of concealment. The HK MP5K is one of the smallest subguns made, and it is over a foot long, without a suppressor.

Recently Magpul Industries recognized this problem and introduced the FMG9 (Folding Machine Gun 9mm) submachine gun to better compete with handguns in the concealment area. Time will tell if this idea catches on. More will be covered on the FMG in Chapter 2.

With these advantages alone, the handgun's future is all but guaranteed. Given the conditions of modern warfare, there will be a definite use for a compact, easy to conceal weapon that can be carried easily, leaving one's hands free to perform other duties, and yet still be able to quickly access the weapon when needed.

As for which pistol designs will dominate, with the exception of the Beretta 92 series and a few others, the Colt-Browning short recoil system has, by far, seen the most use among successful models. Unless a new concept comes along, this recoil system will likely continue as the most common method of operation among modern pistol designs. This method of operation has proven reliable under all conditions. It functions when wet, dirty, muddy, sand filled, you name it. The system has been used on pistol designs the world over. No other method of operation in any rifle or handgun can make this claim. Browning clearly knew what he was doing.

Chapter 2

Submachine Guns

The submachine gun (smg) dates back to the trenches of Europe during World War I. The U.S. Civil War had been bad enough, but the world had never before seen the type of carnage that World War I delivered. World War I was a first for many new weapon systems. Machine guns had their origins in the late 19th century, but their true capabilities became clear during the massed troop charges across "no man's land." Poison gas also made its big warfare debut during this time, but with few exceptions, has thankfully not made an encore appearance. It was in the muddy rat infested trenches of the Western Front that troops soon realized the need for a portable weapon that was capable of the same destruction these men had witnessed machine guns providing above. It was initially known as the "trench broom," and that was its intended purpose. The submachine gun provided mobile, short range firepower. It was intended from the start to quickly clear the way for any advance within the trenches. It was equally useful for defense in these same ditches.

The first true submachine gun was the German Bergmann MP/18.[1] The Italian Villar Perosa was developed a bit earlier (around 1915), but the Italian design was not originally meant for trench clearing, although it was later adapted to this purpose once its potential was realized.[2]

There were other early influential designs like the American Thompson, the German MP40, the British Sten, and the Soviet PPSh-41, but none of these early designs still see military service. These designs used early 20th century technology, and in that they were heavier and longer than today's modern submachine gun designs.

Today's most successful submachine guns are much lighter, though not necessarily any more effective than the earlier designs. The sub-gun's primary purpose has not changed. It was always meant to provide short range automatic fire, and was usually used in the assault role. Traditionally the sub-gun has never been known for great accuracy. This has nothing to do with quality issues but rather design. Most early submachine guns, almost all in fact, were designed to fire from the open bolt position.[3]

What this means is that the bolt is drawn to the rear with the recoil spring compressed, until the trigger releases the sear mechanism. Open bolt firing systems are common on many weapons designed to provide automatic fire. This is necessary to prevent a "cook off," or a chambered round heating up to the point of powder combustion. It is surprising how quickly gun barrels heat up during automatic fire. The accuracy issue stems from the heavy mass of the bolt flying forward after the trigger is pulled. This causes a dramatic shift in the balance of the weapon. It is more noticeable when trying to aim accurately for a first shot. During automatic fire it is less noticeable because so many other forces are acting on the weapon, from recoil, muzzle climb, barrel torque, and the shooter's muscles trying to cope with these forces.

This issue has usually limited the submachine gun's role through the years, and with the development of the modern assault rifle, which has many of the same capabilities, there has been a decreased demand for this pistol caliber weapon. It does not have the same range potential as the assault rifle, nor in most cases, the accuracy. It also does not have anywhere near the hitting power. For most of their history, submachine guns have been chambered in either the 7.62 × 25mm, 9 × 19mm or .45 ACP, all popular pistol calibers as well. These chamberings limit their hitting power and severely limit their range. Most manufacturers list the maximum effective range for submachine guns as 200m. Most modern assault rifles are capable of double this range or better. This power limitation also translates into body armor issues. Pistol calibers generally do not perform nearly as well as rifle calibers on even low threat level body armor.[4]

Due to these shortcomings, the military's use of the submachine gun has gradually decreased for most of the latter half of the 20th century. However, modern warfare has kept the submachine gun alive for a few very important reasons. First, the submachine gun is usually far smaller than the average assault rifle. For example, the Israeli designed UZI measures 17 inches with its stock folded, while the popular M4A1 carbine measures closer to 30 inches with its stock collapsed, even though the UZI weighs roughly 1½ pounds more empty. The submachine gun's use of pistol cartridges allows for shorter actions and much shorter effective barrel lengths. There are short barrel carbines like the Russian AKS-74U and the German HK 53. These weapons fire rifle calibers from barrels under 9 inches in length. This creates many problems. Rifle cartridges were never designed to be fired from such short barrels. The resultant muzzle flash and blast are horrible. Also, the velocities are reduced to the point where effective ballistic data must be re-calculated. In some cases, re-calibrated sights are even a good idea. This is another example of adapting existing designs to fill multiple roles.

The primary job of the submachine gun today is in the role of the counter-terrorist/hostage rescue weapon.[5] It fills this role much better than many short barrel rifles. The rifle's excessive muzzle blast and flash aside, deterioration of hearing and eyesight is reduced with submachine guns, especially if sound suppressors are used. Submachine guns are much easier to effectively suppress than rifle caliber weapons. This is mainly due to muzzle velocity. As mentioned in the chapter on handguns, a bullet must remain at subsonic levels or a loud "crack" will result. Reducing the muzzle velocity of a standard SS109 5.56mm 62 grain bullet to less than 1100 fps means a huge reduction in terminal effect, as well as adding another 5 to 8 inches to the carbine's already longer dimensions. This can become a big problem when attempting to maneuver within the confines of small rooms and hallways.

There is also an advantage to using pistol calibers for hostage rescue work. Again, most modern buildings are constructed with drywall and wood or aluminum framing, none of which can be relied on to stop a bullet. Pistol rounds do not penetrate nearly as well as rifle calibers. This means less likelihood of a bullet passing through a terrorist and hitting hostages or fellow unit members. However if the terrorists are wearing body armor, the situation changes considerably. Good intelligence gathering is a must, helping to better prepare the unit before entry.

Perhaps a final reason for the sub-gun's continued use is that it fits the typical modern warfare scenario quite well. It is compact, usually light weight, especially the newer designs, and despite its range limitations, it can hit a man sized target quite easily at ranges up to 200m. As for its open bolt issues, several popular designs fire from a closed bolt position. In these cases, heat issues can become a problem depending on design. This is a tradeoff some units are willing to live with. More will be discussed on the closed bolt issue as particular models are examined.

While there have been many functional and durable designs made over the years, not all have seen great commercial success. The reasons for this can vary greatly, but common factors in successful submachine gun designs are compact size, good handling characteristics, ease of maintenance, acceptable accuracy, and most importantly, reliability under all conditions. These qualities, in fact, apply to all successful service weapons.

Some of the most successful models achieved their success not because they were superior to all others, but because they filled some particular niche, for example the Colt 9mm submachine gun. It did not bring anything new to this class of weapon, but it did offer simplified training due to its kinship with the U.S. M16. Its controls are identical to those found on its older brother with the exception of the forward bolt assist (more on this later).

As for the models still in use in significant numbers, there are actually not many. Of all the successful models made over the years, only a few still see front line service, although older designs are held in reserve. Good examples of this are Sweden's Gustav m/45B and Britain's Sterling L2A3 (both 9 × 19mm).

Oldies but Goodies

The Gustav is a Swedish design that has also been produced in Egypt, where it was known as the "Port Said" and also saw production in Indonesia. Although no longer standard issue, it was one of the most successful submachine gun designs of the post war era. Estimates are over 300,000 produced.[6] It was popular among U.S. Navy Sea Air Land (SEAL) teams during the Vietnam War. After Sweden stopped supplying weapons to the U.S., the Navy even managed to get Smith & Wesson to produce small numbers of a close copy, known as the M76.[7] The Gustav's reliability is often considered to be because of its 36 round magazine design. The magazine was tapered from rear to front to keep the cartridges better aligned while feeding. The straight sided magazines on many other designs like the Sten were known for jamming on occasion. The British Sterling, while no longer standard issue in England, was one of the most successful designs of all time. It is still produced in India, where it is known as the 1A1. The L2A3 was the primary model in service before its retirement. It has also been produced in Canada as the C1.[8] This version utilized more metal stampings as opposed to the castings employed on the British version.

The Sterling traces its origins to late World War II. It was originally known as the Patchett. The Sterling was far superior in quality of manufacture to the Sten gun it replaced. The Sterling kept the left-side mounted magazine layout of the Sten. It looked awkward and offset the weapon's balance, but the feed rollers built into the magazine follower helped with the extreme reliability of this weapon, though some credit this to the curvature of the magazine. It also had helical grooves cut into the bolt to catch dirt and carbon buildup. These extras, combined with the quality of manufacture, helped make this one of the most reliable submachine guns ever, if more costly than many others. It was only replaced in the late 80s by the Enfield L85A1 (later L85A2) bullpup rifle. This decision has come to be regretted by some within the British military, given the track record of the L85A1. The A2 version was much improved.[9]

The Sterling saw use in many British conflicts over the years, and should the British find themselves in any future large scale urban or jungle conflicts, they will no doubt bring the Sterling out of retirement. It is surprising that it is not still standard issue, as it would seem ideal for British troops serving in the urban areas of the Middle East. The British Special Air Service (SAS) has traditionally used the HK MP5 over the Sterling as their primary counter-terrorist (CT) weapon.[10] This was likely because of the HK's closed bolt operating system and its ability to easily mount accessories. At any rate the Sterling was an iconic submachine gun which served the crown well during the latter half of the 20th century.

The silenced version, the L34A1 (Indian 2A1) has also proven itself over the years. It was used by the British Special Boat Squadron as standard for many years.[11] The L34A1 is built with a ported barrel which lowers the velocity of the standard 9mm round to subsonic levels, making for a very quiet weapon. This is known as an integral silencer, as opposed to an add-on suppressor which requires the use of subsonic ammunition to be most effective.

One of the Sterling's best features was its reasonable rate of fire. Its cyclic rate was 550 rounds per minute (rpm); much higher than this, and a weapon becomes a waste of ammunition. There are different opinions on this, but higher rates of fire do cause a weapon to become less controllable unless fitted with a highly efficient muzzle break. Also any weapon with a very high rate of fire will require a barrel change before too long. This is something most individual weapons are incapable of. Many early medium and heavy machine guns were water cooled to deal with heating issues. This is not an option for a submachine gun, so the Sterling's relatively slow rate of fire worked quite well.

While on the subject of controlling a weapon during automatic fire, there should be an explanation of the proper handling technique for the Sterling. The left side mounted magazine was never meant to be a handhold. The Sterling was provided with a perforated cooling jacket surrounding the barrel. This served as the proper place for the support hand. For right handed users, the magazine would rest over the crook of the left arm to aid in support of the weapon. The Sterling proved difficult for left-handed users, but this was a minor issue (unless you were left handed). Actually, many weapons systems are problematic for left-handed shooters. This was merely exaggerated with the Sterling due to its left side magazine. This was also an issue with the earlier Sten gun. With both designs, the balance of the weapon actually improved as the magazine was emptied. This aside, the Sterling was an excellent design and was very reasonable in weight at 6 pounds empty. The silenced version weighed almost 2 pounds more in the same condition. Both the standard and silenced models are still in production by Indian Ordnance Factories. Being one of the most heavily produced submachine guns of all time, and because they were so well made, they will likely be encountered for many years and in many locations around the world.

The Sterling does have some limitations for urban operations, as it cannot easily mount many of today's popular accessories. Also, its side mounted magazine creates maneuvering issues in confined spaces. As a standard field submachine gun however, it has few equals.

While the Sterling and Gustav are not likely to see much future counter-terrorist work, the next weapon to be covered has seen a great deal of such work, and current versions are still being developed today.

The New Standard

The Israelis had to begin their modern history with a good mix of weapons from various makers. They soon realized that it was not a good idea to rely too much on weapons supplied by outside sources. Luckily for them, the first weapon they designed for mass production has also proven to be one of the best designs of all time. The UZI was one of the first of many successful native designs.

Designed by Uziel Gal, an Israeli officer, the UZI would soon become the standard for the modern submachine gun.[12] It entered service in the mid–1950s, and several versions have been introduced since.

The original model had a crude shaped wooden stock, but a bottom-folding metal stock soon replaced it. This was to become the standard version for many years. It was later joined by the Mini-UZI and Micro-UZI in the 1980s and most recently the UZI-Pro. Some of these are available in both closed bolt and open bolt versions to better fit the needs of today's service units. The original model was only available as an open bolt weapon, though a closed bolt was offered later. Its layout bore a great deal of resemblance to a cz/23, a Czech design from the 1940s which utilized a pistol grip located near the weapon's center of gravity. This was to allow better control of the weapon as well as making it easier to change magazines in the dark, as the magazine well was located within the pistol grip on both designs. This is made possible by using the telescoping bolt concept. This is common today, but was novel at the time. In a telescoping bolt weapon the majority of the bolt wraps around the barrel, allowing for much shorter overall weapon, while still using a standard length barrel. This feature was perfected with the UZI.

It also had many other useful features, including its heavy use of stampings to help lower cost and shorten production time. Since less machining was required, there was a reduction in labor costs, due to less need for skilled machinists. The receiver stampings were designed with grooves to catch sand buildup, a plus for a weapon intended for use in desert environments. The UZI also had a passive grip safety to help reduce the chances of an accidental discharge. This was located at the rear of the grip much like that of the Colt M1911 pistol. The cocking handle was located above the receiver cover, a feature useful for left-handed shooters. The cocking handle was grooved out, as it would otherwise obscure the iron sights.

The UZI's rate of fire is around 600 rpm. This is slow enough to help with controlling the weapon during automatic fire. Later versions have a much higher rate of fire, as the bolts are lighter in weight and all versions operate by the blowback principle, which means the breech is held closed during firing only by the bolt's mass and tension from the recoil spring. The standard folding stocked UZI measures

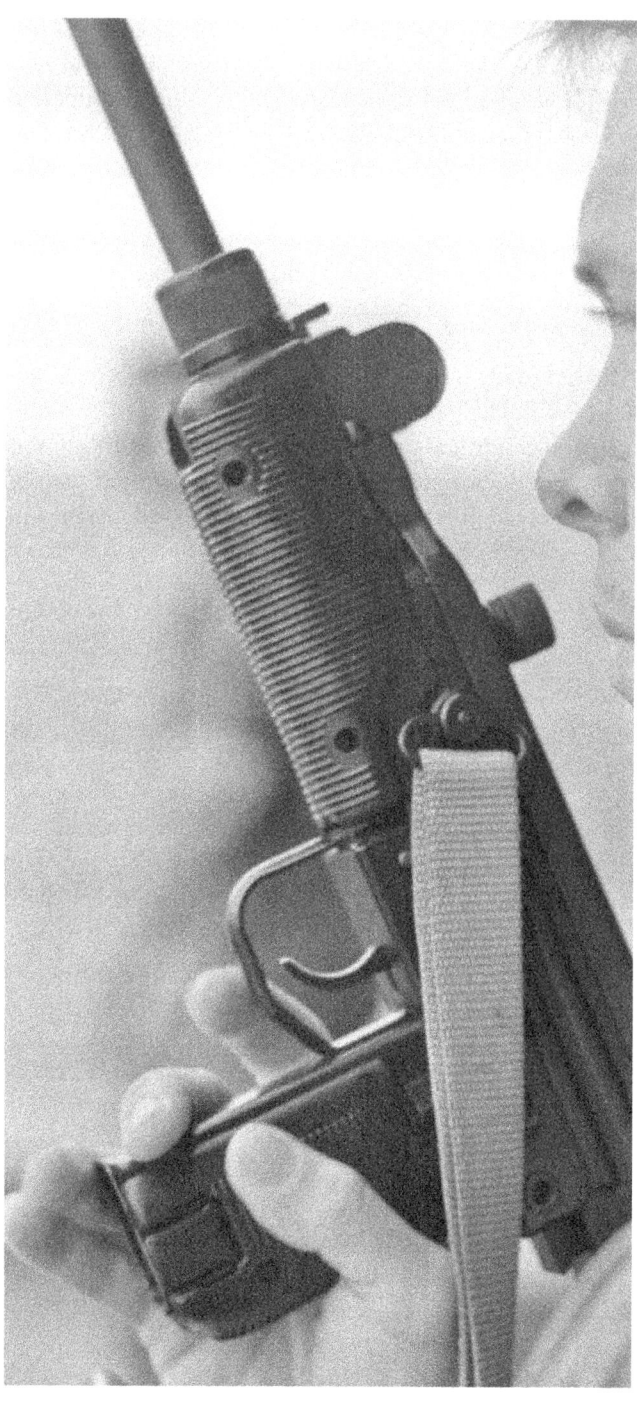

The standard model UZI, an iconic post-war design. This one has had its magazine removed (PH3 T. Olsen, U.S. Navy).

17 inches folded, 25 inches extended. Its weight is just over 7½ pounds empty, not a featherweight, but not unbearable given its reliability in use.[13]

One of the UZI's best qualities is its ease of field stripping. This is a feature common on many better designs. The barrel could be removed by simply unscrewing a collar located in front of the forend. This also allows for easy suppressor mounting, as the suppressor simply screws on in place of the collar. One feature the UZI lacks is a bracket for mounting optics. Some aftermarket companies have designed mounting systems to correct this.

In use, the UZI has proven itself time and again. The near perfect balance due to its centrally located grip allows for easy one handed operation. The Mini-UZI tends to be more popular for counter-terrorist teams due to its lighter weight, smaller size, and higher rate of fire (sometimes preferred by CT units). The Mini-UZI measures slightly shorter at just over 14 inches folded (roughly 23½ inches extended). Its empty weight is nearly 1½ pounds less and its rate of fire is between 950–1100 rpm depending on open or closed bolt operation. The closed bolt version is more likely preferred by CT units for its accuracy potential with first shots. The Mini-UZI introduced cuts in the barrel to help control muzzle climb. It also had a much different folding stock design which can serve as a vertical forward grip when folded. This feature is also seen on the Micro-UZI.[14]

The Micro-UZI is almost too light, being more like a machine pistol with a rate of fire of 1200 rpm. It is offered in closed bolt only, and has tungsten added to the bolt to increase its mass.[15] It would appear that the closed bolt Micro-Uzi version was intended mostly for counter-terrorist operations, but units will no doubt have different views as to which version is best for their needs. For example the Micro-UZI is far easier to conceal. The brand new UZI-Pro model is roughly the size of the Micro-UZI but has a series of accessory mounting rails. It also has a redesigned fore grip and is constructed with far more plastic to help control weight. The cyclic rate is likely similar to that of the Micro-UZI.

The UZI has been offered in several calibers, including .45 ACP, 9mm, .41 AE, and even .22 LR for training purposes. The 9mm is the most common caliber by far, as the magazine capacity of the .45 version is quite limited at only 16 rounds. The 9mm magazines have been offered in several capacities with 20, 25, and 32 round being the most common.

With many different versions offered by the manufacturer, there should be a model to suit any user's needs. The reliability of this design is legendary, and these assets combined should keep this submachine gun around until conventional ammunition is no longer used. When the world stops using the 9mm, then maybe the UZI will die out, maybe.

There was another telescoping bolt sub-gun to enter service in the 1950s. It also proved to be utterly dependable. It had a layout that was different enough from that of the UZI to suit any service unit that did not care for the central pistol grip concept.

The Italian Answer to the UZI

The Italian Beretta model 12 would also serve to set new standards over the years. The model 12 was roughly half an inch shorter than the UZI in its folded position. Its weight was also slightly less at around 6 ½ pounds empty. This model would be replaced in the 1970s by the model 12S. This was improved in some areas. It had a more conventional fire selector lever. The original version used a cross bolt button that was pushed to one side or the other to select between semi and full auto fire modes. There were other minor improvements as well. These were primarily in the area of sights, the folding stock mechanism, the butt catch, and finish. The latest and current production model is the PM12-S2. This version has an added half cock safety as well as a cocking handle safety to help prevent accidental discharge. The model 12 series uses a passive grip safety like that of the UZI, but the one on the Beretta it is located in front of the grip. When the firing hand releases its grip, the safety is activated. The 12S and PM12-S2 also have a tough epoxy coating to help prevent corrosion of the weapon's exterior. The bore and chamber are chrome plated for similar reasons. The Beretta's layout, as mentioned earlier, is somewhat different from that of the UZI. The weapon was designed with a pistol grip as well as a vertical fore grip, where the UZI had a horizontal forend and a centrally located pistol grip for the firing hand. The rate of fire is also slightly lower at 550 rpm. This rate of fire has remained despite each subsequent model increasing in weight somewhat. The model 12S weighed in at just over 7 pounds empty and the PM12-S2 is closer to the UZI in weight at just over 7½ pounds.[16]

The model 12 is produced by Taurus in Brazil, and in Indonesia by PT Pindad. It has proven quite popular, and the latest version can use several useful accessories like a unique light with the battery pack located in the forward grip. Various sighting systems can be mounted as well. A suppressor can also be mounted with relative ease.

In use, the Beretta is reputed to be more controllable than the UZI series, though this would seem to be a matter of personal preference and opinion. With the various modern accessories available, it seems clear that there's no significant chance of the Beretta going

Italy's answer to the UZI, the 9mm Beretta model 12S. This proved to be one of the most dependable post-war designs to see common use (Cpl. D.S. Kotecki, U.S. Marine Corps).

away anytime soon. It fills a void in that it offers reliability on par with the UZI, it offers two vertical grips, which some prefer and claim offers better control during automatic fire.

Magazines have been offered in several capacities over the years, including 20, 32, and 40 rounds. The 32 round seems to be the most common. The corrosion resistant coating on the later models is a plus, reducing the need to constantly wipe down the exterior of the weapon. The model 12 uses primarily stampings and other modern construction techniques to help control the cost just as with the UZI. This allows for easy transfer of technology, which may help explain some of its success in overseas manufacture, though the quality of its design no doubt helped. Much of the credit for the design must go to its chief architect, Dominico Salza.[17]

A New CT Design

The Beretta wasn't the only Italian firm to produce a successful submachine gun in recent years. The Italian firm Societa Italiana Technologie Speciali S.p.A (SITES) had developed a design in the mid–1980s that would be a first on several levels.

The Spectre M4 was a small package with a big bite. Closed bolt in operation, it used a top folding stock that allowed for a short overall length of less than 14 inches, it added almost 9 inches to this once extended. The empty weight was under 6½ pounds, which was fairly conventional. However it utilized a 50 round magazine that was no longer than more conventional 30 to 32 round varieties. It accomplished this by holding the rounds divided into four columns within the extra thick magazine body. This is sometimes called a casket magazine. This style of magazine has a divider in the middle of the magazine body to help with keeping cartridges aligned while feeding. The Russians have recently attempted this with AK magazines, but there have been questions regarding their reliability. With the Spectre, this concept seems to have worked better. Having this much firepower meant fewer magazine changes and fewer full pockets on the user's tactical gear. The Spectre also was a first in that it was designed with a de-cocking lever and double-action trigger mechanism. This allows for a rapid response weapon for counter-terrorism or close quarter operations. The weapon did not have to be carried cocked with the safety on. It merely needed to be brought on target and the trigger pulled. Accuracy was affected slightly by the long, heavy trigger pull, but this was unlikely to be noticed in the middle of a firefight. Another first for the Spectre was its solution to "cook-off" problems usually associated with closed bolt operation. The Spectre was designed to forcefully draw cool surrounding air through its barrel jacket during firing.

In layout, the Spectre was similar to its Beretta cousin in that it was equipped with two pistol grips instead of the more conventional pistol grip/horizontal forearm. The Spectre's rate of fire belies its intended use. Its cyclic rate is roughly 850 rpm.[18] Oddly, the Spectre didn't last in production. It was discontinued after the late 90s and was briefly revived by a new manufacturer for a short period of time.[19] This is unusual given that the weapon was adopted by quite a few European agencies. Perhaps sales numbers just weren't large enough to generate profits. This is a bit of a shame, as the weapon seemed to be a perfect tactical fit for modern urban combat operations. The Spectre's demise is likely another example of the submachine gun's gradual decline among military and law enforcement units worldwide. Many of these units have opted to use PDWs or short barreled carbines firing rifle cartridges.

The Ideal Entry Gun

Perhaps the most successful and certainly most popular submachine gun in use today is the HK MP5. The MP5 has been used by over 40 nations throughout its history.[20] For years it was a standard weapon for counter-terrorist units worldwide. In this role, it was close to ideal. It fires accurately from a closed bolt position, yet due to its fluted chamber, suffers little from the likelihood of "cook off" issues. Its rate of fire is higher than that of the Sterling or UZI at 800–900 rpm, yet this is generally desired in a CT weapon. It can mount many of today's popular accessories. In fact HK has designed several of its own accessories just for the MP5. There are several types of optical mounts offered. HK's quick detach mount was the primary option for many years. Thankfully, this was a well designed mount. It can be easily removed and replaced without disturbing the zero of the sight. This was very rugged and should the optics fail, the iron sights were still visible with the mount attached. A high profile mount like this was required, as a site mounted too close

The original HK MP5A2 9mm, one of the world's all time classics. This model is fitted with the wide "tropical" fore grip, better suited for larger hands (Sgt. L. Bradford, U.S. Army).

to the bore axis would be obscured by the front sight hood. This is a problem with other weapons, including the U.S. M16 and the Russian AK series.

The MP5 series is offered in many versions and was made in .40 S&W and 10mm for law enforcement use as well.[21] It is relatively light, though this varies with particular model. The design of the MP5 was based upon their successful 7.62mm G3 rifle. This rifle itself had its roots in design dating back to the German STG 45 tested during World War II. The roller-locked delayed blowback concept was later developed more fully in Spain as many of the German engineers fled to that country and continued their work. HK later adapted this design to suit needs for a German Service rifle. In effect, the design just came home, as many executives and workers were former Mauser employees during the war. In fact HK's founders were former Mauser people.[22] It is unclear if any lingering attitudes existed over this issue, but the French did insist on a native design and refused the G3 as their service rifle. History aside, the MP5 has become one of HK's cornerstone weapons.

Around 1964, HK adapted the roller locking system to the 9mm round, and soon after, the new submachine gun was adopted by German police agencies. Its real success began after a German CT unit adopted it as its standard submachine gun. When the British SAS chose to adopt it as well, and the world saw it on television during the Iranian embassy siege in 1980, the MP5 became an overnight success. Since then it has become one of the most widely used submachine guns of all time.

The MP5 was originally offered in A2 and A3 versions. The MP5A2 featured a fixed plastic stock much like that of the G3 rifle, while the A3 model used HK's telescoping stock. This latter item was slightly different from that of the rifle. The weight of the collapsible stock version was over ½ pound greater at a little more than 6¼ pounds. Initially only semi or full auto options were available, 2 and 3 round burst options were later offered. Today, various combinations of these are fitted to ambidextrous trigger groups.

The classic counter-terrorist submachine gun, the HK MP5 SD3 suppressed 9mm (J. Yoder, Department of Defense).

HK decided to add an integrally silenced model to the MP5 line in 1974. The MP5SD was similar to the Sterling L34A1 in purpose and its barrel was drilled near the breech to allow for propellant gas to escape, lowering the velocity to subsonic levels. The surrounding suppressor was initially aluminum, though a later U.S. Navy version uses a stainless steel suppressor.[23] This was done to increase its durability in marine environments. The silenced versions are available with the same trigger options as the standard models.

The smallest version is known as the MP5K, the "K" standing for "kurz," German for "short." This model was introduced in the mid–1970s to provide units with a much more concealable weapon. The original MP5A2 measured a bit less than 27 inches, the MP5A3 was just over 19 inches with the stock collapsed. The silenced models were about 4 inches longer. The newer MP5K model had no stock fitted. Instead it was equipped with a flat butt plate that was fitted with a sling swivel. This, combined with a barrel length of only 4½ inches helped make for a very compact submachine gun. It was really more of a machine pistol. Its rate of fire was also higher than the standard model at 900 rpm. The MP5KA1 was equipped with simpler low profile open sights. This was to lessen the chance of the weapon snagging when drawn in a hurry. Some feel that complicated sights on a submachine gun that uses no stock are unnecessary at any rate. This primarily depends on the skill and experience of the user, however.

The MP5K-PDW was designed by HK-USA, which wanted the size of the K model but the option of a folding stock. A U.S. company, Choate Machine and Tool, designed a side folding synthetic stock for this purpose.[24] A small portion of barrel was added to the 4½ inches of the K model as well. This was done to allow for suppressor threading and fitting the lugs of the standard MP5A2. The lugs were there to facilitate attachments like a flash hider, grenade launcher or a blank firing device. As a side note, the same muzzle design is used on the U.S. Navy MP5-N model. This was really just an MP5A3 with a threaded muzzle and a new ambidextrous synthetic trigger group, which later became standard on many versions. The MP5K-PDW measures 14½ inches closed and just short of 24 inches open and weighs roughly 6¼ pounds empty, while the "K" models were 12¾ inches long and 4½ pounds empty.[25]

There were two large caliber MP5 versions made in the 90s. The MP5/10 and MP5/40 were chambered for the 10mm and .40 S&W rounds respectively. These were equipped with straight synthetic magazines as opposed to the curved steel magazines that were standard on the other MP5 9mm models. All magazines had 30 round capacities, though the synthetic magazines had fittings molded into the sides to allow them to be clipped together for rapid magazine changes. These plastic magazines were also translucent to allow the user to quickly see how many rounds remained. On the more common MP5 9mm, a 15 round steel magazine was also offered. This is not seen as often and was probably reserved for the smaller MP5K models for concealment purposes. Early 9mm MP5s had straight 30 round steel magazines, but the design was curved to improve the reliability.[26] There are clamping systems made to allow the 9mm steel magazines to be fitted together like those of the .40 and 10mm models. If so equipped, it is easy to change out an empty weapon; the balance of the weapon is thrown off when these clamps are used as weight is added off center. With the user's adrenaline pumping, this is not likely to be noticed in battle. As a CQB weapon, the MP5 has few equals. It has a fairly high rate of fire but it is still easily controlled. It can easily be fitted with any modern accessory and it possesses rifle type accuracy due to its closed bolt design. It does not have the ability to penetrate body armor as well as a rifle caliber weapon, but often times, this is not needed. The MP5 is relatively light, although there are lighter weapons being made today that are heavily constructed of plastics. These however, often have more felt recoil due to their lighter weight. It is unlikely that any new type of system will come along in the near future to challenge the MP5's supremacy in this role.

Many submachine guns popular today do not have a last round bolt catch. This seems to be more popular with American weapons than with European models. While not a necessary feature, it is useful to know for certain that a weapon is empty, and not wonder if it has misfired or worse, suffered a hang-fire that can go off at any moment. HK has addressed this issue in their MP5/10 and MP5/40 models with the addition of this feature.

The MP5 isn't HK's only design in the submachine gun market. They must have foreseen at least a limited future for this weapon class, as they introduced a more modern submachine gun in the 1990s. HK managed to make good use of recent technological advancements in the area of plastics in particular. They used as many modern polymer components as possible. As a result the entire family is lighter in weight than the standard MP5 series. The Universal Machine Pistol (UMP) is made with a folding stock as standard and is produced in three different calibers: 9mm, .40 S&W, and a slightly heavier model in .45 ACP. The first two models are just over 4½ pounds empty, while the .45 version is roughly ¼ pound more. The .45 version uses a straight 25 round plastic magazine, while the magazine capacity of the other models is 30 rounds, with the 9mm version having a curved pattern. The .45 also has a slightly lower cyclic rate of around 600 rpm vs. 650 for the .40 and 9mm versions. The magazine of the 9mm version is not interchangeable with that of the MP 5. The .40 caliber version was obviously built with the U.S. law enforcement market in mind. Dimensions are the same for all three, roughly 17¾ inches folded, and 27¼ inches extended.[27]

All three can quickly mount accessories due to the rail systems included. The Picatinny rail system is fast becoming standard on many new weapons and older models are often retrofitted with rail systems that match this. A quick attach suppressor is offered for all three models. The .40 UMP is being used by several U.S. agencies and the other calibers are in service with various nations. Time will tell if it can match the MP5's reputation. Given the number of nations using this model, it's off to a good start.

Designs from Around the World

The South Korean Daewoo K7 is a silenced 9 × 19mm design that looks like a Colt 9mm with a sliding wire stock similar to that of the old U.S. M3 "Grease Gun."[28] It was likely meant for special operations use, as the 38th parallel is still a dangerous place.

The Chinese and Russians have also developed their own post war designs. None of these are seen as commonly as the AK family of assault rifles, which have been heavily exported by both nations for years.

The Chinese have two relatively modern and unique designs, the type 79 and the type 85, which is also made in a suppressed version. The type 79 is unusual in that it fires from a locked breech gas operated system. Using a short stroke gas piston, it is quite light at less than 4¼ pounds empty. Also unusual is the choice of the 7.62 × 25mm Tokarev round that the Soviets used during World War II. The Chinese also produce a subsonic version of this cartridge for use in the suppressed type 85. The type 85 reverts to a simpler blowback operation but is still roughly the same weight as the type 79 with a suppressed model weighing about a pound more. It is unlikely that the subsonic 7.62 × 25mm round can perform very well beyond more than 50m as the bullet is fairly light to begin with, and reducing its velocity to less than 1100 fps would destroy its ballistic potential.[29]

The Russians have also done some recent submachine gun design work of their own. Perhaps the most common model in use by the Russians is the PP-19 Bizon. This is chambered for the 9 × 18mm Makarov cartridge and uses a unique 64 round detachable cylindrical shaped magazine that mounts beneath the barrel. When fitted it looks like a grenade launcher attachment. A 9 × 19mm export version is made which has a similar 53 round magazine. There's also a .380 caliber version with a 64 round capacity, as well as a 7.62 × 25mm version which uses a standard 35 round box magazine fed from below the gun in the normal fashion.

The PP-19 uses more than half of the same parts as the Russian AK-74, including the side folding stock. The Bizon-2 is the standard model and there is an integrally suppressed 2-03 model offered as well. All other models can fit a sound suppressor if required. Weight varies with model, but all are relatively light in the 6 to 7 pound range. Length varies a bit from under 18 inches folded, 27¼ inches extended, while the 9 × 19mm is a bit longer at roughly 22½ inches folded and just over 31 inches extended. The design has seen combat use in Chechnya among other places. One final note, the design uses two primary cartridges in 9 × 18mm, a standard round, and a new high pressure round that actually lowers the rate of fire due to longer recoil time. This lowers the cyclic rate from approximately 700 rpm to 650.[30]

The Russians have developed several other new models as well, and some of these, while not widely adopted, have seen combat use. The PP-93, the AeK-919 and the SR2 are all chambered in 9 × 18mm, and there is a new 9 × 21mm round for one version of the SR2. The PP-2000 is a modern design in 9 × 19mm which has seen adoption outside of Russia on a limited basis. None of these designs seem to offer any significant benefit over today's successful models available in the West.

The submachine guns covered here are by far the most common and have proven the most capable in operational use. However there is one new concept that is still in development but may have a future for certain operations.

Russia developed a folding submachine gun in the '90s appropriately named the PP-90. This idea has also been tried experimentally beginning in the 1980s. Recently an American firm, Magpul Industries, introduced a modern version of this concept in 2008.

The Future

The FMG9 is really a housing that holds the Glock 18 machine pistol which can be fitted within the casing, in effect turning the pistol into a folding submachine gun. The housing is largely built of polymer and appears to work quite well. When folded, the package resembles a laptop computer battery. It can be quickly unfolded into a very deadly shoulder fired weapon. This idea has merit for concealment purposes, but anyone attempting to pass the weapon off as anything else would be quickly discovered. However, it does offer the option of being easily concealed, while still being controllable during automatic fire.

There is also a new design in .45 ACP known as the KRISS. It appears to be a well thought out design that redirects the recoil of the .45 in a downward direction to help with controlling the weapon during automatic fire. Similar concepts have been tried in this regard, such as the Finnish Jati-matic developed in the early 1980s. The Jati was another modern plastic design that should have been far more successful. It differed from conventional models in that the bolt recoiled at an upward angle intended to force the muzzle downward, allowing for controllable one handed firing.

Quite a few original ideas show promise but never achieve commercial success. This is unfortunate, as some of the ideas developed in the past performed quite well and would be perfect for urban combat use. While the submachine guns covered so far comprise the majority of those in use today, there is one more that has made some market headway in recent years.

The M16 Submachine Gun

In the late 1980s, Colt decided to produce a 9mm submachine gun based largely on the basic layout of its M16 Commando model. The Colt 9mm submachine gun differs considerably from the M16 in operation. It is a closed bolt, blowback operated weapon, as opposed to the M16's gas impingement system. In terms of fire controls, however, it is almost identical. It does have a large, awkward looking case deflector positioned just to the rear of the ejection port. While this is roughly the same location as the case deflector on the rifle version, it is quite different in size and profile. It is immediately recognizable as a submachine gun when fitted with its standard 32 round box magazine. This magazine is based roughly on the UZI design, but has a different locking notch, as the two weapons did not lock in the same manner. The magazine was fitted into the same port as that of the standard M16 and as a result, it looks peculiar due to the much smaller profile of the magazine. However, these similarities allow for a large degree of commonality. This is true in terms of both parts and training. This makes for very easy transition from rifle to submachine gun and vice versa. The only other noticeable difference is its lack of a forward bolt assist. This was a device forged into the upper receiver of the M16A1 and later models. This device stemmed from the need to ensure the bolt was fully locked as the rifle became fouled. Much more will be discussed on this issue when the M16 rifle and carbine models are discussed in later chapters. As the 9mm model does not possess a locking bolt, this feature was deemed unnecessary. In fact, without a magazine inserted, it will be very difficult to tell this weapon apart from an early M16 Commando model aside from the case deflector.

There are 3 basic versions made. The first is the basic model 635, which has a 10½ inch barrel and a semi or full auto option selector switch. The second has the semi-auto or three round burst option. The third version has a shorter 7 inch barrel with a simpler front sight set up which did away with the large front site post most often associated with the M16. This last model was designed at the request of a U.S. government agency. There is also a unique buffer designed for this model which lowers the rate of fire by 100 to 200 rpm. On the other two models, the standard rate of fire is between 700 to 1000 rpm depending on the type of ammunition used. From this rather high rate of fire combined with the choice of caliber, it seems clear that this was designed from the start as a close quarter battle weapon. It allowed for low cost training for any units that were already familiar with the M16 series. Operational controls are the same, as are most takedown and cleaning procedures. All of this is a plus when trying to issue appropriate weapon systems on a budget.

It is surprising that Colt has not produced a .45 ACP version as well, given the increased stopping power of this round. The physical size of the .45 ACP may have been a limitation, however, as trying to adapt a large caliber to a weapon designed for a small caliber doesn't always go as planned. The size of the magazine well is likely a key issue here. This aside, adapting the basic M16 layout to the 9mm was clearly a success, as quite a few U.S. law enforcement units have adopted this weapon as standard. Dimensionally it is also quite similar to the M16 Commando model. It measures a bit over 25½ inches with its stock collapsed and roughly 29 inches extended. Its weight is less than 6 pounds empty, making it just a bit heavier than the MP5A2, a model it often competes with for market share. This weapon isn't really an example of a better mousetrap, just one that is convenient for training purposes. Having backing from a defense firm the size of Colt doesn't hurt either. This may have been partly responsible for its success, but to be fair, it has proven itself in operational use.

The submachine gun is kept in reserve by many units and is still used as standard by some, as it does fill the close quarter battle role perhaps better than any other weapon available. It does this by being powerful enough to do the job without the severe over penetration that tends to result from the use of rifle calibers. Most 9mm submachine guns also tend to have less recoil than these short rifles. While there is often concern over the 9mm's ability to stop an opponent, the use of high performance rounds can make the smaller caliber submachine guns more than adequate for the task at hand. With the current trends in warfare conditions, they may very well see resurgence in use. They are still popular among one group in particular due to the small size of certain models.

A Budget UZI

Organized crime has always made good use of modern weaponry. The submachine gun offers what many criminal groups desire, high firepower in the smallest possible package. The historical connection here explains the popularity of the Thompson, the Ingram Mac 10, and the UZI among members of organized crime. The Mac 10 was used on occasion by U.S. military units, but its rate of fire was generally considered too high. It looked very much like a low cost version of the Micro-UZI, though the Micro-UZI fires from a closed bolt and the Mac 10 was an open bolt weapon. The even smaller Mac 11 was offered in .380 ACP. None of these models saw widespread tactical use and have died out due to several issues. They do show up from time to time among various criminal organizations, however. The Mac 10 probably sees the most use in the entertainment industry. From the tactical perspective, the Mac was really too light (just over 6 pounds empty) and had a rate of fire that was far too difficult to control. The Mac never saw a great deal of use or widespread adoption and with the introduction of the Micro-UZI, its days were numbered. Its production first ended when the initial manufacturer went out of business. It has been revived from time to time through various manufacturers, though none saw great commercial success. It could possibly show up again due to its ease of production, low cost, small size, and firepower. All of these fit with today's production goals of getting the most for one's dollar or investing very little and getting an adequate weapon for your return. In terms of quality, the Mac 10 was never much more than a modern Sten gun. It was constructed primarily from stampings and welding and had few extras.

There is an ironic connection here, however, in that modern warfare conditions often parallel those seen for years within the underworld. This comparison refers to choices of preferred weaponry as well as combat environment such as city streets and building interiors. These conditions of fighting are not new to criminal groups and it is here that many of the same tactics and methods apply. In some cases, there is much that can be learned from the methods and tactics that successful criminal groups have practiced for years.

Chapter 3

Personal Defense Weapons

This will be a rather short chapter as there are not many weapons within this class either in active service or in development. This new class of weapon is the result of the submachine gun's inability to defeat body armor, combined with the failings of short-barrel assault rifles for counter-terrorist operations given their severe muzzle flash and blast. Initially the short barrel carbines looked set for a beautiful future. They simplified logistics by using the same ammunition as the standard service rifles, yet offered the compact size of the submachine gun with far greater power. These rifle calibers were able to punch through body armor where pistol calibers were often stopped cold. Also given the limited effective range of submachine guns, their ability to engage enemy troops beyond 200m was questionable at best.

What was desired was a weapon with the size of the submachine gun and the ability to penetrate body armor in a manner similar to what the short barrel carbines could do. The solution was the personal defense weapon (PDW).

There are actually two different fields of thought here. The first resulted in the HK MP7A1 and the FN P90, two systems that have already been adopted by various military and law enforcement units around the world. These were both built around the concept of a lightweight, high velocity bullet that had a similar effective range as the submachine gun, yet could defeat most body armor far more easily. Such a lightweight bullet rapidly loses velocity, and it would pose less threat beyond 200m. This was clearly designed for urban environments. This concept held appeal to units in law enforcement, for the safety factors involved.

A New Approach to a New Approach

There is a second train of thought regarding PDW class weapons. Why not create a weapon that uses a conventional rifle bullet in the 60 to 70 grain range moving at velocities similar to what was seen from the short barreled carbines, but without the muzzle flash associated with these weapons? This is a newer concept that would appear to hold more promise for military units, as the effective range is greater than that offered by the light weight bullets of the P90 and MP7A1.

3. Personal Defense Weapons

The PDW developed by Knight's Armament Company (KAC) is built around this newer idea. It is chambered for a new 6 × 35mm cartridge developed by KAC. The round has a bullet weight similar to the 5.56mm NATO cartridge. Knight's wanted to keep the same velocity that was generated by the short barreled carbines it was going to be competing against. At the same time, they made sure the entire powder charge was consumed before the bullet leaves the barrel, eliminating the deafening blast and blinding muzzle flash that are present with the short barreled carbines.

The controls of the Knight's PDW are quite similar to those found on the M16, making for easy familiarization with this new weapon, as well as lowering the cost of retraining personnel.

There are a great many advantages to this concept. The velocity is only marginally lower than the Colt M4, yet the weapon is much shorter. The Knight's PDW measures less than 20 inches folded with a 10½ inch barrel and measures close to 27 inches with its stock extended. KAC achieves this by using a conventional folding stock as opposed to the telescoping stock found on the M4 series which only reduces overall length by a few inches. The Knight's PDW is also lighter at just under 4½ pounds empty. The 11½ inch Colt Commando is nearly a pound heavier. The U.S. M4A1 carbine is longer and heavier still, though with its 14½ inch barrel, velocity is improved over the Commando model. The effective range of the M4A1 is usually accepted as roughly 550 yards against point targets. The Knight's PDW doesn't reach out this far, but it does provide a big advantage over the effective range of submachine guns. KAC claims the effective range of the PDW is 300m. Given its advertised muzzle velocity and bullet weight, this seems likely. Since the Knight's PDW was primarily designed for issue to support troops, this is a big improvement over what they have traditionally been given for weaponry, which was usually a handgun or submachine gun. KAC also claims that recoil is 50 percent lower than for the standard M4A1 carbine.

This weapon is operated by a unique two piston system which is supposedly far more reliable than the M4's gas impingement action. There are several other unique features, from a dimpled barrel designed to decrease weight while maintaining rigidity as well as increasing cooling surface area, to improved magazine geometry for enhanced reliability. The Knight's PDW concept has great potential given today's combat environment.

The Reigning Champs

Within the PDW class there is another more tested field of thought. While the Knight's PDW has not seen any adoption as of yet, the FN P90 and HK MP7A1 have been serving for several years now, including some combat use. While similar in concept, these two weapons are very different in operation.

The FN P90 is the older design dating back to the mid–1980s. It went into production in the early 90s, but the initial design was changed somewhat. The P90 uses a 5.7 × 28mm cartridge designed specifically for this weapon. The same cartridge is also used in the FN Five-seveN semi-auto pistol mentioned in the chapter on handguns. The first variant of the new cartridge utilized a 23 grain projectile with a synthetic cored bullet and as opposed to the usual lead or steel core. The standard round was later changed to a 31 grain bullet that used an aluminum core with a steel penetrator. The velocity was lowered from a listed 2800 feet per second for the initial SS90 cartridge to 2350 feet per second for the current SS190 cartridge, which has become standard. The round is also a shorter than the earlier SS90 pattern so as to make it easier to adapt it to the companion pistol.[1]

In operation, the P90 is a blowback weapon of bullpup configuration, meaning that the trigger group lies forward of the action, placing the breech mechanism near the shooter's face. With most people this is a problem, as the weapon must be set up either for left or right hand users. This has always proven to be a major tactical shortcoming of the bullpup configuration. With the P90, ejection is straight down rather than to the side, making for a truly ambidextrous design. All controls are accessible for either left or right hand users with equal ease. The P90 comes with several sighting options, including the standard model with optical sight. There is also a rail equipped tactical model, and models equipped with either visible or infrared laser. Iron sights are fitted should the optics fail during use. A suppressor is available and there is a special subsonic cartridge for use with this accessory. This weapon uses a unique detachable magazine that mounts horizontally in line with the top of the receiver. The 50 round magazine is transparent and holds the rounds at a right angle to the weapon's bore axis. The magazine feed well rotates the rounds in line to allow for feeding into the chamber. There have been some complaints about rounds spilling out of the magazine if dropped.[2] This is likely not a serious issue, as the P90 has seen service with quite a few military and law enforcement units, and is still being used without modification.

The production model of the P90 weighs approximately 6½ pounds empty, depending on model. Its overall length is close to 20 inches with a barrel length of roughly 10¼ inches. The cyclic rate is 900 rpm. As mentioned, the effective range is listed as 200m and given the weight of the bullet, this seems quite reasonable.[3]

The advantage of such a light weight projectile is the reduced possibility of ricochet and should the bullet miss its intended target, its energy is quickly dissipated. This is an important consideration in heavily populated areas and structures with thin wall construction.

One of the P90's most recognizable features is its grip layout. It has two radically curved, forward angled pistol grips, giving the weapon a distinctive look and making it instantly recognizable. The FN P90 has strong competition from the other PDW currently in service today.

The HK MP7A1 differs little from the original version of the MP7. The A1 model has added a safety trigger similar to that seen on Glock pistols. There are other minor changes, mostly cosmetic.

HK introduced the MP7 early in the 21st century. It uses its own 4.6 × 30mm round, very similar in concept and performance to the FN 5.7 × 28mm. The standard service cartridge is the German DM11. This features a 31 grain bullet that has a muzzle velocity of 2250 feet per second. This is a bit slower than the SS190 5.7 × 28mm round, though the penetration is claimed to be a bit better, most likely due to its smaller diameter. Which caliber is superior is still debatable.

The MP7 (MP7A1) is very different in operation from the P90. In terms of appearance, the MP7 seems like a modern version of the UZI. It feeds from a box magazine inserted into the pistol grip. Capacities are 20, 30, or 40 rounds, though HK currently lists the 30 round only. The stock slides straight into the receiver, shortening the weapon's length from just over 25 inches, to roughly 16¼ inches. The empty weight is 4.4 pounds The rate of fire is slightly higher than the P90, at 950 rpm. Effective range is also 200m.[4]

The MP7 is not a blowback operated weapon like the P90. Instead, the MP7 fires from a locked breech and uses a short-stroke gas piston similar to that of its big brother, the HK G36. The German army uses the MP7A1, and it has seen combat service in the Middle East. A suppressor is offered and iron sights are standard, though these can be easily removed and replaced with any type of sighting system in use today, as a rail system is standard. There is also a folding vertical grip mounted near the front. The MP7A1 must perform fairly well if it can serve in a harsh climate like the Middle East.

As for the tactical potential of the PDW as a weapon class, there is much left to be learned. The KAC concept seems to offer the most for military applications. This is likely to be debated hotly by fans of both the P90 and the MP7A1. There are concerns within the law enforcement community that the 5.7 × 28mm and the 4.6 × 30mm are not suitable calibers for police use. There is much to be resolved regarding the stopping power of these calibers. True, these lightweight, high velocity bullets do offer better body armor penetration and increased safety. Yet they are not winning heavy support for their ability to quickly stop a suspect. The concept of such a lightweight bullet being used to stop an opponent is not likely to win many votes among police officers. Reports on caliber performance in Iraq and Afghanistan are, in fact, supporting the old school thought regarding bullets. The hard hitting, heavier bullets appear to be preferred by troops, the 7.62mm over the 5.56mm, the .45 over the 9mm, the Mk 262 Mod 1 77 grain bullet over the M855 62 grain bullet, etc. Troops like to know that the enemy will stop fighting once hit. The tradeoff for this will always be increased recoil and greater ammunition weight, resulting in fewer rounds being carried in the soldier's combat load. These weapons do offer reduced recoil when compared to short barrel rifle caliber weapons as well as submachine guns. As for the subsonic rounds and suppressors, this combination would appear to offer even less stopping power. As these are intended for very close work, this is not likely a big issue. The ability to protect the user's hearing is a bigger issue in this regard. From a cost perspective, it would have been far cheaper to have done more work on a workable armor piercing pistol round for existing submachine guns. This would have allowed units to keep the greater hitting power of the heavy standard bullets and use the armor piercing ammo as needed. There have been some armor piercing pistol rounds used over the years, but they may not have offered the desired performance.

Chapter 4

Carbines/Rifle Caliber Submachine Guns

This class of weapon is difficult to classify. Some closely resemble submachine guns in size but are quite different in design and performance. While submachine guns often operate via simple blowback, short barreled rifles usually operate by locked breech mechanisms identical to their full sized rifle variations. There are a few exceptions to this. For the most part, however, these are nothing more than chopped versions of their standard rifle length counterparts. Some do have slight modifications in order to achieve their short overall length and yet maintain reliable functioning.

These also differ from the PDW class in that they utilize standard rifle calibers and use the same magazines as their service rifle equivalents. This class of weapon is fast becoming the largest group of small arm in service today. Most manufacturers offer either one or more compact versions of their standard service rifles. Many companies offer several different models designed to meet varying mission requirements. These vary from standard rifles to carbines, to compact models with barrels under 10 inches long. It is primarily this last group that has largely replaced the submachine gun within the arsenals of many nations. The initial reason for this move had to do with the increased use of body armor by groups other than law enforcement.[1]

As already mentioned the 9mm and .45 pistol cartridges simply move too slowly and have poor bullet design when it comes to penetrating Kevlar and other modern ballistic materials. Kevlar is still one of the most common choices for body armor, but there are even more effective materials being used today. Many vests also now use hard trauma plate inserts to increase the vest's ability to stop high performance rounds. The most advanced designs like Dragon Skin are designed to take multiple hits without any degradation in performance.

One of the advantages rifle bullets have over pistol calibers is their much smaller diameter combined with a far more aerodynamic profile. There are many other factors involved here, but these characteristics help to make it easier for the bullet to upset the integrity of the thread structure present in the vest. Basically fewer threads are being impacted at the same time. The ballistic material is designed to spread the force of the

4. Carbines/Rifle Caliber Submachine Guns

The Belgian designed FN FAL 7.62mm NATO 50.63 carbine, a very handy version of this popular rifle design (SSgt. K.R. Thomas, Department of Defense).

bullet's impact over a large area. The rifle bullet simply does a better job at preventing this. The typical rifle bullet is more adept at cutting through any medium. Contrary to some views, Teflon coatings on bullets do not allow them to penetrate body armor. There may be some reduced friction due to the coating, but the original Teflon coated ammo was designed for law enforcement to reduce barrel wear. The harder the bullet, the better it penetrates body armor, tungsten being the most popular insert material today. Also, standard rifle bullets tend to have hardened penetrator inserts that do not readily deform.[2]

As for stopping power, the typical rifle round has much more kinetic energy than any submachine gun caliber. This is true even when the rifle's barrel has been cut back to less than 10 inches. For example, the standard 20 inch barrel of the U.S. M16 rifle achieves a muzzle velocity of roughly 3000 feet per second with the M855 cartridge.[3] When this round is fired from a barrel of less than 10 inches, the muzzle velocity can be reduced by as much as 700 feet per second. Even at these reduced velocities, there's still an advantage over the submachine gun with regard to kinetic energy.

Ahead of Their Time

Most of the carbines and rifle caliber submachine guns are chambered in either 5.56 NATO or 5.45 Soviet calibers. From the early 1950s up until the 1980s, there was not a large variety of service rifles to choose from. The 7.62mm NATO that was standard at the time was far more powerful than the intermediate cartridges popular today. During this time there were only three rifles adopted in any significant numbers. These were the FN FAL, the HK G3 and the U.S. M14.[4] There were a few other good designs, like the SIG 510-4, a variation of the standard Swiss service rifle, the Stg 57. But until the Israeli Galil was available in 7.62mm starting in the 1980s, these three rifles were pretty much it. The FAL was available in two versions with carbine length barrels of either 17 or 18 inches, but the standard barrel length for the FAL was closer to 21 inches. The M14 had a 22 inch barrel, and the only one of the group that was available in short barreled models was the HK G3. This was available in a version known as the G3K, which had a barrel close to 12½ inches in length. This was probably far too short for effective use of the 7.62 NATO round. While having never seen this weapon fired, it is a safe bet that its muzzle blast and flash must have been intense. The 7.62 Galil was available in the Shortened Assault Rifle (SAR) version, which had a barrel length of close to 16 inches. This model appears to have been more successful than the HK G3K. There have been variations of the M14 with barrels shorter than 18 inches, like the La France M14K.[5] Currently the

The Galil SAR in its larger 7.62mm NATO chambering, a very powerful caliber for such a short barreled rifle. This example is using the early pattern magazine; later mags have a waffle pattern body (credit: PV2 A.W. McGalliard, U.S. Navy).

commercial firm of Springfield Armory offers a 16 inch barrel copy of the M14 known as the SOCOM 2. This weapon, however, uses a cast receiver in place of the usual forged receiver of the true M14. This weapon is semi-automatic only and is available to civilians.

The limited selection of carbines in this caliber over the years is due to the nature of the round. It must be remembered that 7.62 is a far more powerful round than any of the intermediate calibers usually associated with this weapon class. This explains why compact 7.62 NATO caliber weapons are rare. However, once the intermediate rounds were widely adopted as standard calibers, this scene changed a great deal. Over the years, many nations have designed carbines alongside rifle counterparts. The shorter, lighter weapons were often issued to non-commissioned officers, vehicle operators, ordnance disposal personnel, etc. The U.S. military used the M1 carbine for years in this role. During the Vietnam War, several short barrel versions of the M16 were tried. The 10 inch models were the first ones issued in this role. The original version was lengthened a bit and the 11½ inch versions became the primary model seen, though they still had severe fouling issues in addition to the muzzle blast and flash issues already covered.[6] For years, HK marketed the chopped model 33 5.56mm rifle known as the model 53. This was one of the first of this short class of weapon to prove successful, as it did not suffer the reliability issues of the short barreled M16s tried during the Vietnam War. It did, however, suffer from the same muzzle flash problems. HK redesigned the flash suppressor for this weapon prior to halting production. At the time of the HK 53's introduction, the motivation was the desire for greater stopping power in a compact weapon, as body armor was not yet widely used by criminal or terrorist groups. The HK 53 used a barrel of less than 9 inches in length and with the standard flash hider used at the time, was not likely very efficient at controlling the muzzle flash.

The End of the Rifle

Despite the shortcomings of these short assault rifles, they are likely here to stay. One of the more popular weapons in this class is the Russian AKS-74U. This is probably the most likely weapon of this type to be encountered worldwide. Despite this, there have been complaints regarding overheating during automatic fire for this small rifle.[7] Since the barrel of this weapon is nearly 8 inches in length, it probably suffers from even worse ballistic reduction than the M16 Commando models. As a result of the shortcomings of this weapon, Russia has recently begun to issue the AK-105 intended to replace this very compact weapon.[8] The reduction in velocity likely results in a decrease of effective range somewhere in the neighborhood of 50 percent. For example, the standard 20 inch barrel of the M16 delivers an effective range of around 600 yards against point targets, using the standard M855 62 grain cartridge. The new Mk 262 Mod 1 77 grain bullet does increase this range considerably, however. Some reports claim engagement beyond 700 yards is possible.[9]

The ultra short AKSU-74 (also known as AKS-74U) 5.45x39mm is Russia's equivalent to the Colt Commando, though far shorter due to the folding stock (LCpl. M.A. Sunderland, U.S. Marine Corps).

By comparison, the M4 and M4A1 carbines have an effective range of roughly 50 yards less than the standard rifle model. The ultra short M4 Commando with its 11½ inch barrel has an even shorter effective range than these other weapons. Most likely, it has an effective range of less than 350–400 yards. Colt's Manufacturing lists the effective range of the M4 Commando as 400m. Some feel this is optimistic. It is generally regarded that weapons in this class have a maximum effective range of less than 400 yards and this would be in the hands of very skilled shooter. This is not really much of an issue tactically, as these weapons were intended for use at much closer ranges. Given that iron sights are not very useable beyond 500m and some feel this is being generous, the popular use of these carbines makes a good deal of sense. They are far more compact given their shorter barrels. Many also have folding or collapsible stocks. However, reducing the 5.56mm rifle barrel below 14 inches tends to create much more intense muzzle flash, as well as drastic velocity loss.

Quite recently, an announcement was made that the M16A2 would be replaced by the M4 carbine as standard U.S. Army issue. While surprising, this is likely a sound move, as the shorter weapon is far more versatile and it gives up little in terms of effective range. The 11½ inch M4 Commando model will probably see some limited use as well. There has even been a shorter Close Quarter Battle Receiver (CQBR) version to enter service recently, known as the Mk18 Mod O.[10] This model was intended for use by counter-terrorism (CT) personnel. It appears that quite a bit of design work and money went into this model to make it function reliably. I am not sure this was worth the cost, as the overall length of this weapon is only about an inch shorter than that of the M4 Commando.

The more practical M4/M4A1 carbine series uses a 14½ inch barrel, as previously mentioned. This length appears to be a good compromise, as it offers reasonable ballistics with flash characteristics far less severe than that seen in shorter barrels. For CT units, it is understandable why they would want the smaller CQBR or Commando versions. While the CQBR is only about 4 inches shorter than the M4 carbine, this can be a big deal to CT units with regards to maneuvering in confined spaces.

From examining most data, it appears that the 5.56mm does not suffer severe loss of muzzle velocity until the barrel length is reduced to below 13 inches. After this, there is drastic degradation of velocity, as too little time is allowed for pressures to build before the bullet leaves the barrel.

While these carbines and submachine gun derivatives are becoming the new standard issue weapons for many troops, the question is which ones perform best.

The New U.S. Army Standard

The Colt M4/M4A1 is one of the most common Western shoulder arms seen since the original M16 entered service. It is the most common weapon to be encountered in current U.S. operations in Iraq and Afghanistan. Large numbers have been sent to Israel as well, though many of these were earlier versions like the Colt model 653. The primary visible difference between this weapon and the current M4 is the smaller diameter barrel of the 653. The M4 carbine has a distinctive larger diameter barrel with a step cut into it a few inches from the muzzle, which was necessary to allow for fitting of the M203 grenade launcher.

The difference between the M4 and the M4A1 is in fire control features only. The M4A1 is either semi-auto or full-auto, where the M4 carbine is either semi-auto or three round burst only.[11] Opinions on the three round burst feature differ. Special operations units in particular tend to prefer the M4A1 with its full-auto capability. The likely reason for this is the understanding that automatic fire from a lightweight weapon tends to be ineffective at all but the very closest ranges. With a three round burst, even the third round tends to go high. This is why the two round burst feature is offered on HK weapons. Two rounds can usually be kept on target, vastly increasing the chances of quickly stopping an opponent. Placing two rounds on target in rapid succession is often referred to as a "double tap." This is common practice with many CT units and SWAT teams. Having a weapon do this automatically makes perfect tactical sense.

However, if ranges are extremely close, such as breaking contact after an ambush, or if a defensive position is being overrun, automatic fire tends to be more effective. There have been complaints against the three round burst feature of the M16A2. Well disciplined troops are aware of the effectiveness of automatic fire and when it is needed. However when it is needed, automatic fire is what is desired, not a three round burst. There are, no doubt, those who will argue against this point. The initial U.S. decision to eliminate the full auto option on the M16A2 had to do with trying to reduce the amount of ammunition wasted. Someone in charge must have felt that a mechanical control device was superior to proper training with regards to fire discipline. When the Swedish military adopted their version of the FNC rifle, the AK5, they requested the three round burst option be removed. Given the introduction of the M4A1 and the M16A3, both full-auto weapons, it would appear that others in the U.S. military feel the same way.

The M4 series will likely become the most common version of the M16 for the remainder of this design's service life. The M16 is far from perfect, and around 2004, the U.S. Army's Delta units replaced the M4A1, which had been their standard weapon, with the HK 416, and there is a slight chance that this may become the next U.S. service rifle. From a cost perspective, this is a good move as it affords far greater reliability than currently offered by the M4 for relatively little cost, as the upper receiver of this weapon can be installed on the existing lower receivers of the M4/M4A1. This is speculative, and to be fair, there are excellent commercial designs that can also achieve this result. Excellent gas piston conversion kits are available from several companies. Many of these can be purchased as complete weapons as well. Good examples are companies such as Land Warfare Resources Corporation, Lewis Machine and Tool, and Patriot Ordnance Factory, among others.

In 2007, the U.S. military conducted a test on the reliability of the M4 carbine. It finished last in a group of weapons that included the HK 416, the XM8, and the FN SCAR.

4. Carbines/Rifle Caliber Submachine Guns

U.S. Air Force Combat Control Team with a 5.56mm Colt Commando, foreground. This is the 11.5 inch version that experienced severe fouling issues due to its short barrel (Sgt. R. Dorscy, Department of Defense).

While the M4A1 is likely the most versatile M16 variation, its reliability record will probably be the cause for its eventual replacement. This applies to all M16s, however. Recently some U.S. special operations units fielded another weapon, the FN Special Operations Forces Combat Assault Rifle (SCAR). This rifle is being offered in 5.56mm and 7.62mm versions. It was recently announced that the 5.56 version is not likely to be purchased in large numbers. The 7.62 version may still have a future, as it offers greater range potential and versatility. Given the current situation, the HK 416 seems to have the brightest future with the U.S. military. More will be covered on the HK 416 in Chapter 5.

The Compact AK

The compact version of the AK-74 was first publicly seen in the early 1980s after the U.S.S.R. invaded Afghanistan. This is a highly compact version of the AKS-74 rifle, which in turn was a folding stock variation of the standard AK-74. While similar in appearance to the standard AK-74, there were quite a few differences. The smaller model had a faster barrel twist, a shorter gas system, different sights, and a new muzzle device which combined a flash hider with a gas expansion chamber to improve reliability. There was also a change in the receiver cover, which was now hinged at the front end. The expansion chamber on the muzzle device was necessary for reliable functioning of the gas system. While very compact at close to 19 inches long with the stock folded, and slightly more than 5½ pounds empty, the ballistics of this weapon severely suffered just as with other short barreled rifles like the Colt Commando.[12] The sights on this weapon are calibrated for up to 500m. It seems unlikely consistent hits can be made with this weapon at that distance. As mentioned, there were complaints about this weapon overheating when fired on full auto. Despite this weapon's compact size, the slightly longer AK-105 is meant to be its successor.

As it has seen service for over 25 years, the AKS-74U is likely to be encountered in a great many locations around the world. The Bulgarian firm Arsenal, Inc., offers several high quality variations of this weapon chambered in 5.56mm NATO. The Bulgarian models, however, use a machined receiver as opposed to the stamped receiver of the Russian model. As the machined receiver would likely perform better as a heat sink, these versions should deal with the overheating issues somewhat better. There are some differences with these variations. The AR-SF model has an older pattern bottom folding stock. The AR-M4SF model uses a right side folding stock as opposed to the left side folding stock seen on Russian versions. This latter model has also added a left side thumb safety lever much like that found on the Israeli Galil rifles. This was necessary, as the conventional safety on the right side is inaccessible with the stock folded. This model also has a fitting for a tactical flashlight in the forend. The AKS-74U is not Russia's only current compact assault rifle.

Russia's New Urban Combat Caliber

There is a relatively new caliber to see service in Russia. It is, in fact, one of the first original ideas to come along in the small arms industry in recent years. The submachine gun by definition uses a pistol round. The compact rifles that largely replaced the submachine gun are most often chambered in either 5.56mm NATO or 5.45mm Soviet calibers, these rounds utilizing much lighter bullets at a far higher velocity than conventional submachine gun chamberings. The Russians decided to take a new approach with their 9x39mm cartridge. They decided that a very heavy bullet, moving at a subsonic velocity, would be just as effective as an intermediate caliber, and it would be far easier to effectively suppress.

This new round entered service in the 1990s, and has obviously been successful, as there are now at least six separate weapons used in this chambering: the AS, VSS, SR3, 9A-91, VSK-94, and the newer Kalashnikov AK-9. For this chapter the compact SR3 and 9A-91 are of particular interest. The AK-9 is a quite new design that should prove successful given its powerful chambering and its rugged heritage.

The 9 × 39mm cartridge utilizes a 250 grain bullet moving just below the speed of sound. The cartridge case is derived from the 7.62 × 39mm Soviet cartridge which has been opened up at the case mouth to accept the larger 9mm bullet.[13] There are two primary versions of this cartridge, the SP5, and the armor piercing SP6. A training round designed to be lower in cost was tried, but was found to create excessive barrel wear. The SP6 is said to be able to defeat the standard Russian Kevlar vest composed of two titanium plates and multiple layers of Kevlar, at a distance of 400m.[14] This is also considered the maximum effective range for this caliber. The 9 × 39mm has seen combat use in Chechnya, and has developed a reputation as being very effective in stopping targets quite quickly.[15] While this caliber has a subsonic velocity, it's extremely heavy projectile combined with its rifle bullet geometry allow it to keep its momentum for a good distance. Its effective range is the same as for the 7.62mm AK round.

The most remarkable aspect of this new caliber is the selection of weapons available in this chambering. As mentioned, the SR3 and the 9A-91 are especially useful. They are highly compact and do not generate the firing signature of the intermediate calibers in a weapon this size.

The SR3 is sometimes also known as the MA, and weighs less than 4½ pounds empty, has a top folding stock, and measures less than 14½ inches folded. Its rate of fire is 900 rpm. The detachable magazines used are either 10 or 20 round curved plastic boxes that can also be used in the AS and the VSS weapons. In fact the SR3 is closely related to both models and all three were developed as a system at roughly the same time. The SR3 is used by Russian executive protection personnel, and is really just a streamlined modification of the AS. The changes made from the AS were in the areas of stock design, as the AS has a side folding stock. Changes were also made to the cocking lever. The traditional right side cocking handle of the AS has been changed to small projections located over the gas system near the muzzle on the SR3. The safety layout is also different. On the AS, the safety is more along the lines of that seen on an AK rifle. This model does not normally use a sound suppressor.[16]

Of even greater potential is a rival model, which was also developed in more than one version. The 9A-91 is available in conventional form, or as a silent sniper rifle meant for paratrooper use, known as the VSK 94. The VSK 94 does not have as many modifications as found on the SR3. The 9A-91 parent model is the tactical equivalent of the SR3 and the VSK-94 version was seen in use by the military during the 2004 Beslan hostage crisis. Dimensions for the 9A-91 are similar to the SR3, roughly 15 inches folded, and just over 4½ pounds empty. The rate of fire is somewhat slower than the SR3, at 600–800 rpm. The detachable magazine for the 9A-91/VSK 94 is a straight 20 round metal box that is different from that used on the AS family. The 9A-91 and the SR3 are considered to be some of the smallest assault rifles in the world. The 9A-91 can use a detachable suppressor and a special PK-01 optical sight, as well as a recoil pad over the buttplate of the top folding stock. The recoil pad must be removed before folding the stock back to its closed position. The recoil pad is meant for use when the final accessory is attached. The 9A-91 has one big advantage over the SR3 in that it can also mount the GP95 40mm single shot grenade launcher.[17] This weapon has a 400m range, and can fire an assortment of standard 40mm Russian grenades. It is basically the standard GP30 grenade launcher with a modified mounting bracket for use with this particular weapon.

It is odd that the West has no equivalent to any of these designs or even an equivalent to this caliber for that matter. There's been some testing with the Whisper series of cartridges from SSK Industries, but these have yet to see any adoption. As a practical matter, the suppressed 9A-91, combined with GP95 grenade launcher and PK-01 sight, is quite possibly one of the most lethal weapon systems available for the modern combat environment. With the grenade launcher attached, the weapon only weighs in the neighborhood of 7½ pounds empty, although the sight and suppressor will add to this weight. As both rifle and launcher offer an effective range of roughly 450 yards, they should be able to handle most urban situations, and provide a great deal of lightweight firepower in the process. The magazine capacity for this new family of weapons seems limited to 20 rounds. This is most likely due to the weight of the ammunition itself. Thirty or more rounds of such a heavy cartridge will most likely overstress the magazine spring and lead to malfunctions.

The final weapon to be introduced in this caliber is the new Kalashnikov AK-9. This weapon also uses a different plastic magazine from the other two systems offered in this caliber. It also appears limited to 20 rounds. Outwardly this new carbine closely resembles other carbines in the AK-100 series such as the AK-102, 104, or 105. A detachable suppressor is offered, and it appears that this weapon was intended for use with the suppressor installed. Dimensions are similar to other AK carbines in this series. It will take time to see if this model can achieve the same success as the previous 9 × 39mm designs. It should do quite well given its Kalashnikov origins. All of the weapons in this new caliber utilize Kalashnikov based gas operated actions, modified for a reduction in size. The fire controls on the SR3 and 9A-91 are somewhat different from that seen on the AK family, and appear to have been better placed for easy operation.

The Hungarian AMD-65 is an AKM derivative that is very compact and effective. This model was originally intended for use by armored crew members. It uses the standard AK action with a barrel several inches shorter than the normal 16 inch rifle version. It is mounted with a unique pattern flash hider–muzzle brake. It also uses two vertical

A compact copy of the AK-47/AKM, the Hungarian AMD-65. This weapon is popular for close combat due to the power of the 7.62 × 39mm round, which is considered a good stopping round inside 200 yards. Some have been modified by private security contractors to make them better suited for modern urban fighting, as large numbers of these are in service in Afghanistan (SrA. N. Callon, U.S. Air Force).

grips that are identical. The front grip is simply mounted in reverse to give it a forward rake to allow for easier magazine changes. The folding stock is a simple single strut steel design. The forend is sheet metal and no wood is used on the weapon, unusual at the time of its introduction. While no longer standard in Hungary, large numbers were sent to police units in Afghanistan. Some of these rifles were used by private security units operating within that country. These were modified for close combat missions. The stock was reshaped to allow for the use of the 75 round drum RPK light machine gun magazine. The sheet metal forend also made for easy rail mounting to attach accessories. Other minor modifications were also made. This was done because many prefer the heavier 7.62 × 39mm caliber for close combat, as it offers good stopping power.[18]

Many former communist nations that have their own AK variations have also developed short versions of the same designs. Romania offers the md 86, which is a derivative of the AK. This is offered in a short although seldom seen carbine model. Poland offered the Tantal and later Beryl.[19] Both are close AK-74 copies with some minor changes added and short models were offered as well.

Building on a Good Idea

Since the long stroke gas piston system has proven very reliable over the years, it has been widely used in many designs. Many of the better Western designs have copied the long stroke AK gas system and the AK bolt design as well. The Belgian FNC, the Italian AR70/90, the Swedish AK5, and the Swiss SIG SG550 all copy the AK action in this regard. All of the models listed have carbine versions and some offer even shorter models as well.

The FNC is made in a carbine version that uses a 14¼ inch barrel. The Swedish AK5D Mk2 is the current short model for that country. This uses a very short barrel of less than 10 inches. The AR70/90 is made in a short barrel SCP70/90 version that uses a carbine length barrel of just over 14 inches. The SG550 series is available in the largest selection of variations. The SG550 is the rifle version and is covered in Chapter 5. The SG551 carbine is offered in 14.3 or 17.9 inch long barrel variations. The SG553 is a highly compact model that is intended for special operations use. This is made in a standard 8.9 inch model or a 553 LB version with a 13.7 inch barrel. The LB variations are intended to allow for the use of rifle grenades and can mount a bayonet.[20] What good a bayonet is on a carbine is anybody's guess.

The Israeli Galil is offered in the SAR short model in either caliber. The 5.56mm SAR uses a 13.1 inch barrel, while the 7.62mm NATO SAR is equipped with a longer 15.7 inch barrel. This appears to be the minimum that can be chambered for this powerful round. A much more recent design appeared in the mid–90s. The MAR or Micro-Galil uses a barrel length of less than 8 inches and a new forend design that helps keep the support hand from sliding forward towards the muzzle. The South African R4 copy of the Galil is also offered in the compact R5 (13.1 inch) and smaller R6 (11 inch) versions as well. There was even an R8 ultra compact version developed.[21] This version may have been too short and little is seen of this weapon today.

The New HK

With regard to other new Western designs, the short HK 53, briefly covered earlier, has been discontinued in favor of the G36C.[22] This is very similar in concept to the model 53. In terms of operation, however, the HK G36C is very different. The HK 53 used the traditional HK roller locking system while the G36 uses a short stroke gas piston system very similar to that found on the old Armalite AR-18 design that was supposed to offer improved performance over the M16.[23] Many view both the short and long stroke gas piston as more reliable than the gas impingement system of the M16. They are certainly cleaner in operation. They also keep the breech area cooler during use. The rifle version of the G36C has done quite well. The G36 has been adopted by several nations as a standard service rifle and is still seeing adoption by others. The G36C model is primarily the same weapon with a barrel of less than 9 inches. The cyclic rate is the same as for the rifle version, at 750 rpm. The current G36 series is offered with the popular Picatinny rail system to allow for different sighting and accessory options. The flash hider is a different pattern than that found on the rifle version. This pronged flash hider is apparently more effective at reducing the rather severe muzzle flash. It is also found on the 12½ inch G36K carbine. This slightly longer model has improved ballistics over the G36C, but also has an increased weight of close to 7½ pounds. The rate of fire is also the same as for the other models.

The G36 series has gained a good reputation for reliability. When combined with its excellent handling characteristics and a reasonable cost, this has created a capable design that is becoming popular worldwide. The right side folding stock shortens the length of the weapon by roughly 9 inches. The smallest version, the G36C, measures less than 20 inches folded.

As with many modern designs, the G36 uses a great deal of modern plastics in its construction. A vertical foregrip can be mounted on all models. This accessory is becoming popular, as it offers greater control of the weapon.

There is one final design that is not widespread but should be mentioned. The South Korean K1A1 carbine is a short model that uses a gas impingement system similar to the M16. This is unusual in that the K2 Korean service rifle uses a more conventional gas piston system. The K1A1 is the older of the two designs. While it is a compact design, it is not widely used by any other nations. This is also true of other Daewoo designs. This is a shame, as these designs show some promise. It is odd that many of the South Korean models use the same wire sliding stock design. This was closely copied from the M3 submachine gun which was used for years by the South Korean military.

Accessorize

Most of the modern carbines mentioned in this chapter were originally meant to use iron sights. However, optical sighting devices are much more likely to be encountered today. Luckily, many were capable of accepting some type of mounting base or have been modified

An Israeli made Galil SAR in 5.56mm, perhaps the finest made AK-47 variation (Sgt. D. Foley, U.S. Army).

to do so. As with modern handguns, many other accessories are available for these weapons. Small image intensifier night scopes are common, as are thermal imaging sights, compact scopes like the U.S. Advanced Combat Optical Gunsight (ACOG), Holographic Weapon Sights (HWS), and infrared laser pointers like the U.S. AN/PEQ-2. Even visible lasers, flashlights, and red-dot sights are common today. Many modern sights are a combination of a red-dot sight for close work combined with a more conventional scope for longer range shooting. While most of these sights use batteries, some are illuminated by radioactive elements or use fiber optics for improved light gathering. The M4 series is often fitted with the Knight's Rail Interface System (RIS) to facilitate mounting these add-ons. The advantage of these new aiming systems is primarily in their speed of use. They do a better job at helping the user engage their targets.

Suppressors are becoming quite common for today's urban combat weapons. In the not too distant past, suppressors were thought to be used only by spies or professional killers and organized crime. These attachments offer many useful advantages for troops operating in an urban area. A suppressor does a fantastic job at helping to minimize flash and can preserve the shooter's vision in poorly lit areas. They also make it very difficult to determine where the shot came from. The traditional method for fitting a suppressor is to remove the flash hider from the barrel and screw on a suppressor with the proper thread pitch. Many are still attached in this manner. Some newer models offer faster and more convenient methods of attachment. Gem-tech offers the HALO model for the M4 carbine series. This model simply fits over the barrel without modification and quickly locks into place. The Russian AK-100 series rifles are fitted with a scope mount bracket on the left side of the receiver for mounting a variety of sights, something the original AK-47 usually lacked. The suppressors for most AKs are threaded on in the traditional manner. Suppressors are made for all the primary rifle calibers in use worldwide.

While this chapter did not examine every carbine design in use, it should provide insight into the most common models out there. While these short barreled weapons do suffer from some loss in ballistic performance, they are very handy in use and this seems to outweigh the shorter effective ranges offered by their abbreviated barrels. This is clear from the number of different models currently in service. These shorter versions of the assault rifle are clearly pushing the traditional longer barreled service rifle aside as the preferred issue shoulder arm. Given the time and money spent developing these weapons, it is obvious they are here to stay. As the typical urban environment tends to involve residential or commercial structures, the shorter effective range of these weapons should pose no real problem. Their shorter barrels and folding stocks make for a much shorter overall length, and the shortest models with the 7–10 inch barrels are limited to around 400 yards at best. This is still double the effective range of the pistol caliber submachine gun. This combined with their superior performance against body armor has created a much better all around weapon. The only real drawback is the severe muzzle flash and blast. While this may not seem like a big problem, it must be remembered that these weapons will often be used indoors. The first round will destroy both the user's night vision and his hearing. If ear plugs are used, unit communication and situational awareness are drastically limited. As the electricity is likely to be out in many structures during fighting, this will only make it that much worse with regards to readjusting one's vision.

There are cost advantages with these weapons in that many parts used are identical to those of the rifle version, including the magazines. For some special operations units, pistol caliber submachine guns will continue to be used for certain jobs, usually those involving the use of sound suppressors. This is something for which the rifle calibers are ill suited. Overall, the carbine/rifle-caliber submachine gun has a great deal to offer for the urban combat environment. The U.S. Army clearly feels the same.

Chapter 5

Assault Rifles

The story of the assault rifle is well documented, so will only briefly be covered here. The STG 44 was a German rifle generally regarded as the first true assault rifle designed as such from the start. After the war, the Soviets closely studied the design and the AK-47 bears some external resemblance to the German design, though bolt operation was somewhat different, as the AK uses a rotating bolt vs. the tilting design of the STG 44. At any rate, while the Russians were still perfecting the AK-47, the West had been developing a new standard cartridge, the 7.62 × 51mm. This was developed by the United States and was based on the .30-06 that had been successfully used in two world wars. The reason for NATO adoption of the new round had more to do with the power position of the United States at the time than with the superiority of the cartridge. Repeated tests over the years have shown that the 7mm bullet is superior as a combat caliber. Why one has not been perfected and adopted in nearly 100 years of study is still a mystery to many. Regardless, the 7.62 × 51mm, also known as the .308 Winchester, is an excellent round that is well known for its accuracy. This would be the NATO standard cartridge until 1980, when the 5.56 × 45mm was added as NATO standard caliber.[1] Both are current NATO standard rounds today.

During the 1950s, three primary rifles in 7.62 × 51mm would see widespread adoption. The FN FAL was by far the most widely used of these three. Roughly 90 different countries have used this weapon at some time, with around a dozen producing some version. The HK G3 was almost as successful with roughly 40 nations adopting it over the years, with production continuing even today. Few others chose the third model, the U.S. M14. One of the reasons for this may have been the cost of the rifle, as the M14 used very few stampings and was constructed primarily from expensive forged and milled parts. Although the end result was a very accurate and reliable rifle, it never enjoyed the popularity of the first two designs. The reason for its mention here is that it is currently seeing a revival in use by U.S. troops in the Middle East, where the longer range of its 7.62mm round is being appreciated. With an effective range roughly double that of the 5.56mm NATO, it is far better suited for desert warfare, and at close range, offers a great deal more power. The reliability of this rifle compared to that of the M4A1 carbine is also superior, especially in sandy environments. It is far better at punching through the con-

The U.S. 7.62mm M14 in its target shooting role; another mission at which it excels (SSgt. K. Walker, U.S. Air Force).

struction materials commonly used in Iraq.² The 7.62mm has a disadvantage in that the ammunition weighs a great deal more. There is another tradeoff in that the recoil of the 7.62mm is far more punishing and the M14 weighs over 3 pounds more than the M4A1 in empty condition. It would appear that many troops are willing to live with these tradeoffs versus the alternative. With the new Mk 262 Mod 1 5.56mm cartridge now seeing service, things may change a bit, as this cartridge is reportedly performing much better than the standard M855 62 grain bullet, and is reportedly capable of engaging enemy combatants out to 700m.

The M14 Finally Finds Its Place

There are currently several versions of the M14 serving in the Middle East. There is the standard M14, which is issued with a wooden or fiberglass stock, the M21 and M25 sniper variants, the Designated Marksman's Rifle (DMR), and the Mk 14 Mod 0 Enhanced Battle Rifle (EBR). The Mk 14 Mod 0 is perhaps the most heavily modified version. It uses a new telescoping stock design equipped with an assortment of rails for accessory mounting.³ This version weighs far more than the original M14 with its standard wooden stock. The original M14 with fiberglass or wood stock weighs slightly over 9 pounds. Once scopes, mounts, and bipods are added, the weight can quickly increase. However, an optical sight is beneficial in this caliber, to take full advantage of its lethal range.

In operation, the M14 was never effective when fired in the automatic mode. Its rate of fire was far too high given the weight of the rifle, the design of the stock, and the power of the 7.62mm NATO round. Many were altered to provide semi-auto fire only. However, in semi-auto, the M14 has long been respected for its excellent accuracy. The M14 uses a detachable box magazine, with the steel 20 round being the most common by far. There have been some plastic versions made recently which perform fairly well. Some 25 and 30 round steel magazines are also on the market.

A drawback to the M14 in the past was the lack of a well designed folding stock. Today there are a few rugged and functional stock models that telescope a short distance to help with the overall length of the weapon. The standard M14 is quite long at 44 inches with the original stock design. Its barrel, however, was also long at 22 inches. Its rather lengthy flash hider didn't help much.

The M14 has been used to good effect by the U.S. military as a sniper rifle. Commonly known as the M21, the sniper variant has recently been joined by the M25 variation. The M21 was nothing more than a highly tuned M14 with no provision for full automatic fire, and was traditionally fitted with a 3–9 variable power scope named the "Leatherwood," after its designer.[4] It had an effective stadiametric range finding reticle. The mount was quickly and easily detached through the use of a large thumb screw, though a newer version offers two screws for more secure attachment. If needed, the flash hider could be removed and a suppressor installed in its place to help mask the origin of the shot.[5] The U.S. produced close to 1.4 million M14s and then sold the tooling to Taiwan, which continued production as the type 57.[6] Springfield armory currently manufactures an investment cast receiver model in semi-automatic with several barrel length options. Mainland China also has produced copies for the export market. The commercial copies from Springfield armory are available in handy variations. The 18 inch Scout Sniper model is equipped with a forward mounting rail for optical sights and this is fitted with a lightweight folding bipod. The 16 inch SOCOM and SOCOM II versions are fitted with even more rails, and both of these models would likely perform quite well in the harsh environment of the Middle East, as well as being very convenient in use.

Given recent complaints regarding the reliability of the M16/M4 series and the power of the 5.56mm cartridge itself, U.S. troops are once again learning to appreciate the M14's qualities as a combat rifle. It does have one advantage over other 7.62mm NATO service rifles, in that it can be reloaded through the top of the receiver with the use of stripper clips. This allows a soldier to carry fewer detachable magazines which are bulky and add unnecessary weight to their combat load. Once the standard scope mount is used, however, access to the stripper clip guide is no longer available. The M14 was issued during the first Gulf War and some troops wrapped the action in cloth in an attempt to keep out the fine sand. This was done due to the belief that because the M14's action is wide open, sand could easily enter the mechanism. While this is true, at the same time, it makes the weapon far easier and faster to clear. Often merely using the index finger to wipe out the locking lugs is enough to keep the weapon functioning.

Should an FAL or G3 experience a stoppage, it is unlikely they can be returned to action as quickly. To clear a more closed mechanism usually requires partial disassembly, which is inconvenient in combat at best, and out of the question at times. While the 7.62mm Galil would also probably require partial stripping, the Galil's AK based action is not known for being sand sensitive. The G3 has a fairly good desert reputation, but the locking rollers and recesses must be kept clear at all times, not always easy to accomplish during a sandstorm. However, the FAL is known for being rather sand sensitive in harsh desert climates, and this was the primary reason for the Israeli development of the Galil rifle.[7] In sandy conditions, lubrication must be kept to an absolute minimum, and graphite powder should be used whenever possible. This is not something that is easily accomplished with the M16/M4 series, which is recommended to be kept well lubricated with oil at all times.[8] Aside from the extra power of the M14 rifle, its superior reliability, when compared to the M16, is likely one of the reasons for its resurgent use among U.S. troops.

The M14 will no doubt remain in service for the remainder of U.S. operations in the Middle East. It is quite likely that it will also be kept as a reserve weapon, should future desert combat require its presence once again. Many stockpiled M14s have been given away or sold to other nations over the years, depleting the U.S. inventory, however. Should the new FN SCAR-H rifle prove a successful weapon system, it may eventually replace the M14, but that would be a much more costly solution, and may not be economically feasible at this time.

The World Standard

The next weapon to be covered is the Fusil Automatique Léger (Light Automatic Rifle) or FAL. The FAL was by far the most successful of the 7.62mm NATO combat rifles. Not only was it adopted by a large number of nations, it was manufactured in several of them as well. There are a great many versions of this weapon worldwide, from standard rifles to 17 and 18 inch barrel carbines and heavy barrel rifles designed for use as squad automatic weapons. The squad auto models had a reputation for jamming after firing the first couple of rounds in a full magazine for some reason. Many of these versions were available with either fixed or folding stocks. The FAL pattern folding stock is one of the better designs and is also used on the Israeli Galil and the South African R4 rifles as well as the FAL's replacement, the FNC.

The FAL dates back to the end of World War II. The same designer that had completed the design of the Browning High-Power also had much to do with the development of the FAL.[9] The FAL is a short-stroke gas operated weapon, as opposed to the long stroke gas system of the M1 Garand or AK-47. Unlike the M14, the FAL has an adjustable gas regulator. This allowed a badly fouled weapon to continue to function reliably. The regulator could also be turned down to minimize felt recoil. While somewhat sensitive in sandy conditions, the FAL does possess excellent balance and handling qualities, and many

5. Assault Rifles

felt it was superior to the other 7.62mm NATO rifles in this regard. The FAL has few equals in any environment other than the desert. It proved reliable in the jungle, snow, mountains, and most other conditions worldwide. For years it was one of the most widely used weapons on the African continent, and it has seen a great deal of use in that region's many conflicts.

The FAL was initially offered with wooden furniture. This was soon changed to plastic to reduce weight and maintenance requirements. Wood tended to warp or swell in jungle conditions and dry out and crack in desert conditions. The M14 had similar issues during the Vietnam War and a fiberglass stock was later developed for the M14. Some FAL variations have grooves cut in the bolt to help maintain reliability in sandy conditions. This no doubt helped somewhat, but the FAL will never perform as well as an AK action in desert conditions.

The standard FAL was 1 to 2 inches shorter than the M14 depending on model. Its weight is similar, but again this depends on the particular version. However, the FAL is offered in a folding stocked carbine known as the 50.63, which could be had with either 17⅛ inch or 18 inch barrel, and weighed around 8¼ pounds. empty.[10] The FAL also had an advantage over the M14 in that it could be fitted with a lightweight folding bipod that was far more convenient than the clamp on steel bipod developed for the M14. Most M14s in use today use a much handier Harris lightweight folding bipod. For years, the FAL 50.63 was one of the most compact 7.62mm NATO rifles. For 7.62mm NATO caliber weapons, this carbine along with the HK G3K and Galil SAR 7.62mm all offer excellent qualities for modern combat conditions. The barrel of the G3K is probably a bit short, however.

The M14 in its new configuration, the Mk 14 Enhanced Battle Rifle (GSgt. J. Frank, U.S. Marine Corps).

The FAL suffered from the same full auto control issues as the M14, or for that matter, any 7.62mm NATO rifle in this weight range, although the pistol grip likely afforded somewhat better control than was possible with the M14. Many versions, however, were modified for semi-auto fire only. The British L1A1 model was a semi-auto only rifle. This model also had a longer flash hider, which increased its overall length somewhat. There are so many variations of the FAL that it becomes difficult to classify them. However, the basic operating system for all remains the same.

The FAL could mount a scope with minor modification, and was sometimes set up as a sniper rifle. In this role, however, it was not usually as accurate as the sniper variant of the M14. The folding stock variation of the FAL was somewhat different in design than the original fixed stock version, as the recoil spring had to be relocated to be fully contained within the receiver. On the fixed stock model, the recoil spring is located within the buttstock. This change required other minor modifications as well but did not reduce the reliability of the rifle, as is usually the case with modifying an existing design. The FAL is an outstanding combat rifle to this day, the carbine version in particular. The carbine's lighter weight and overall length of less than 30 inches folded make for a very maneuverable and handy rifle with great power. The FAL originally used a forged receiver, which made for a fairly expensive weapon, though it used more modern production techniques as the years went by to help with cost control. There were also some versions made with alloy lower receivers to reduce weight. Oddly, the 5.56mm FNC rifle, intended to replace the FAL, is no lighter or more compact than the 7.62mm 50.63 carbine.

The standard version of the FAL. These appear to be British L1A1 variations, judging by the long, slender flash hiders (J. Bonet, CIV).

5. Assault Rifles

The HK G3A3 7.62mm NATO. This was the second most popular Western rifle of the post-war era after the FAL. This model is fitted with the wide "tropical" foregrip. Early versions usually used a smaller sheet metal handguard (LCpl. P.M. Johnson-Campbell, U.S. Marine Corps).

The Second Standard

The second most common 7.62mm NATO combat rifle of the post-war era was the HK G3. This was the father of the MP5 submachine gun covered in Chapter 2. The G3 was the first of the HK roller-locked weapons. Its CETME heritage and the history of the rifle have already been covered in many other works so I won't do it here. It is enough to describe its basic operating system. The HK roller locking system is actually a delayed blowback device. It is not truly a locked breech weapon as are most 7.62mm NATO rifles. This is the reason for the fluted chamber present in all HK roller-locked weapons. The purpose of the flutes is to keep the case from being ripped apart as the bolt is drawn violently to the rear during recoil. The brass case floats on a cushion of gas before it is extracted from the chamber. This is the reason for the dark lines present on the spent cases from HK roller-locked weapons. Shooters sometimes complain of the HK system having rather sharp recoil compared to gas operated rifles. The recoil forces are the same. They are merely being applied over shorter period of time.

HK weapons are sometimes said to have poor, heavy trigger pulls. Its trigger was designed for safety and combat reliability, not for target shooting. HK uses polygonal rifling which is claimed to provide higher velocity and better accuracy due to less bullet deformation. HK rifles are certainly known to be accurate. The G3's balance is often judged as inferior to that of the FAL or M14. This is a matter of personal preference. The G3 has established a reputation for reliability matched by few other rifles, in spite of how some feel about it. It does not have a last round bolt catch like the FAL or M14, but again this is not a required feature. The G3 is usually seen with a 20 round box magazine made of either steel or aluminum. Other magazine capacities are seen on occasion and a large 50 round drum magazine has been offered for this rifle. This is likely a very heavy magazine when loaded, though its firepower would certainly be appreciated in combat use.

The G3 was made in a short 12½ inch barreled version known as the G3K, as mentioned earlier. This was likely too short a barrel for this caliber. However, when combined with HK's telescoping stock design, this would have made for a very compact and powerful carbine. The standard G3A3 fixed stock version was roughly 40 inches in length, shorter than both the FAL and M14 standard models. HK also offered the G3A4 version with its telescoping stock, which reduced the overall length from roughly 40½ inches, down to just over 33 inches. This model was about ½ pound heavier, however. Since the G3 was already the heaviest of the 7.62mm NATO rifles, this extra weight was undoubtedly not welcome. The cocking handle of the G3 is located on the forward left side, as are all HK roller-locked weapons. As mentioned, there was no bolt catch, but the cocking handle could be retracted and locked into a small notch to keep the bolt open. The original forend of the G3 was a narrow sheet metal fitting; a wider plastic forend, commonly known as the "tropical" version, was later offered.[11] The excellent HK claw type scope mount could be fitted as with other HK weapons of this type. There were special sniper variants produced. These will be covered more in Chapter 6.

The G3 not only had a good reputation for reliability, it was cheaper to manufacture and required fewer machining operations than either the M14 or FAL. Despite the modern production methods used in its manufacture, the G3 has a reputation for longevity. These rifles just don't seem to wear out quickly. This is likely due to a combination of factors, low stress on the parts, barrel making techniques, polygonal rifling, and quality of design. For whatever reason, the G3 is known to have a fairly long service life.

As for modern use, the G3 is available with new low profile rail mounts and rail equipped forends as found on some Norwegian military versions. These added features have allowed the G3 to keep pace with other modern modular rifle designs. The power of the 7.62mm NATO round combined with the rugged dependability of this rifle will keep it in service for years to come. HK has halted production of this weapon, but it remains in production in other locations around the world. As with the FAL, this weapon has been produced in a number of nations. As the G3 requires less machining than the FAL, setting up production was likely less difficult for the G3.

The Swiss SIG 510-4 was an excellent weapon that was roughly similar in operation to the G3, but as this weapon was extremely expensive,[12] it never sold in large numbers and is seldom encountered today. Since this book is meant to cover only the most successful and common weapons in current service, I will move on to the next 7.62mm NATO design.

5. Assault Rifles

The AK Bulks Up

The last 7.62mm NATO to be covered is possibly the most combat worthy of all. The AK action has usually been accepted as the world standard for reliability. Mating this design to the power of the 7.62mm NATO cartridge would seem to be the best of both worlds. The Israelis did this with the 7.62mm NATO Galil rifle in the early 1980s. This rifle was likely designed for the U.S. market more than anything else. The Israelis had been using the 5.56 Galil since the early 70s, and it has proven to be one of the most reliable weapons ever made. The Galil, along with its South African R4 variation, can be considered the "Rolls Royce" of AK-47s, or if you prefer, an AK-47 with all the bells and whistles. Despite all it has going for it, the Galil is not a perfect design. It lacks a bold hold open device, it is extremely heavy, and the safety, while better than that of the AK-47, was still rather awkward to manipulate.

The 7.62 Galil was offered in the same three basic versions as its smaller brother. The ARM was considered the light machine gun version. It was equipped with a 21 inch barrel, 18 inches for the 5.56mm version, a rugged folding bipod, which could double as a bottle opener and wire cutter, and a folding carrying handle (not used on the R4). On the Israeli made versions the original forend was made of wood, which supposedly absorbed the heat created by automatic fire better than the plastic present on the other models. All models use the FN pattern folding stock, which reduces the length of the weapon by over 9 inches. The cocking handle could be easily accessed by left or right handed users and the standard AK type safety lever remained, although a thumb operated safety was connected to it on the opposite side just above the pistol grip. The magazine capacity in 7.62 is normally 25 rounds and most seen are made of steel, although in the 5.56 version, 35 round synthetic magazines have been encountered. The R4 uses a synthetic magazine as standard. Originally 12, 35 or 50 round steel magazines were the only ones offered for the 5.56mm models. The current 7.62mm magazines have a waffle pattern designed to increase rigidity somewhat. Galils are made with a groove on the left side of the receiver to allow for fitting of a quick detach scope mount that automatically returns to zero after being removed and re-installed. This feature was probably more beneficial for the 7.62mm model due to its increased range when compared to the 5.56mm.

The AR model had the same barrel length but lacked the folding carrying handle and bipod, and the forend was made of plastic instead of wood.

The final SAR model was far more compact. The 7.62mm SAR was fitted with a barrel of just under 16 inches, and the 5.56 SAR had a barrel just over 13 inches long. These models were fitted with the same synthetic forend as found on the AR. While ballistics suffer with the shorter barrels, these models would seem to fit modern urban warfare conditions the best, allowing for better maneuverability in tight quarters.

It is strange that the Galil has not enjoyed the commercial success one would have expected from such a design. Although it has been sold to several nations, these were generally smaller purchases from developing countries, the South African R4 version being an exception, although this version was not widely used outside of South Africa either.

While on the subject of the R4, it was never manufactured in 7.62mm NATO caliber. This weapon was offered in the compact R5 and R6 ultra short versions, the R5 being very similar to the Galil SAR 5.56mm. The R6 is an even more compact version, with the barrel length reduced to 11 inches. The manufacturer of the R4 series also offered a heavy barrel R7 squad automatic version, as well as a highly compact R8, very similar to the Micro-Galil, although there has not been much publicity regarding the last two variations. The R4 series had minor improvements in some areas, including some internal mechanisms being altered. The most noticeable changes were the elimination of the carrying handle, the synthetic being used on all models including the bipod equipped model, and a folding stock being made of plastic instead of metal. The stock was lengthened somewhat as well. Recent Galils have been seen with synthetic forends on the ARM models, and the Micro-Galil uses a synthetic stock instead of the usual metal version normally found on Galils.

The 7.62mm ARM Galil was tried as a light machine gun for some time, but as it lacks a quick change barrel, its success in this role was likely limited. The Israelis have long used the FN MAG machine gun as their normal squad automatic weapon, as it offered a quick change barrel and belt fed mechanism, giving it a much better sustained fire capability. Recently the 5.56mm Israeli designed Negev belt-fed squad automatic weapon has taken over this role. Both of these will be covered more in the chapter on machine guns. As a service rifle, the 7.62mm Galil is about as good as a rifle can get. While not perfect, it has the AK's reputation for reliability, combined with better quality of manufacture, although some nations produce excellent quality AKs. The Galil also used a strong machined receiver and an excellent folding stock design, and it has vastly increased range over the 7.62 × 39mm Soviet cartridge. The 7.62 SAR model offers great power for close range use, and would no doubt make a lethal modern combat weapon.

There is a new series of Israeli/Colombian rifles known as the ACE. These appear to have been heavily influenced by the Galil, but have considerable differences, and are also available in 7.62 × 39mm Soviet as well as 5.56mm and 7.62mm NATO. These are quite new and it remains to be seen how successful they will be. The nation of Colombia has used the Galil in several versions for many years, and the Indumil factory in that country was at least partially responsible for the inspiration of this new series of rifles.[13]

More recently, the 5.56mm Micro-Galil was introduced. This model is vastly reduced in size over the SAR version. It was likely designed for Israeli CT units that required more firepower than the Uzi family could deliver. The Micro-Galil has a barrel length of around 7¾ inches, and measures 17½ inches with the stock folded. This is a considerable reduction in size when compared to the 7.62 ARM Galil, which measures close to 32 inches folded, and the 5.56mm ARM which measures just over 29 inches folded. The Micro-Galil also weighs considerably less at 6½ pounds empty, where the original ARM models weigh between 9½ and 10 pounds depending on caliber, the 7.62 model weighing closer to 10 pounds. The SAR models are considerably lighter, with the 7.62 SAR weighing close to 8½ pounds and the 5.56 SAR closer to 8¼ pounds.

Short Rifles with Long Barrels

For all it has going for it, the Galil was never widely used by the Israelis, most likely due to the large number of M16s supplied by the U.S. government.[14] The Israelis began to issue their latest design starting in the mid–2000s. This is a bullpup design known as the TAR21, a compact and reliable weapon. However, the Micro-Tavor MTAR21, also known as the Tavor-2, has recently been selected as the standard Israeli service rifle.[15] The Tavor-2 appears to be very similar to the Steyr AUG bullpup design in concept, in that it can be easily converted to a 9mm submachine gun. The Israeli decision to adopt the bullpup as a standard weapon was rather surprising, given the tactical shortcomings of the bullpup configuration. While most bullpups are convertible for either left or right hand use, switching a borrowed weapon over is not something one wants to do in the middle of a firefight. This also creates problems as a weapon setup for right handed shooters cannot be fired around the left side of a building without the user being exposed to enemy fire, unless the user wants to turn the weapon upside down and forget aiming. Given the vast experience possessed by Israeli troops regarding urban combat, the move to adopt a bullpup is rather surprising. Its tactical weaknesses aside, the bullpup concept makes a great deal of sense. By placing the action behind the trigger, the overall length of the weapon is greatly reduced, while maintaining a conventional length barrel. The new FN 2000 may be more successful in this regard, as it addresses the issues of cartridge ejection by directing the empty cases forward. This new design has yet to see any adoption by a major service and as of now should still be considered unproven. Since bullpups appear to be here to stay, let's cover perhaps the most successful model of bullpup manufactured to date.

Way Ahead of Its Time

The Steyr AUG was ahead of its time when first introduced in 1977. It was quickly adopted by its native Austria as the STG 77. The AUG utilized modern high quality plastics for much of its construction. The standard rifle uses a chrome lined 20 inch cold hammer forged barrel to increase its service life. Other barrel lengths offered are a 16 inch carbine, 13¾ inch submachine gun barrel, and a 24.4 inch heavy barrel fitted with a recoil brake and folding bipod. These barrels are offered with rifling rates of 1 to 9 inch as used by the Austrians, though other twist rates are available.

The AUG is unique among service rifles in that its barrel can be quickly changed by the operator. Easy barrel change systems are becoming more commonly seen, but this is still an operation usually performed by armory personnel. This unique feature gives the AUG the ability to provide continuous fire support as long as a cold barrel and loaded magazines are on hand. The AUG can also be fitted with any sighting system desired by using an alternate receiver cover. The most recent AUGA2 and A3 models have rail systems installed. The original AUG has an excellent standard sight in its own right. It is a 1½ power scope with a centered circular reticle which doubles as a range finder, as an average size man just fits within the reticle's circle at 300m. Some versions of this scope have

Australian F88. This is the Steyr AUG made "down under." This model has a rail system in place of the usual scope, along with an M203 grenade launcher (MC1 [SW/AW] J. Collins, U.S. Navy).

a dot centered in the reticle for more precise aiming. The AUG can be set up for semi-automatic closed bolt operation, closed bolt semi/full automatic, and semi/full auto firing from an open bolt position as a light machine gun.

There is also a three round burst option, but the user does not have the option of firing full auto and burst. To select between full-auto or burst the trigger mechanism has to be removed and a lever shifted. Like many modern rifles, the AUG uses a translucent plastic magazine that was very original at the time. These were available in either 30 or 42 round capacities. The smaller magazine is better suited for use with the bipod due to its smaller profile; while the 42 round was designed for the light machine gun role, it is likely to bump the ground. When fired from the prone position, the longer magazine interferes with elevation adjustments.

The AUG uses a short stroke gas piston system that is offset to the right side, where it serves as one of two guide rods for the bolt carrier. The gas piston and cylinder are contained within the barrel assembly in a fitting that is shrunk fit over the barrel. The barrel assembly is equipped with a folding vertical grip, which is fixed on the 13¾ inch barrel. The bolt is very similar to that of the M16 with 7 radial lugs that rotate into a locking collar fitted into the aluminum receiver.[16] Large numbers of small locking lugs generally make for difficult cleaning, especially on dirty functioning weapons like the M16. The Steyr AUG however, is far cleaner in operation and has proven very reliable in use.

Were it not for its bullpup configuration, this would be perhaps the most effective service rifle in use today. As it is, it suffers from the same tactical shortcomings of all bullpups. The AUG has also been produced in Australia, where it is known as the F88 or the Austcyr. This variation has an automatic locking device fitted similar to the AUG version adopted by Ireland.[17] This device was installed to prevent the trigger of the AUG from being depressed fully to the automatic mode. The AUG uses a two position trigger with the first pull delivering semi-automatic shots, while continuing to depress the trigger will deliver automatic fire unless setup for burst. Other weapons have used this type of trigger in the past, and it takes some getting used, to but appears to work efficiently. As it does not have a fire control lever, the AUG uses a cross bolt type safety located above the grip. This is an excellent quality, well designed system, especially considering that it was first introduced in 1977. The cocking handle does not move during fire but can be used as a forward assist device if needed. Current versions have a bolt release feature although original (A1) always had a last round bolt catch. In the original version it was necessary to slightly pull back the cocking handle to release this. The trigger guard covers the entire hand which makes this design suitable for use with heavy mittens in cold climates. As a side note, many rifles designed for use in cold weather have trigger guards that can be pivoted out of the way. Takedown is easy and there is a 9mm conversion kit available. The magazine for the 9mm version is interchangeable with that of the Steyr MPi 69 and MPi 81 submachine guns. These are UZI lookalikes using a great deal of plastic in construction, and were supposedly quite reliable and simple, but never very popular in use.

There have been three versions of the AUG, the A1, A2, and the A3. The A2 version added a folding cocking handle and an integral rail system on the receiver cover. The A3 is similar, but has additional rails for accessory mounting with the addition of the bolt catch device. Recent A3s have a magazine well that uses the M16 pattern magazines. The A3 model looks a bit different from the earlier versions but it is still recognizable as an AUG. The AUG can also be used with the M203 grenade launcher with very little modification. For those that did not like a separate grenade launcher, rifle grenades can be fitted to the NATO standard 20 inch barrel. The overall length with 20 inch standard barrel is just over 31 inches, with a weight of around 7.9 pounds. empty. While it has the same layout as other bullpups, it is often considered the finest design in this rifle class, certainly the most versatile given its modular makeup. Where its bullpup layout is not an issue, it makes for an outstanding rifle, being a rifle, carbine, submachine gun, and light machine gun all in one. The Israeli Tavor-2 may give it some competition in the modularity department, however.

The Other Bullpups

The other two well known bullpup designs are the French FAMAS F1/G2 and the British SA80 (L85). Neither of these designs has matched the AUG for ruggedness or reliability. In fact, initial models fielded were not entirely satisfactory. The FAMAS reportedly had trouble with plastic strength and magazine failures. This has not been well documented, however. The FAMAS was originally meant to use a disposable magazine. This

The French FAMAS F1 5.56mm bullpup, standard rifle of the French army until the updated G2 version was adopted. These drill rifles have magazine blocks fitted (SrA. E. Berrios, U.S. Air Force).

5. *Assault Rifles*

This is the newer FAMAS G2; the new triggerguard shape can be clearly seen (LCpl. K.J. Launius, U.S. Marine Corps).

British L85A2, a vast improvement over the original A1 variation, which developed a poor reputation during the Gulf War (MSgt. S. Faulisi, U.S. Air Force).

was probably not a good idea, as the magazine is a key component in the reliable functioning of any self-loading weapon. The G2 version has been improved and strengthened and has been recently adopted by the French military. The G2 version now has a trigger guard very similar to that found on the AUG, which covers the entire hand. Time will tell if this makes for a more field worthy weapon.[18]

The British SA80 (L85) was a fiasco. The Enfield, as it is sometimes called, quickly developed a reputation for parts breakage, jamming, and accidental magazine release. The L85A2 is supposedly vastly improved, having been extensively reworked by HK. Reports are that the newer version is far better than the original model, both in terms of parts durability and reliability.[19] The main disadvantage of the L85 when compared to other bullpups is that it is not convertible to left-side ejection, meaning the weapon can only be fired from the right shoulder. It is doubtful, given the track record of both of these rifles, that either will see any significant adoption or use beyond what they currently enjoy, though the current versions appear to be performing well enough.

Israel's New Rifle

As briefly covered earlier, the Israelis have recently adopted the MTAR-21 Micro Tavor as their new standard rifle. The Tavor will likely prove a more successful bullpup than either the L85A2 or the FAMAS G2. To quickly cover its history, the Tavor design began in the early nineties. It had its share of initial problems. It began to replace many U.S. made M16s starting in 2003. The Tavor is a modern bullpup and operates via the proven long stroke gas system which uses an M16 style rotating bolt. It was also designed to use the M16 magazine which has become standard for many modern rifle designs, unfortunately. The compound curve of the M16 magazine has never been known for its reliable feed characteristics. There have been many attempts to correct this, some more successful than others. The Tavor will be replaced by the improved Tavor-2, which offers greater modularity and has hopefully corrected the initial problems, though the original Tavor appears to be performing quite well, after its early minor issues were corrected. The newer model has a different sight than the original, along with the normal rail mounting options available.[20] Like most bullpup designs, it can be converted to left or right hand use.

The standard Tavor weighs 7¼ pounds. and measures just over 28 inches in overall length. The recently selected Tavor-2 will likely be similar dimensionally, depending on which barrel is chosen as standard. India has reportedly been using the Tavor to a large extent.

Bullpups Are Not the Only Option

Bullpup models aside, the vast majority of rifles most likely to be encountered worldwide are still conventional in layout. Starting in the 1970s, several new designs began to hit the market. Many of these models were heavily influenced by the AK-47. One of the earliest models to enter service was the Beretta AR 70. This first saw use in the early 1970s and borrowed considerably from the AK. The bolt and gas system was very closely related to the Kalashnikov system. In use, the AR 70 showed several major flaws, and an improved and strengthened version was adopted in the mid–1980s by the Italian military. The new AR 70/90 still kept the same operating mechanism. The receiver was changed in geometry to increase rigidity as the earlier rectangular shape was found to suffer from bolt binding under severe stress. Despite its AK origins and quality construction, it has not sold as well as many other modern rifle designs.

The Belgian FN Fusil Nouveau type Carabine (FNC) is another rifle clearly derived from the AK. This design was meant to correct the flawed FN CAL design of the 1960s. The FNC was meant to provide reliability under extreme conditions, to be inexpensive and use modern manufacturing techniques, and to be a worthy successor to the legendary FAL. While the FNC has been relatively successful, the most modern version of this rifle is not the original Belgian model, but rather the Swedish AK5C and its shortened version, the AK5D Mk 2. These differ quite a bit from the original, but most of the changes are for increased modularity and user convenience.

Sweden decided to manufacture its own version of the FNC in the early 1980s, known as the AK5. This replaced the earlier AK4, the Swedish designation for the HK G3. The initial AK5 performed well, but the Swedish must have felt it could be improved. They began developing a heavily modified version and adopted it in 2005. This version is what the FNC should have been from the start. It is fitted with rails on the receiver top and forend, a vertical grip can be attached up front, and a last round bolt catch has been added, something the original lacked. The standard magazine is a translucent plastic model designed for reliable feeding, although standard M16 magazines can also be used, as with the FNC. An improved folding stock is fitted. This stock not only folds like the original, but can be adjusted for length of pull as well. Other minor improvements were made to the pistol grip, flash hider, and forend. Folding iron sights can be fitted to the rail system, although optical units were clearly meant to be the primary sighting method. The end result is a rifle with a reputation for top reliability, which possesses all of today's desired features. This is one of the more modern rifles currently available. The compact model AK5D Mk 2 is likely meant for use by Swedish special operations units and elements within their law enforcement community. The end result is perhaps one of the finest service rifles ever designed. The AK5C offers the reliability of the AK-47 along with a more convenient safety, a bolt catch, and the simple and fast magazine release of the M16, all of which are the usual gripes against the AK. The rifle offers all this in addition to the variety of accessories or sighting options that can be mounted. This makes the Swedish service rifle a very lethal urban combat weapon system.

Another AK derivative is the Swiss SIG SG 550 series. Some authorities consider this to be one of the best, if not the best assault rifle in the world. This is the end result of a series of earlier models, the SG 530 and SG 540. The SG 550 was originally known as the SG 541, but was later renamed. These were intended to be lighter weapons meant to replace the Swiss Stgw 57 service rifle of the post-war era. Though the 57 was an excellent service rifle, it was extremely expensive and a bit heavy.

The SG 550 uses a long stroke gas operated action with a bolt design that is obviously borrowed from the AK-47. The gas system of the SIG is far more refined and uses an adjustable regulator that allows for reliable functioning in the event of severe operating conditions. The plastic magazines are translucent like many other modern designs and are of a unique pattern that is not interchangeable with any other popular design. Standard capacities are 20 and 30 rounds, though smaller capacities are also offered. The 550 series is capable of three round bursts in addition to full auto, and the cyclic rate is roughly 700 rpm. There is a last round bolt catch as well as a right side folding plastic stock that reduces the overall length by roughly 9 inches. The standard rifle version is roughly 39 inches overall and weighs 9 pounds empty with its lightweight folding bipod, which can be removed if desired. The rifle version uses a 20.8 inch barrel. Several smaller versions are also made. The SG 551 uses either a 14.3 inch or 17.9 inch LB (long barrel). The LB version is capable of using both rifle grenades and a bayonet, which cannot be used on the 14.3 inch version. There are also two versions of the SG 553, as mentioned in the previous chapter. These replaced the earlier SG 552, which did not function as reliably as hoped.

Available rifling is either 1–10 inch (standard) or 1–7 inch. The SG 550 is one of the most accurate service rifles made. A great deal of this has to do with the quality of manufacture. The shorter barrel models do not give up much in this regard either. There are two basic receiver versions made. One uses a standard diopter rear sight, and the other uses the popular rail system (flat-top). Night sights are fitted as standard, as with several other modern rifles. Although the standard iron sight receiver can fit a scope mount, a detachable cheek piece would likely be required to bring the eye and scope into proper alignment. This cheek piece is one of many accessories offered for this family of weapons. The flattop version is better suited for optics use. A magazine loading tool is stored in the pistol grip on all models. SIG offers the GL5040/5140 40mm grenade launchers to fit the 550/551. This is a single shot launcher of high quality. There was a sniper variant of the SG 550 made, which had no iron sights fitted. This model has been discontinued, likely due to lack of demand for a sniper rifle in the 5.56 NATO caliber. The SIG SG 550 series are arguably the finest assault rifles in the world, and they should be given their price tag, which exceeds that of most service rifles currently in production.

The First 5.56mm HK

While many of today's best assault rifles are based on the AK-47 to one degree or another, they're not the only successful designs. While no longer produced by HK, the 5.56mm HK 33 series has done quite well worldwide, and production continues outside of Germany. The HK 33 is basically a smaller version of the popular G3 7.62mm NATO rifle. The HK 33 was used on a limited basis by U.S. special operations units during the Vietnam War. It was identical in operation to its bigger brother, but the overall length and weight are considerably less. The HK 33A2 was the standard fixed stock model. It weighed just over 8 pounds. empty and measured slightly over 36 inches in overall length.

5. Assault Rifles

The new 5.56mm HK G36, which uses a gas operated action, unusual for HK designs (SFC J. Cervantez, U.S. Army).

The magazine capacity was initially either 25 or 40 rounds, but 30 round versions were later available. The 40 round magazine capacity was the reason for the 33's use by U.S. units. This was a considerable improvement over the 20 round, then available for the M16. The telescoping stocked model 33A3 reduced the length by over 7 inches, but weighed a bit more. This rifle was also offered in two short barreled models, one was the HK 33K with a 13 inch barrel. The other was known as the HK 53, which had an 8.8 inch barrel.[21] These were some of the first "chopped" assault rifles, aside from the Colt Commando models, though the short HKs didn't suffer from the reliability issues that plagued the Commando. This was due to use of the delayed blowback operating system which is not as touchy regarding barrel length.

The final production version was the model 33E. This was basically the 33A2 with a new designation. The same applied to the carbine version which became the model 33EK. Either weapon could be ordered with fixed or telescoping stock.

There was an updated model introduced in the 1980s that was meant to meet NATO standards. This was known as the G41. This new model offered a bolt catch, dust cover, and quiet bolt closure device among other improvements. This was supposed to become the next German service rifle but was apparently too expensive. There was also a carbine version but these did not succeed in keeping the HK 33 line going, and HK instead turned to a new idea altogether.

Plastic Is King

The HK G36 was the result of Germany's need for a new service rifle. The German re-unification created budget problems for the nation. As a result, the G11 caseless rifle program was cancelled.[22] At the same time the modernized HK G41 was not going to happen. It was even said that the AK-74 was being considered as a service rifle due to the huge number the former East Germans had in stockpile. This would have been the least expensive approach. Germany still wanted a modern 5.56mm rifle and HK took a new approach with the G36. They gave up the roller locking system and decided to go with a short-stroke gas piston system that borrowed heavily from the Armalite AR-18 rifles developed in the 1960s. The G36 gas system is self regulating, and once enough gas has been used to operate the carrier, the supply is cut off.

The rifle uses a great deal of polymer construction. Optical sights are standard, and on the newer G36A2, a rail system is standard and a new model red-dot sight has been adopted. For those not already familiar with the G36 sight, the system is actually two sites combined with emergency iron sights for backup. For close range, the red-dot sight is used, and a three power optical scope is used for longer ranges up to 800m. This scope uses a built in range finder and is matched to the ballistics of the 5.56mm NATO standard round. The G36E export model uses a simpler 1.5 power scope without the red-dot sight.[23] Interestingly, the dual sight system is proving popular. A similar scope is commonly used on the Colt M4/M4A1 series. The U.S. sight is made by Trijicon and is known as the ACOG which was mentioned in Chapter 4.

The G36 has all the other features of today's big sellers. It can fire NATO standard rifle grenades, mount a 40mm single-shot launcher (the AG36), and a bayonet can be fitted. The weight of the standard German model is 8 pounds empty, with the export model weighing just over 7¼ pounds. The overall length is approximately 39¼ inches extended, and just under 30 inches folded. It is designed to be fired with the stock in either position. There are two short models made as well as the standard rifle version (see Chapter 4).

It is claimed that the gas system of the G36 can handle 5000 rounds before cleaning is required. This is encouraging but probably not recommended in operation. Carbon deposits seem to work better than glue, especially after they have cooled and hardened.

The G36 has sold very well worldwide. Spain adopted the export model shortly after Germany adopted the original version. Mexico had planned to manufacture the rifle locally but this deal has been shaky, likely due to cost issues in setting up production. The G36 is used by at least 20 nations in one form or another. It has proven to be a rugged, dependable weapon with good handling qualities. There have been some complaints that if the weapon becomes too hot, the accuracy decreases due to the synthetic housing softening. As the barrel is free floating, the validity of this complaint is questionable, but possible, as the entire action is housed in a plastic casing. This aside, the G36 is often considered to be one of the best of the current 5.56mm NATO rifles. The gas system works so well, in fact, that it has been duplicated in the HK 416 and 417.

These are important designs, as there is a chance that the HK 416 may replace the Colt M4 series as the next U.S. service rifle. This is only speculation, but it is a well founded guess.

The M16 Gets a Heart Transplant

The HK 416 and 417 are identical in operation. The 417 is chambered for the 7.62mm NATO caliber and is larger dimensionally. The 416 was developed to be a fix for the M4/M4A1 carbine. It was originally offered as an upper receiver conversion for the M4. It is still offered as a retrofit, but is marketed as a complete weapon in a variety of barrel lengths. The 416 was adopted by the U.S. Army's Delta Force around 2004.[24] It was recently tested by the U.S. Marine Corps for possible adoption as the M27 Infantry Automatic Rifle (IAR).[25] This testing parallels the testing of the FN SCAR-L by the U.S. Army, although this model has been turned down in favor of the 7.62mm NATO SCAR-H, as it is felt that the larger caliber offers greater versatility.[26]

The 5.56mm HK 416 (foreground), the choice of the U.S. Army's Delta Force. This weapon uses a gas system similar to that of the G36 (PH3[AW] S. Hussong, U.S. Navy).

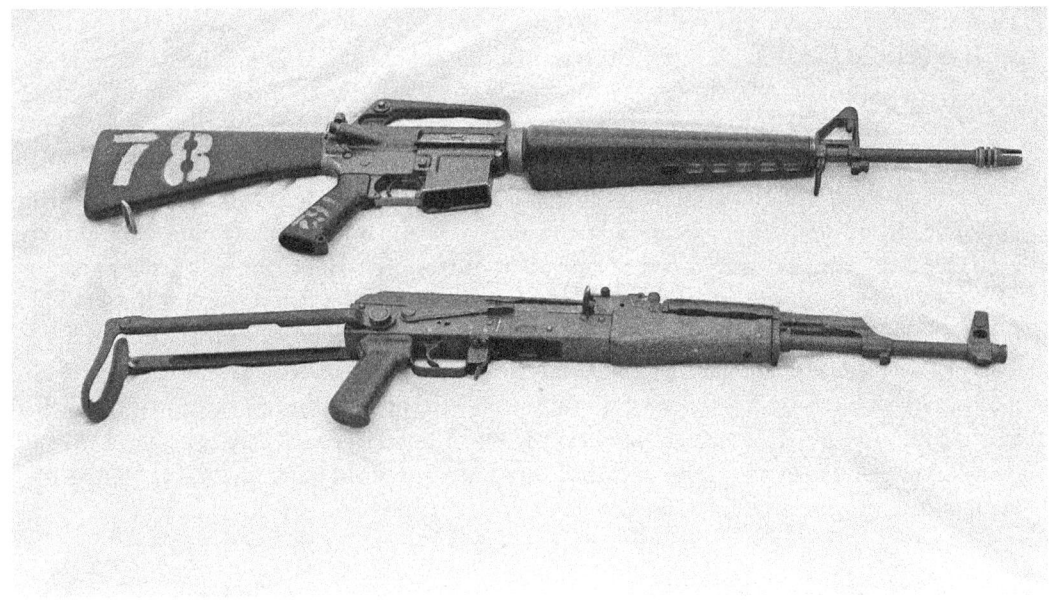

5.56mm M16A1 (top) compared to the 7.62mm AKMS. The flash hider on the M16 is the early pattern open prong type. Later models were closed to prevent snagging on foliage (Sgt. B. Bethune, Department of Defense).

The Norwegian military has adopted the HK 416 as their standard service rifle. The 416 and 417 offer cold hammer forged barrels that have twice the service life of the standard M4 barrel. The 416 can be fired after being submerged in water without completely draining the barrel,[28] something that can usually cause a burst barrel. If acquired as a complete rifle, a new grip design and improved buttstock are fitted.

The 416 offers a significant increase in reliability over the M4 carbine and there is a chance this could be the U.S.'s next service rifle.[27] Land Warfare Resources Corporation offers a somewhat similar design known as the M6. This is often considered to be one of the finest gas piston derivatives of the M16. Some even consider it superior to the HK 416. There are many other commercial gas piston rifles based on the M16 layout. Many of these are of excellent quality.

Heavy and Slow, but Still Deadly

While the rifles covered in this chapter have so far been chambered for NATO calibers, there are other popular and effective calibers being used. One of the most lethal was introduced in Chapter 4. The 9 × 39mm Russian subsonic cartridge has proven very reliable as a stopping round. This is no doubt due to its bullet weight, as it is even heavier than that of the .45 ACP, as well as being slightly higher in velocity. While the compact 9×39mm models covered earlier are almost ideal for modern urban combat, the larger

Russian AS suppressed assault rifle offers many desirable traits for similar fighting conditions. It is reportedly popular among Russian troops. The AS is one of a family of weapons and design work began in the late 1980s. Other models related to the AS are the VSS sniper variant, and the compact SR3, which is more heavily modified. While these are different weapons, they are all based on the same basic action.

The AS was designed from the start as a suppressed assault rifle. This should not be fired without the suppressor installed, as the shooter could be severely injured. The action is roughly derived from the AK and the safety lever greatly resembles that of the AK-47. The fire selector design is original and is separate from the safety, whereas the AK uses one lever for both jobs. The AS uses a side folding wire steel stock that reduces the overall length from almost 34½ inches down to just over 24 inches. The rate of fire is considerably higher than that of the AK at 900 rpm. The AS is also quite light at 5½ pounds. empty. Plastic 10 or 20 round magazines are standard, and the same magazines can be used on the VSS and SR3.[29] As already mentioned, magazine capacity is most likely limited due to bullet weight combined with spring tension issues. A sight mounting bracket is standard on the receiver as with most modern AK variations. Open notch iron sights are standard. Maximum effective range is claimed to be 400m, though this weapon is most likely meant for use at much closer ranges. It has seen combat use in both the Chechen and Georgian conflicts with favorable performance.

As an urban combat weapon, its folding stock is a must and its AK based action is likely appreciated for its reliability. The power of the 9 × 39mm cartridge, even at its subsonic velocity, exceeds that of short-barreled assault rifles, and offers considerably more power than any submachine gun. Reliable and consistent stopping power is always favored by troops, especially a close range. These are qualities that this round seems to possess in spades. The suppressor of the AS keeps things quiet and helps eliminate flash at the same time, both big advantages for indoor operations. With an effective range of over 400 yards, the AS is more than adequate for most urban operations. The standard sights are not very effective beyond this range anyway. Beyond this distance, open notch iron sights become very slow to use and hits become inconsistent as the sights begin to blur. This family of rifles — including their competing models, the 9A-91, VSK-94, and AK 9 — are likely to see continued service, as they appear to be tailor made for modern warfare environments. It seems that the 9 × 39mm cartridge is here to stay.

The World's Most Common Firearm

The two final rifle designs to be covered in this chapter are without a doubt the most prevalent combat rifles in the world. They are usually recognized even by those who are not at all familiar with firearms. The Kalashnikov AK-47 has become the definitive assault rifle. It will probably see use in every conflict the world experiences for the next 50 years, unless there is a technological breakthrough in the small arms industry. It has been estimated that over 50 million AK rifles have been produced.[30] Some estimates are as high as 100 million. If these numbers are even close then nearly one in five firearms in the world is some form of AK. No other modern small arm in the world has even come close to achieving this kind of success. The U.S. M16 is the second most common assault rifle in the world and not even 10 million have been produced.[31] The previous record holder was the model 98 Mauser bolt action rifle, with roughly half the production numbers of the AK.

Why this rifle has proven so successful is due to several factors. First of all, it is the oldest assault rifle still in production, so it does have a good head start. As it was the standard Soviet service rifle for many years, a great many were handed out to nations that supported the socialist cause, either for free or at very low cost. China also chose this design as the type 56 and with the world's largest army, a great many had to be produced just to equip the People's Army. Probably the main reasons for the AK's success are its low cost and relative ease of production. The AK is a very simple weapon design, and minimal machining is required for the stamped AKM version, which is the most common.

The AK-47 is a long stroke gas piston rifle. This was not a new concept, even at the time of the AK's introduction. However the AK added to this a very reliable rugged curved steel magazine design which almost never fails to function properly. And one of the key components in any automatic weapon is its feed system. The most perfectly engineered self-loader is useless without an equally trustworthy feed system. The AK was also designed

Field stripped M16A1 (top) compared to the AKMS for comparison. Both weapons are easily broken down for cleaning but use very different technology (Sgt. B. Bethune, Department of

with the minimum number of parts. This created a great deal of space within the rifle's action. This, plus the designer's forethought of allowing for plenty of clearance between components, gives the AK very little sensitivity to sand and mud. Fine sand is the worst enemy of any firearm.

The AK-47 also uses chrome plating on many key internal components. Chrome plating on bores and chambers has long been a military practice to reduce corrosion. A great deal of older ammunition uses corrosive priming compounds and chrome plating helps keep this corrosion at bay. Some newly manufactured ammunition still uses the same ingredients, but for the most part current production ammo is generally non-corrosive. The residue from this corrosive priming compound would quickly pit any non-chrome plated bore if not cleaned regularly. As many Soviet military personnel were conscripts, rifle maintenance was not always done on a regular basis. Many of these troops just wanted to go home as quickly as possible. The AK's generous amount of chrome plating kept these issues to a minimum.

The AK's 7.62 × 39mm cartridge was designed late in World War II and was first used in the Simonov SKS carbine, another very rugged rifle, but one that lacked a full auto option and was limited in firepower with its 10 round fixed magazine. This round was clearly inspired by the German 7.92 × 33mm short round used in the STG 44. The Germans had studied the ranges at which most rifle fire took place and determined that cartridges with effective ranges of over 300m were overly powerful and led to unnecessary resource consumption. Using a round with just enough power to be effective at the observed combat ranges allowed for a lighter cartridge that generated less recoil. This meant less wear on parts, a lighter rifle, and the ability of troops to carry more ammunition into combat. The Soviets were impressed by this logic and it also fit well with their infantry doctrine. The Soviets had made heavy use of submachine gun fire during the war, and the idea of a lightweight automatic rifle suited them well. The 7.62 × 39mm cartridge was also well suited to automatic rifle designs. The cartridge case had a gentle shoulder angle which did not stick in the chamber as readily as cases with sharp shoulder angles. This case geometry reduced accuracy somewhat, but the Soviets were not looking for a target grade rifle. Once Kalashnikov had perfected the design, the rest fell into place. The initial version was meant to use a stamped receiver, but this did not work out as planned. As a result, the first service models used a machined receiver instead. Finally the stamped receiver version was perfected in 1959, and the AKM, as it was known, became the standard version until replaced by the AK-74 in the mid-1970s. The AKM differed little from the original AK in overall length, but was far lighter. It usually weighed between six and seven pounds depending on the density of the wood used. The original AK-47 weighed somewhere in the neighborhood of 9 pounds empty.

The New AK

The Soviets had studied the M16's performance in Vietnam and were impressed by the concept of the 5.56mm round. They decided it was a sound idea and developed their own version, the 5.45 × 39mm. The AK-74 was first seen in service in the 1970s and was used heavily during the invasion of Afghanistan. The AK-74 was basically the AKM in a smaller caliber. It did have a newly designed muzzle break which outperformed anything previously seen. This device redirected the muzzle gases to counteract the recoil and muzzle climb forces. It is claimed that the recoil was cut in half, and that muzzle climb is almost nonexistent when fired on auto.[32] Some have said it is like firing a .22 rimfire automatic rifle. The side effect was that anyone standing next to the rifle would receive a very harsh blast. Most current production AK models use this device. The stock design was new for the folding variant. Original Soviet AK-47s and AKMs usually used a bottom folding stock similar to that used on the German MP 40 submachine gun. The new stock looked more like the skeleton version of a normal rifle stock. It folded to the left side when not in use.

During the Soviet invasion of Afghanistan, a highly compact version of the new rifle entered service. The AKS-74U was smaller than many submachine guns. The barrel was cut down from over 16 inches for the standard rifle to roughly 8 inches. As with all short barreled assault rifles, the usual problems arose with regards to muzzle flash. To deal with this, a different type of muzzle device was needed. The new device was a combination bell shaped flash hider mounted ahead of a tubular expansion chamber that helps keep gas pressures up to aid in reliable functioning. This was needed as the barrel was so short that the gas pressures didn't have time to build in the cylinder to properly propel the piston rearward. As mentioned in the previous chapter, this very short weapon had some overheating issues and it looks as if the longer barrel AK-105 carbine will become its replacement. The AK-105 has a barrel length of approximately 12½ inches, but still uses the same type muzzle device as seen on the AKS-74U.

While on the subject of the AK-105, the current production series is known as the AK-100 generation. These stem from the AK-74M, which is considered to be the parent model. This is the standard Russian service rifle at the present time, although an AK-200 model has been revealed. The 100 series isn't much different from the previous AK-74. The furniture used is no longer wood and the side folding stock mechanism is standard. The stock, however, now resembles a conventional rifle stock as opposed to the earlier skeleton model. Also a sight mounting rail is fitted on all models. Replacement forends with rail systems are available, and these appear to be standard on the newer AK 200 series. The Russians have developed a 60 round casket magazine that was roughly the same length as the standard 30 round AK-74 magazine, but it appears that this magazine doesn't perform as well as hoped.[33]

As for the AK magazines, the original 7.62 × 39mm steel magazines are widely encountered, although many newer versions are made of plastic. Most AK-74 magazines are made of plastic, although Polish and Romanian steel 5.45 × 39mm magazines have been encountered in 30 and 40 round capacities. The standard light machine gun magazine in 5.45 × 39mm is usually a 45 round plastic version. For most 7.62mm models 30 and 40 round steel magazines are used, although there is a 75 round steel drum magazine offered. Some steel 20 round magazines in 7.62mm are seen on occasion, usually intended for use within armored vehicles that had small entryways. As AK rifles do not have a last round bolt catch, some AK magazine patterns, such as those from the former Yugoslavia, have a follower design that catches the bolt as it is returning to battery. This served as a crude form of bolt catch, but made magazine removal more difficult as the recoil spring was pushing in the opposite direction.

AK rifles, especially the folding stock variations, are ideal weapons for the modern combat environment. They are compact, light, and can easily mount modern optics. Most models can mount suppressors, once the normal muzzle device is removed. The full length AK can also mount the GP30 40mm single shot grenade launcher. The GP30 and GP34 are the most recent versions of this launcher. While the carbines and short AKS-74U cannot mount these launchers, there is a 30mm silent single shot launcher made for these weapons, known as the BS-1 (GSN-19). This combination makes for a very powerful, quiet, compact, and deadly combination for city fighting.

U.S. troops first gained respect for the AK when these rifles often outperformed the M16 series during the Vietnam War. This was primarily because the M16 kept failing to function. The AK has continued to show its reliability in other conflicts since. It is generally accepted that the AK is far more reliable than the M16. There are those who would dispute this, though it is generally a wiser practice to accept the word of the troops in the field, as they have the most experience in dealing with these weapons in combat conditions. One of the former security firms to operate in the Middle East had a great deal of respect for the AK. It was so well respected that a number of Hungarian AMD 65s were refitted for close combat operations. The 7.62mm AK round is reputed to be more deadly than the 5.56 NATO when used for close combat.

With regard to caliber choice, the 5.45 × 39mm AK-74 cartridge closely approximates the 5.56 NATO cartridge not only in bullet diameter, weight and muzzle velocity, but it also did a good job of copying one of the 5.56mm's other traits. The original U.S. M193 cartridge used during the Vietnam War utilized a 55 grain lead cored bullet that was stabilized by a 1–12 inch twist. This was just enough to be stable in flight, but once the bullet hit something, that changed dramatically. This led to horrible wounds being created. The original 5.45mm Soviet round reportedly does an even better job in this regard. The original AK-74 bullet had a center of gravity located far aft. The round was reportedly so deadly that the Afghan freedom fighters took to calling it the "poison bullet" because of the nasty wounds it created. Both the M193 and the pattern 74 cartridges would seem to be in direct violation of international agreement, but the matter has never been fully resolved.[34]

The Russians also make use of more modern tungsten cored armor piercing bullets in both the 7.62 × 39mm and 5.45 × 39mm rounds. These are likely similar in performance to equivalent U.S. bullets such as the 5.56 × 45mm bullet of the M995 cartridge.[35]

The AK-47 family has seen more combat use than any other modern service rifle for several reasons. One is because it is so common in areas of recurrent fighting. It is also common because it was relatively cheap for the Soviets to supply these weapons on a widespread basis. The versatility of the assault rifle itself has made it the ideal weapon

The 7.62 × 39mm AKMS without the muzzle brake usually seen on the AKM series rifles (SSgt. J. Swafford, U.S. Air Force).

for the conditions of modern warfare. The typical assault rifle has more than enough range for most urban conditions. They are horribly destructive at close range. They can be used to provide limited fire support, and are usually accurate enough to hit individuals out to the limits of iron sight capability, usually 400 to 500 yards, perhaps a bit more in the hands of an expert. Combined with the ability to mount single shot grenade launchers, this gives most forces a tremendous amount of firepower in units of any size. While some assault rifles are more reliable than others, it is not surprising that many of the best performing weapons seem to be derived from the most successful rifle in history.

The Black Rifle

The final rifle to be covered in this chapter is the AK's primary competition, the U.S. M16 and its variations. This has been the standard U.S. service rifle in one form or another since 1967. It was first purchased by the military for trial issues several years prior to its adoption. One of the latest announcements regarding the M16 series is that the M4/M4A1 will be the new standard issue "rifle" for the U.S. Army. These will replace the M16A2 rifle. This very recent decision is evidence of the military's knowledge of the

5. Assault Rifles

current trends in modern warfare. The M4 is far more compact with its shorter 14½ inch barrel and collapsible stock. The weight is also reduced by approximately 1½ pounds. compared to the standard M16A2 rifle.

The history of the M16 is probably better known than that of many of today's rifles, so I will keep to the essentials to aid better understanding of the current issues involving the M16 and its performance in the Middle East.

The M16, originally known as the AR 15, was primarily designed by the late Eugene Stoner in the mid–1950s. It used a completely original approach to rifle design. The heavy use of aluminum in its construction stemmed from Stoner's experience in the aircraft industry. Such heavy use of aluminum had never been attempted in rifle design prior to this. Steel was still used in the construction of necessary parts such as the bolt, barrel and bolt carrier. Stoner decided to use an aluminum receiver in order to save weight. He also decided to use another weight saving measure in his choice of operating system. He chose a direct gas impingement action that utilized a stainless steel gas tube to provide the needed force to the bolt carrier. Direct gas action was not new and had been done successfully in other designs prior to this. It was efficient at saving weight in that it did not require the use of a gas piston and cylinder which would have added to the overall weight of the rifle.

The M16 was known as a straight line rifle in layout. This meant that the stock/cheek weld was in line with the bore axis, which tended offer better control during recoil and allow for faster follow up shots. To accomplish this, raised sights were necessary. This is why the M16 series has a rear sight located within an integral carrying handle, as well as a distinctive "A" frame front sight bracket, very much like that of the AK-47. The rifle was certainly light at less than 6½ pounds for the original model. The M16 performed well during testing, but once it entered service, major issues began to show up. The rifle rapidly acquired a reputation for jamming quite easily, and this has been well documented.

The cause of this change in performance was later found to be due to two primary issues. The first was the lack of chrome plating within the bore and chamber. This created corrosion issues which were accelerated in the jungle climate. A chrome plated bore and chamber were previously requested and denied. Some genius thought they knew better than experienced military ordnance personnel. The reason for the denial was that since the designer didn't include a chrome plated bore and chamber, the rifle didn't need them.[36] The second reason behind the jamming was a change in the type of propellant used for the ammunition. The original powder used was an older stick powder form, while the new powder used was a ball power which burned dirtier and left behind a greater amount of residue and carbon buildup. No one told the troops that there had been a change in powder and the rifle quickly fouled. This was aggravated by the initial claims that the M16 was a self cleaning rifle, something that does not and never will exist.[37]

The M16's problems were seriously addressed and some of the problems went away, while others persisted. These fixes were quickly handled but that didn't help the U.S. troops that had been killed as a result of the initial problems. The M16A1 that was to become the standard version finally had the chromed bore and chamber which it should have had in the first place. A device called a forward bolt assist was also fitted. The housing for this device was integral to the upper receiver and this allowed the A1 model to be readily distinguished from the earlier standard M16. The purpose of the forward bolt assist was to ensure that the bolt was fully locked prior to firing. In reality the usefulness of the device is questionable, but the reason for the addition of this device still remains to this day. The M16 uses a bolt with a large number of small radial locking lugs that are difficult to properly clean. By itself this is not a problem, as it results in a strong bolt design that does not have to rotate very far before unlocking occurs. The problem arises when this bolt is combined with the increased fouling that results from the M16's direct gas action. Here lies the heart of many complaints surrounding the M16 rifle system, as well as the many attempts to fix the problem. Some of these attempts were more successful than others.

Whether or not one is a fan of this design does not change the fact that the gas impingement system is dirty in operation. True, it is simple and results in a lighter weapon than more conventional gas operated systems. However, it cannot be denied that the system creates an excess buildup of burnt powder residue and carbon. The issue is made worse from the heavy use of aluminum in the M16's construction. Gases tapped from the barrel are directed into the receiver area in order to operate the carrier. This gas contains a great deal of carbon residue from the powder combustion which is then deposited on all components within the operating mechanism. Not only does this quickly foul the action, the residue hardens after the weapon cools, and then acts as a form of adhesive. Another harmful side effect of this design is that the superheated gas drastically heats the components in the receiver. Some of these parts are plastic and some are heat treated for hardness. If these parts become too hot, their service life is severely shortened, resulting in parts breakage. This heating is made worse by the aluminum receiver which does not act as a very efficient heat sink. None of these problems can be fixed without changing the gas system itself. This is just a tradeoff for the designer's choice of action and desire for a lightweight rifle.

Matters are worse for the M4 and M4A1 carbines. The shorter barrel on the M4 series creates even greater temperatures in the receiver area due to a shorter gas tube. This is due to a shorter delay before action unlocking resulting in higher heat and pressure, which results in faster wear of the gas port area. As the gas port erodes, the pressures build even more, as it allows for the passage of an even greater amount of combustion gas through the port. The pressure issues are worse when the M4 is fired in full auto mode, with the pressures and temperatures building at an even faster rate.[38]

As mentioned earlier, a test was conducted in 2007 where the M4 carbine finished last out of the several rifles tested. Among the other weapons tested were the XM8, the HK 416, and the FN SCAR-L. The SCAR and HK 416 were closely related in performance and reliability. As a side note, both of these rifles use a short-stroke gas piston operating system. As previously stated, the HK G36 and HK 416 use almost identical operating systems.

Since the M4 has just taken the place of the M16A2, this does not bode well for the troops. The M4 series is a better overall choice, as it allows for far more versatility, while only sacrificing roughly 50 yards in effective range. However, the fact remains that the M4 suffers from issues that cannot be easily fixed. For troops serving in the Middle East, problems are worse. The fine sand works its way into the action and accelerates wear of the parts. In desert conditions, it is best to avoid the use of excess lubricating oil, and this issue has long been understood by troops. The problem here is that it is recommended that the M16 series be kept well lubricated for reliable functioning. This creates a Catch-22 for U.S. troops operating in desert environments.

Another major issue is with the U.S. standard ammunition and not with the M4 carbine itself. The 1–7 inch barrel rifling of NATO standard weapons does a very good job at stabilizing the 62 grain standard bullet. It does such a good job, in fact, that the bullet punches a small hole in targets without doing much damage at ranges beyond 200 yards.[39] At close range the round seems to perform fairly well. This effect is less pronounced when the round is fired from the longer 20 inch rifle barrel of the M16A2 or A4. However, in the 14½ inch barrel of the M4/M4A1 carbine, the M855 cartridge does not have a good reputation. A heavier 77 grain bullet is being issued in limited numbers (proof of complaints against the standard round). This is known as the Mk 262 Mod 1, and it appears to be performing better than the M855 standard round. Standardization of this round would certainly be a cheaper solution than adopting a new standard caliber such as the 6.8mm Special Purpose Cartridge (SPC). This caliber appears to be the most likely candidate for replacing the 5.56mm NATO. Several quality rifles are currently offered in this caliber, such as the LWRC M6 and the Barrett REC-7, both reliable gas-piston M16 pattern rifles sold commercially.

For the time being, it looks as though the U.S. will have to make do with the M4 carbine. Current economic conditions make any other option unlikely. The current version of the M4 is a 6 pound weapon with an effective range of roughly 550 yards. Most current versions use a detachable carrying handle with an integral M1913 Picatinny rail as standard. This allows for a wide selection of sighting options, including flip up emergency iron sights. Knight's Armament makes a rail equipped forend that adds roughly ½ pound to the overall weight of the weapon. This Rail Interface System (RIS) is fast becoming a standard fitting for the M4. A detachable suppressor is available and there are several new magazine designs to help improve upon feed reliability. Some perform quite well. HK designed a reliable but expensive steel model, and Magpul has a couple of good plastic designs as well. Even the current standard aluminum version of the M16 magazine has been improved over previous models.

Thirty rounds is the standard capacity usually seen today. Troops have learned over the years to load between 27–29 rounds to improve feed consistency, as the original fully loaded 30 round magazine had a tendency to jam within the first few rounds.[40] A 100 round plastic dual drum magazine known as the Beta-mag is also offered for the M16 series and for other rifle designs as well. This magazine performs quite well and offers superior firepower to the standard 30 round clip. Many clamping systems are made to allow magazines to be held side by side for quick reloading. This is a modern version of the practice of taping M1 carbine magazines back to back, as was done during World War II. The overall length of the M4 has already been given and with the reduced 30 inch length offered by the collapsible stock, a slight increase in handling quality is gained. While the stock doesn't offer much reduction in overall length, the large diameter buffer tube that makes up part of the stock offers a comfortable cheek weld for more accurate shooting.

One thing the M16 has always been respected for is its ergonomic design. All fire controls are within easy reach and are convenient to operate. The bolt catch, fire selector lever/safety, and magazine release are all within easy reach. In fact, the magazine release is one of the M16's best features. It is a simple push button design that is quick and easy to use. Magazines are inserted straight into the well until they lock into place, which does away with having to pivot the magazine into engagement as with many other rifle designs. This also reduces the chance of the magazine being improperly inserted and dropping out of the bottom of the magazine well at the wrong moment. More than once, with traditional magazine latch designs, a magazine appears to be inserted properly, only to fall out after the first round is fired. Despite its excellent handling qualities, the M16 would be better served by using a more reliable system of operation. One unusual feature of the M16 is its ejection port cover. While this cover does a good job of keeping out debris when closed, it must be closed manually after firing. The cover pops open after the first round is fired and remains in the open position. More functional designs return to position after every shot. It is likely that the designer was trying to reduce wear on this component by going with this design, but this is just speculation.

While the M16 performs its duties, it cannot be counted on as consistently as more conventional designs. It has a great many weaknesses in design that cannot be remedied easily or inexpensively. It was a good idea in theory, but as with so many other theories, they don't always work as well in practice. Should U.S. economic conditions improve, it is likely that the M16 series will be looking at a limited future and rightly so. It does offer many good features, but reliability under combat conditions is not one of them. As this is the primary requirement from any service rifle, it is possible that the M4 carbine will not long remain as the standard U.S. Army service rifle.

The assault rifle has been the primary battle weapon for the last 40 to 50 years, and until something new takes its place, it will remain so. Larger caliber, long range rifles like the U.S. M14 or HK G3 will likely continue to serve on a limited basis as needs warrant, but by and large most military units will continue to use some form of small caliber assault rifle as their standard weapon for most combat situations. The need for the 7.62mm NATO as an option is shown in the recent decision to go with the SCAR-H (7.62mm) instead of the SCAR-L (5.56mm) as a limited issue weapon.

CHAPTER 6

Sniper Rifles / Precision Tactical Rifles

Sniper rifles and precision tactical rifles do not comprise a new small arms category by any stretch, but it is a type of weapon that is finally coming into its own. For many years the sniper was the leper of the battlefield. No one wanted to deal with that type of soldier. The sniper has always been an essential soldier during war. Things are beginning to change with regards to the general attitude towards snipers. While they have always been very useful on the battlefield, snipers are an absolute necessity in today's urban combat environment. This is often because specific individuals must be targeted and the target may be using some type of hostage as cover. In these situations, top notch shooting skills are called for. Specialist training is also sometimes a must. Not to go too much into the sniper's mission or training, they are not just first rate shooters, they are also trained in intelligence gathering and reconnaissance missions, woodcraft, recognition of high value equipment, and related expertise. The sniper is no longer viewed as a cold-blooded killer, but one who brings a great many needed skills to the battlefield. His role in modern combat is in no way diminished due to the nature of his mission. If anything the sniper will see an increase in duties in future combat. However, at the heart of any sniper program is the rifle.

Dedicated sniper rifles have been used since the Revolutionary War. At the time sniping was not the term applied. They were previously called sharpshooters. Sniping as a dedicated job became common around the turn of the century during the Boer War.[1] During World War I, sniping rifles were fairly common. At the time these were usually standard service rifles equipped with early optical sights, and sometimes even standard iron sights were used. After 1918, more specialized sniper rifles began to appear. Most of these were still the standard service rifle, but were usually issued with optical sights. By the time of World War II, the U.S. decided to go a step further and began to issue the M1903A4 Springfield sniper rifle. This was basically the M1903A3 without the iron sights and a high quality Weaver scope was issued as the standard sight.

The First Modern Sniping Rifle

Truly dedicated and purpose built sniper rifles began to see adoption following the

Small Arms for Urban Combat

Above: 7.62 × 54mmR SVD sniper rifle, a very common rifle in terrorist hands (Cpl. D.J. Schalue, U.S. Marine Corps). *Below*: A U.S. Marine firing the Dragunov SVD. This rifle is one of the deadliest threats to U.S. troops serving in the Middle East (LCpl.N. McCord, U.S. Marine Corps).

Korean War. The former Soviet Union was actually one of the first nations to build a sniper rifle from the drawing board and take it to the battlefield. The SVD or Dragunov, as is often called, is a semiautomatic 7.62 × 54mmR rifle equipped with both iron sights and a specialized range finding sniper scope. The scope used an infrared filter that could detect infrared light sources. This scope could also be used in conjunction with an infrared light source, although this did not turn it into a night sight. The SVD uses a detachable 10 round magazine and has a skeletonized stock fitted with a cheek piece to allow for proper eye alignment with the scope. The SVD weighs 9½ pounds empty (with scope), making it lighter than most current sniper rifles such as the U.S. M21 sniper variant of the M14. The SVD is several inches longer than the M21 at just over 48 inches in overall length. This design was heavily influenced by the AK-47, though the gas system was far different. The SVD uses a short-stroke gas piston as opposed to the long stroke system of the AK. The purpose of this is to help keep the weapon balanced better during recoil, as a long stroke system would have a heavy bolt carrier and piston rod traveling over a much greater distance due to the length of the 7.62 × 54mmR cartridge. A bolt catch was fitted unlike the AK.

Not only did this rifle system work well, it was made in large numbers and is probably the most common semi-auto sniper rifle likely to be encountered in the world. It is especially common with terrorist groups operating in the Middle East.[2] The precision of this rifle is not equal to many more expensive Western sniper systems, but it is far more prevalent, meaning several sharpshooters operating in a specific area could very well be armed with an accurate long range rifle, creating a great deal of trouble for troops operating in the area. The SVD has proven highly effective at its job. The 7.62 × 54mmR is approximately equal to the 7.62 NATO in terms of maximum effective range. This seems reasonable given similar velocities, bullet weights, and diameters. However, the 7.62 NATO round is renowned for its accuracy. At any rate the SVD has proven a low cost sniper system which vastly increases the range at which Soviet supplied military units or terrorist groups can engage. It offers roughly 2–3 times the effective range of the AK-47 7.62 × 39mm cartridge.

There are several new versions of the SVD in production. The SVDS is a side folding stock variant that is made in both 24¾ inch and 22¼ inch barrel versions with the shorter model being the preferred standard. These rifles have also been offered in 7.62 NATO for export. Oddly, the stock on this rifle folds to the right side, which prevents access to the safety. The SVDS uses a shorter flash hider design than the original. Newer scopes are also offered, although these are similar in mission to the original PS-01 scope. A longer 15 round magazine is also offered in addition to the original 10 round version. The longer magazine was designed for the SVU bullpup sniper version to be covered shortly. The weight of the SVDS is increased by under a pound, and the folding model would seem ideal for an urban sniper system. It offers good range capabilities combined with compact dimensions, allowing for easy transportation within military vehicles.

There is also a 9.3 × 64mm SVDK model which is slightly larger overall, due to the larger caliber for which it is chambered. This round is far more powerful than the 7.62 × 54R of the standard SVD or SVDS. The rifle itself resembles an enlarged SVDS, as it uses a folding stock. All three variations can mount a variety of new Russian optics and can be fitted with a bipod as well. The SVDK appears to have been designed with the intention of competing against a similar new western cartridge, the .338 Lapua. These calibers vastly extend the range of sniper systems without drastically increasing the weight of the rifles. For example, the SVDK weighs in at just over 10½ pounds empty. The U.S. firm of Dakota Arms makes the T-76 "Longbow" .338 Lapua bolt action, which weighs roughly 13½ pounds without scope. These are not light weapons, but they are within reason, and are far lighter than the excellent Barrett model 82 series of .50-caliber anti-materiel rifles, which weigh between 25 and 30 pounds. At the same time, new long range calibers offer 2–3 times the effective range of the more conventional 7.62mm sniper cartridges. The .338 Lapua is, in fact, becoming the sniper round of choice for many Western nations due to its effective range and accuracy potential. Some tests have shown consistent hits with a .338 Lapua at ranges of up to 3000 yards, which is more than possible with the correct load and with modern computerized sighting systems. One of the most effective sniper cartridges in this caliber is the 270 grain Lost River bullet, which remains supersonic to 2000 yards, and it is claimed that a new bullet design will extend this capability out to 2200 yards. Should this go into production, it places the .338 Lapua very close to the capabilities of the current long range kings, the .416 Barrett and .408 Chey-Tac. The Russian 9.3 × 64mm is not quite as effective but it does give the Russians an alternative before going to the heavy recoil of the 12.7mm or 14.5mm heavy machine gun calibers used in anti-materiel rifles.

There are other versions of the SVD, including night sight equipped models and a bullpup with selective fire capability. Oddly, this weapon still uses the standard 10 or 15 round magazines. The Russians have advanced considerably in the area of small arms development, especially since the end of the Cold War. In fact, there are now far more Russian designs produced than were ever made during the Soviet era. The AS suppressed assault rifle mentioned in Chapter 5, is offered in a sniper variant known as the VSS. This is the same rifle as the AS, but with a detachable stock very closely patterned after that of the SVD. This rifle is meant to be carried in special hard case for transport. As a result, the entire system breaks down into several sub assemblies: the receiver, stock, sight and suppressor. When assembled the overall length of the VSS is just over 35 inches and its empty weight is close to 6 pounds. Sight and mount add to this weight a bit. Various day or night optics can be fitted, such as the standard PSO-1-1 which can be stored in the carrying case as well. This provides a convenient urban sniping system useful for ranges up to approximately 450 yards. The Russians have also added some new bolt action designs that were meant for use where greater precision of fire is required. The SV 98 is a modern design offered in 7.62 × 54R or a 7.62 NATO and is supposedly going to be available in .338 Lapua shortly. A forend mounted bipod and suppressor are available, as are a variety of day or night optical systems. This rifle is heavier than the SVD and offers an adjustable trigger pull, a precisely manufactured barrel, and more stock adjustment options. This is clearly designed to compete with comparable Western designs. The SV-98 is reportedly based on Russian competition rifles. There is also a .22 rimfire sniper rifle, the SV 99. This weapon is meant for close range work, as a suppressor is normally fitted. The SV 99 is likely equipped with a very efficient suppressor, and it can be broken down in much the same way as the VSS. The small components can be easily stored in the case for transport without drawing undue attention. Both of these systems are in use but not widespread.[3]

The SVD semi-auto sniper rifle is without question the most common sniper rifle worldwide and it has spawned a great many copies, either very similar or identical. The Chinese type 79 and also type 85 variants are very close copies, though the 79 has a shorter stock fitted, most likely to better suit the smaller stature of the average Chinese soldier. Other similar models include the Romanian FPK and Zastava M76. These resemble the SVD but utilize the long stroke system of the AK-47 rifle. The Zastava, in particular, has a reputation for being a quality weapon in terms of manufacture. This also applies to their AK copies the M70 B1 and folding stocked B2. These are almost identical to the Soviet AKM with the exception of the integral grenade launcher sight which cuts off the gas supply when flipped up for use.

European Designs

Regarding Western sniper systems, the Austrian Steyr SSG 69 is a successful bolt action design that has been used for many years. It uses a rotary drum detachable magazine with a five round capacity, a cold hammer forged barrel, and a rigid six lug bolt for secure lock-up. The SSG 69 is standard for the Austrian army. It has been offered over the years in several calibers but the 7.62 NATO is by far the most common for most service work. There are several options offered, stocks are adjustable, some have iron sights, or barrel threaded for suppressor use. Any number of optical devices can be fitted, and the weight of the standard model is less than 9 pounds empty.

The British firm of Parker-Hale has a long history of building sniper systems for military use. These are based on the old model 98 Mauser bolt action system. For anyone not familiar with the model 98, it was the most produced firearm in history until the arrival of the AK-47. It is often considered the pinnacle of bolt action designs. Its reliability is better than perhaps any other rifle ever made. One of the keys to this design's popularity and success was its controlled feed mechanism. The cartridge was under the control of the massive claw extractor from the instant it was free of the magazine. This feature prevented double feeding rounds during a moment of panic. Double feeding refers to attempting to chamber a round while there is already a round in the chamber. On some rifles the bolt must be completely closed before the extractor fully engages the case rim. If the user was to forget to lock the bolt after chambering a cartridge and not engage the extractor, he could easily forget and cycle the bolt again, sending the pointed bullet of the second round into the primer of the chambered round and possibly detonating the chambered round. This would obviously lead to disastrous results. With the Mauser model 98 this is not possible, and many modern commercial bolt action weapons have opted to use the controlled feed concept for safety purposes.

Two popular Parker-Hale designs for sniper use were the model 82 and 85. The model 85 was primarily the same as the model 82, but utilized a detachable box magazine in place of the model 82's internal magazine. As with many bolt action sniper systems, these were available in a variety of configurations and sighting options. They could utilize night scopes, sound suppressors, etc. Adjustable stocks were an option as well. The model 82 was the standard Canadian sniper rifle for some time, and was designated the C3 in modified form. The C3A1 model was fitted with several improvements but the basic Mauser action was the same. Primary changes to the A1 model were a new stock, magazine design and a better trigger. The Canadians have recently adopted a form of the U.S. M24 sniper system but still have numbers of C3A1s, as the Mauser action does not quickly wear out.

The Remington M700 in Uniform

The U.S. Army M24 is the current standard sniping system, with the U.S. Marine Corps choosing the M40A3. Both of these rifles are derived from the bolt action Remington model 700. The M24 uses a longer action to allow conversion to the .300 Winchester Magnum round which extends the reach by over 300 yards when compared to the 7.62 NATO standard caliber. The .300 Winchester Magnum began to see more use as a sniper caliber starting in late 1980s, but it has recently lost ground to even more effec-

U.S. M24 Sniper Weapon System. This can be chambered for either the 7.62mm NATO or the longer range .300 Winchester Magnum (SSgt. S. Pearsall, U.S. Air Force).

6. Sniper Rifles/Precision Tactical Rifles

The 7.62mm M14 was adopted in 1957, though this photograph is quite new. Classics just never seem to die. This model is fitted with a Harris bipod (very popular), and the improved 2-screw scope mount to secure the fiber-optic scope (SFC M.H. Robinson, U.S. Army).

tive calibers such as the .338 Lapua, .416 Barrett and .408 Chey-Tac.

The M24 is issued as a Sniper Weapons System (SWS). This is issued as a complete system including scope, mount, sling, tools, etc., along with the standard issue carrying case. It has reportedly performed well in operations in the Middle East. This is not a surprising, as the earlier U.S.M.C. M40A1 was based on the same action, and the older rifle has done well for many years. While the Remington 700 action does not use the controlled feed extractor of the Mauser model 98, this does not seem to have affected performance in the field. The M24 weighs around 12 pounds empty. This weight can rapidly increase depending on the choice of sights and accessories. The M24 system was meant to be used in conjunction with the M118LR 7.62 NATO cartridge. This is the standard U.S. sniper round and was designed with a heavy 175 grain bullet to provide reduced wind sensitivity. Another popular cartridge is the 168 grain match grade hollow point bullet as used by Federal in their Premium cartridge lineup. The hollow point in this design is not for expansion purposes but is a byproduct of its manufacture.[4]

The U.S.M.C. has a long association with the Remington 700 action. The M40A1 sniper rifle has been U.S.M.C. standard since the 1970s. The current M40A3 uses the same basic Remington 700 short action. The A3 version has added several modified features, mainly it to allow for easy suppressor use and user adjustment. The same basic

The Knight's Armament 7.62mm M110 rifle is an updated version of the old Armalite AR-10 from which the M16 was derived. This model is fitted with a Quick Detach suppressor (Sgt. M.J. MacLeod, U.S. Army).

scope is used as on the A1 model, the Unertl 10 power. No doubt other scopes can be fitted if desired. The popular 1913 rail system is used but is mounted at a shallow angle to allow for better long range engagement. While these are the two primary U.S. sniper weapons systems, there are others in use.

The U.S. M21 is a sniper variant of the M14 and is still useful for times when a semi-auto is needed. The M25 variant is also used, and is quite similar to the original M21. KAC offers the Mk 11 Mod 0, also known as the SR 25 and M110 in slightly different form. This is a semi-auto 7.62 NATO rifle based on the much earlier Stoner AR 10 design. This was the original big brother of the M16. Each of these rifles has its good points and bad points. A standard sniper system for the entire U.S. military has yet to appear.

England's Winning Design

The UK's standard for many years has been the Accuracy International (AI) L96A1. This bolt action system is now offered in both magnum and super magnum variations as

6. Sniper Rifles/Precision Tactical Rifles

well. The standard model is also known as the Arctic Warfare (AW) and was designed to perform reliably in very cold climates without freezing up. Sweden has chosen this and designated it the PSG 90. The British, among others, have adopted the super magnum version in .338 Lapua and the British designation for this rifle is the L115A1 or L115A3, depending on variation. The AI AW model has proven one of the most successful modern bolt action sniper systems in recent years. Its larger caliber versions also appear destined for success.

The AW50 is an enlarged version of the AW, which is chambered for the .50 Browning machine gun (BMG) round. This model is used in Germany as the G24. A folding variant of this weapon is used by the Australians as the AW 50F. There is a new AX .338 that may take the place of the AWSM model. This new version differs visibly in the stock and forend designs. The AI weapons vary in weight depending on model. The standard AW model weighs 13 to 14½ pounds depending on barrel length. Use of a suppressor adds to this weight. The AWM magnum version weighs just over 14 pounds with a 26 inch barrel and the AWSM super magnum .338 Lapua is just over 15 pounds with a 27 inch barrel. The newer AX .338 Lapua weighs just over 17½ pounds with a 27 inch barrel. The AW .50 weighs far more as most .50 caliber rifles do, at roughly 30 pounds.[5] This design will be covered more in the next chapter.

The standard scope used by AI is the Schmidt and Bender, and there are several options. Operators will no doubt choose their favorite scope, however. Many popular scopes now use the mil-dot reticle pattern, although other range finding reticles are gaining in popularity. The mil-dot system is used as a form of range finding and trajectory compensation, as there is a fixed distance between the dots superimposed on the scope's reticle. By sighting on the target through the mil-dot scope, the range can be determined after using a fixed mathematical formula. The "mil" in mil-dot is short for miliradian, an angular unit of measure. While this system has been popular for some time, other range finding systems are faster in use.

One of the fastest range finding reticles was developed by Shepherd Enterprises. The reticle used on the Shepherd scopes has a series of circles that are each centered on crosshairs that begin at the center of the reticle and progress downward with each circle slightly smaller in diameter. The user simply places the target within the appropriate circle and fires. If the target doesn't quite fit one of the circles, the user simply extrapolates and places the vertical stadia line somewhere between the two best fitting circles. This sounds imprecise but works quite well. Each scope model must be matched to a specific bullet weight and velocity range. However, this is true of many other range finding scopes as well.

Finland Is In the Game

The Finnish Sako TRG is another popular bolt action sniper rifle. This is reportedly less costly than the AI series but performance is similar. The TRG is available in TRG-

22 and TRG-42 configurations. The TR-G22 is a smaller action for the 7.62 NATO, while the TRG-42 is for the longer .338 Lapua and .300 Winchester Magnum chambering. Traditionally most sniper rifle actions were glass bedded. That is, the action was custom fit within the stock using a soft compound that later hardened. This provided a perfect fit with minimal play after installation. The AI and Sako systems are fitted to aluminum chassis to achieve even better rigidity. This is increasingly common with modern sniper bolt action systems.[6]

Semi-Autos Are Accurate Too

While bolt actions dominate the sniper rifle field, the SVD is not the only semi-auto sniper rifle to achieve success. Part of this is because a sniper rifle must be highly accurate but still be reliable enough to be field worthy. There have been some semi-auto sniper rifles that were equal to many of the better bolt guns but they didn't have the needed reliability to make it as a service weapon. The Walther WA2000 is a good example.[7] This was an excellent weapon with regards to accuracy, but was never truly accepted as a field-worthy service rifle. Nations that use self-loading sniper systems have gone a different route in general. What most services have done is to take a proven rugged design and accurized it significantly. This has been done with most of the popular 7.62 NATO combat rifles. There are scoped versions of the FAL in use by several countries. The HK G3 has been seen in the G3A3Z scoped configuration, and occasionally in a more specialized G3 SG1 version. The G3 SG1 is much closer to being a true sniper rifle in design. This version is basically a standard G3 that uses a select quality barrel, and is then fitted with the HK folding bipod and tropical forend, followed up by the HK claw mount usually fitted with a Zeiss variable power scope.[8] Finally a special set trigger mechanism is fitted and a cheek piece is attached to the fixed buttstock to help with better scope-eye alignment.

The U.S. uses several sniper variants of the M14. However, Israel took the M14 a bit further as a sniper rifle. The M89SR is an Israeli M14 sniper model that has been converted to a bullpup layout. This actually makes much more sense for an urban combat rifle, as it results in a much shorter overall length. This allows the M89SR to be far more portable and maneuverable in the tight streets and alleys present in many older Middle Eastern cities.

However, the best example of reworking a service rifle into a sniper's weapon is the Israeli Galil sniper rifle and its updated variant, the SR 99. As already covered, the Galil is one of the best combat rifles made in either caliber. The 7.62 NATO model was the perfect starting point for building an excellent sniper rifle. To make the sniper variant, they started with the basic 7.62 Galil and added a 20 inch heavy barrel fitted with a new pattern muzzle break and flash hider combination. This could be removed and replaced with a sound suppressor if needed. The trigger group is limited to semi-auto fire only. An adjustable wooden buttstock was standard, though it was still capable of being folded. Newer models are synthetic and metal. The forend is a bit different in shape, and finally, the bipod has been moved to just forward of the receiver, as it can be easily adjusted from this position by the shooter. Also, a bipod mounted to the barrel tends to shift the point of impact when used. A specially designed range finding scope with interchangeable filters for varying light conditions is fitted to a quickly detachable scope mount. The entire system is issued in a special case along with other accessories.

The updated SR-99 version has even more features. A strap is mounted above the barrel to lessen optical distortion caused by heat rising from the barrel. The forend is now plastic and is of a different pattern, as is the buttstock. A monopod has also been fitted to the buttstock for added stability. The overall weight has been reduced to roughly 12 pounds, where the original Galil sniper rifle weighed 14 pounds when equipped with scope. There is much to be said for using an existing design that has already been proven in the field. While the end result may not have the same degree of accuracy as a bolt action, a semi-auto can provide much faster follow up shots or shots at a separate target. There are times when this is preferable. Where stealth is required, a bolt action is usually the first choice, as there is no cycling of the action or brass case flying through the air to give away the shooter's position.[9]

A Whole New Ball Game

While the 7.62 NATO and 7.62 × 54R Russian calibers dominate the sniper rifle world, there are several new calibers that can achieve hits at far greater ranges. While the need for these extreme ranges is not likely to be in great demand for many urban conflicts, the open desert terrain of the Middle East is made for these ultra long range sniper calibers. While the .300 Winchester Magnum did see an increase in use as a sniper caliber in the 1980s, it only achieved this with an increase in recoil and required a longer action length for proper functioning. The most recent .300 Winchester Magnum loads offer about 400 yards greater effective range than the best 7.62 NATO sniper rounds. This does not compare to the newer calibers that are gaining in popularity as sniper rounds. We're primarily talking about the .416 Barrett, the .408 Chey-Tac, and the .338 Lapua. From the look of things, this last round is the new standard sniper caliber for most Western nations.

The capabilities of these new calibers allows for engagement distances that would've been unimaginable more than 15 years ago. These new calibers are even more lethal when combined with the new computerized sighting systems, range finding scopes, wind meters, and the new high quality sniper rounds. These new systems offer shooters the potential to make hits up to 3500 yards on a good day, and 3000 yards on most days. The current world record for consistent shot placement is held by the 408 Chey-Tac with three rounds falling into a circle less than the width of the average man's shoulders. This was done at a range of over 2300 yards. Based on sheer velocity, the 416 Barrett should actually outperform the .408 slightly, as the Barrett offers roughly 200 feet per second more velocity and similar bullet weight. The .408 Chey-Tac is known for having one of the most aerodynamic designs ever produced in a bullet. This allows for superior stability throughout the bullet's flight path, resulting in lower shot dispersal down range.[10]

Sniper capabilities have greatly improved in recent years, largely due to rifles like this one from Accuracy International, the L115A3 .338 Lapua (Sgt. M. Downs, RAF).

6. Sniper Rifles/Precision Tactical Rifles

British Secretary of State for Defense John Hutton examines the AI L115A3. This design holds the current world record for the longest sniper shot in combat (MC2 [SW] A.X. Ramirez, U.S. Navy).

The big rifle that started it all, the Barrett .50 BMG. This is a recent M107 version, though an even newer M107A1 is now available, which is lighter and more easily suppressed (LCpl. K.J. Keathley, U.S. Marine Corps).

The current weapon system that Chey-Tac has had success with is the M200 Intervention system. It is called such because it is a system and not just the rifle and scope, similar to the M24. Barrett has a similar capability with its .416 caliber model 99 single shot rifle and its BORS sighting system. This caliber is now available in the Barrett semiauto design as well.

The .416 Barrett maintains supersonic velocities at 2500 yards, but this comes with greater rifle weight and more punishing recoil. By comparison, there are many .338 Lapua rifles that weigh little more than some 7.62 NATO Service rifles. The C14 Timber Wolf is Canada's new standard sniper rifle. This is replacing the C3A1 7.62mm NATO. This is a bolt action weighing in at roughly 15 pounds and measuring 49 inches overall. It uses a detachable magazine and the fluted barrel design helps reduce weight and increase surface area for cooling, while maintaining barrel rigidity.[11]

The AI AWSM along with the AX .338 will likely be popular .338 Lapua rifles and will prove successful systems just as most of the other AI designs have proven to be. There are several other .338 Lapua rifles being offered as well. There are designs being offered by Erma of Austria, Blaser of Germany, Truvelo in South Africa and Armalite from the United States, just to name a few. It seems quite likely that this caliber will be around for some time to come. The Dakota Arms T-76 Longbow combines the Mauser model 98 action with this effective cartridge. An updated version known as the Scimitar uses the same basic action with a detachable box magazine in place of the fixed internal magazine of the T-76.

Many of the long range systems are available with suppressors as with standard rifles and carbines. While standard optical scopes are the usual sighting device, these weapons often make use of passive thermal and image intensification sights as well. These are certainly not cheap, especially in the case of thermal sights, but they give the sniper vastly improved capability.

The new long range systems are here to stay, but will likely be limited in use, as the extra range is not always needed for much of the urban battlefield. Right now, these calibers are in their element with the wars in the desert going into their 10th year. Barrett has been happy enough with its .416 to adapt it to its M82 semi-auto design. The M99 bolt action .416 held a 1000 yard record with a shot group of just over 4 inches.[12]

These newer ultra long range calibers have brought the ability to reach out well beyond 2500 yards. When these rifles are combined with the new computerized sighting systems like the Barrett BORS and the Horus Vision system, ranges of over 3000 yards are well within their reach. While these rounds do not quite have the long range hitting power of the larger .50-caliber rifles, they offer better consistency within their effective range.

Despite their outstanding performance, their future is set, but on a limited basis. It is unlikely that these larger calibers will come anywhere near the production numbers of the Russian SVD. However, the war in Afghanistan provides the perfect battleground for these calibers with its vast mountainous terrain and large open valleys. The fighting in Iraq likely provides shorter shooting distances than Afghanistan. For most urban fighting, the capabilities of the 7.62 NATO and other similar calibers are more than adequate. That is not to say that a unit operating within a given area should not have access to one of these bigger calibers. These weapons should be maintained within any arsenal for units that may require the range capabilities these weapons can provide.

Given the typical urban setting, it is understandable why a 1000 yard rifle is more than enough for most sniping needs. Any experienced combatants will use the structural layout of their environment to their advantage. This becomes an even bigger problem if they are the defenders and are familiar with the area of operation. Some may even be knowledgeable of actual internal structural layouts and will be able to move under the protection of the structures. On the rare opportunity a target presents itself, it will be for brief moments. If such a shot is even attempted at an extreme range, the target is likely to be gone by the time the bullet arrives. The open desert and mountainous terrain in the Middle East does not afford this type of cover in most instances, with the possible exception of caverns. However, movement within these caverns is largely limited. Urban fighting tends to involve far closer engagement ranges and shooters are often afforded very little time in which to pull off an accurate shot. It is for these reasons 7.62 NATO rifles will continue to see service, in spite of the superior capabilities of these newer long range sniper calibers. The semi-automatic sniper rifles in particular will be highly valuable for future urban conflicts, as they allow for very fast follow up shots. The most valued will be compact as well as accurate, reliable and fast shooting.

Chapter 7

Anti-Materiel Rifles

The previous chapter covered sniper rifles in both standard service calibers as well as the newer long range calibers that are bringing a new dimension to sniping. The development of these highly effective calibers might not have taken place were it not for several factors.

During World War I, the gas operated French Hotchkiss machine gun was produced in a large 11mm caliber. This large caliber was meant to provide the reach needed to hit observation balloons. After the war the U.S. wanted a caliber capable of similar range for anti-aircraft use. Once again J.M. Browning proved to be the best man for the job. What he designed was a new .50-caliber machine gun cartridge and the M1921 machine gun to chamber it. The classic M2HB version was to show up in the 1930s. The heavy barrel of the HB model was designed to eliminate the need for a water cooling jacket. This machine gun has become the longest serving small arm still called standard in the U.S. arsenal. More will be covered on the M2HB in Chapter 8. For the purposes of this chapter, we are more concerned with the .50 Browning Machine Gun (BMG) cartridge than with the M2HB machine gun.

Origins of the Anti-Materiel Rifle

One unique feature of the M2HB is its ability to fire single shots through the manipulation of a bolt latch mechanism located in the center of its butterfly trigger. This feature was used in combination with a mounted scope during the Korean War. This created one of the first .50-caliber sniper rifles. Although anti-tank rifles have existed since World War I, no one ever really considered them as sniper rifles. No doubt some were used for this purpose at times. During the Vietnam War shots were made with the M2HB set up as a sniper weapon, at ranges of over a mile.[1] A firearms designer name Ron Barrett took this idea one step further and in 1982, introduced the Barrett model 82 semi-automatic. The model 82 weighed around 30 pounds and was nearly 6 feet long. It uses a short recoil operating system which helps to absorb some of the harsh recoil of this massive cartridge. While recoil operated guns are usually not as accurate as bolt action designs, the Barrett did well enough. It was its reliability, power and relative lightweight that brought it to the attention of the U.S. military, although this took nearly seven years. Luckily the rifle entered service just before the first Gulf War. During operation Desert Storm, they proved their worth. Since that time many other designs have entered production. These large caliber weapons don't quite possess the accuracy potential of the .408 Chey-Tac or .416 Barrett. However, the .50-caliber and similar heavy machine gun calibers like the 12.7mm and 14.5mm Soviet use bullet weights that are far greater. The result is a far greater lethal range. At ranges out to 1000 yards, the effects are similar. The .416 Barrett actually possesses greater energy at 1000 yards.[2] This begins to change further down range, however. The heavy machine gun calibers represent the apex of small arms capability. The only option for greater power is to step up to a cannon round. In fact, this has been done recently, as there now several 20mm anti-materiel rifles presently offered.

The anti-materiel rifle is kind of another dual purpose weapon, although in this case it wasn't intentionally adapted to fill multiple roles. It merely offers great versatility due to the nature of its design. These large caliber rifles were initially designed as a means of providing heavy long range firepower without the weight of a heavy machine gun. While it can provide excellent sniper capabilities, the .50-caliber round was never intended to be a sniper cartridge. The ability of these rifles to be used as sniper weapons is merely a useful byproduct. Many of these rifles performed quite well as ultra long range sniping rifles. The world record for a combat sniper shot was held by the Macmillan Tac-50 bolt action for several years. The recorded distance of the shot was 2430m. It has recently been broken by the AI .338 Lapua L115A3 bolt-action.[3] Despite their outstanding performance as sniper weapons, they truly shine in their anti-materiel role.

The extreme bullet weights used in these calibers allows for considerable down range energy retention. This makes this class of weapon ideal for taking equipment out of service. Favorite targets include parked aircraft, lightly armored vehicles, generators and radar and air defense installations, along with stores of munitions. The performance of anti-materiel rifles has always been good in this role with conventional armor piercing incendiary rounds. In recent years, however, newly designed explosive bullets have brought this rifle class to a new level of performance. New cartridges, like the Raufoss Mk 211, have turned the .50 BMG round into a small cannon shell in terms of performance. The Mk 211 projectile is a clever mix of an armor piercing insert combined with a small explosive charge that is delayed to allow the bullet time to penetrate the surface before detonation, enhancing the explosive effect.[4]

Shoulder Fired Cannon

With the recent development of the 20mm anti-materiel rifles, the explosive effects are greatly enhanced along with the recoil. Since the cannon rounds are fuse armed, magazine design has to protect the nose of the shell during recoil. The modern urban applications for these weapons are perhaps more numerous than for long range sniper rifles due to the superior penetration and destructive effect of the 20mm. Given the use of reinforced concrete in the construction of many exterior urban structures, the capabilities of the larger round are easily understood and appreciated.

While these guns excel at material destruction and perform reasonably well as sniper rifles, they've found a third use as well. The 20mm offers an explosive effect that should make it quite good at detonating explosives from a considerable distance. The .50 rifles are often used for this purpose. If an unexploded bomb or improvised explosive device (IED) is located during a patrol, these rifles are often used to detonate the device from a safe distance.[5]

The First of a New Breed

As these high power weapons have demonstrated their ability on more than one occasion, they will remain in service for some years. The Barrett model 82 was probably the first modern anti-materiel rifle made and was the first successful new rifle in this class. The original Barrett model 82 offered an efficient arrow shaped muzzle brake which was claimed to cut recoil forces by over 50 percent. The newest version, the M107A1, has a new cylindrical shaped brake designed for mounting a suppressor without modification. The weight has also been reduced considerably to around 25 pounds empty.[6] The use of saboted rounds is not possible on the Barrett, as with many rifles equipped with muzzle brakes. The sabot breaks up as it passes through the brake. This is not of great concern, as the Mk 211 round is one of the most effective ever devised for the .50 BMG. The model 82 series has many useful design features. It can be easily field stripped for cleaning and transport, the folding bipod can be removed if needed, and the rail system allows for mounting any type of sighting system. Some models offer a rear monopod for increased stability, and the rifle can be pintle mounted for shooting from vehicles. The short recoil system of this weapon requires some barrel play by design. This means the barrel is not rigidly fixed in the receiver. This limits its ability as an anti-personnel sniping rifle. As a result Barrett, among others, has designed bolt action .50-calibers to improve on this a bit.

A bullpup version of the Barrett model 82 was also developed to reduce the overall length of the rifle, creating a somewhat more compact weapon. Even in bullpup form this is not a compact weapon by any means, and the military is continuing to use the standard version.

Bolt Actions Still Do the Job

The Barrett model 95 is a bolt action .50 BMG that did not receive the standard issue nod, but offers good accuracy potential due to its rigid barrel/receiver link. While repeating weapons are the norm for service rifles, they are not necessarily a must. In Chapter 6, a Barrett single shot bolt action design was introduced which has set accuracy standards. The model 99 is also available in .50 BMG, and the extra rigidity offered by this weapon helps it in the accuracy department, due to its lack of a magazine well cut out in the bottom of the receiver.

McMillan is a name that has long been associated with sniper systems. The Macmillan Tac-50 bolt action has set standards for accuracy as well. As mentioned, this rifle held the world record for a recorded sniper shot in combat for several years. The McMillan TAC-50 uses a detachable box magazine and an efficient muzzle brake, and can mount a variety of optics. It is popularly known as "Big Mac." The McMillan Tac-50 measures 57 inches overall with 29 inch barrel and weighs 26 pounds empty.

These proven designs are likely to see some competition in coming years from Accuracy International's designs. The AW50 is manufactured to the same standards as the other AI models and they now offer a semi-auto AS50 that may give the Barrett M107 some stiff competition. Unlike the Barrett, the AS50 is gas operated and as such it is made with a fixed barrel rather than having a moving barrel, as required in the recoil operated system of the Barrett. AI has no doubt taken great care in the design of its gas system to minimize any effects on the accuracy of the rifle. Time will tell if it can take the place of the Barrett model 82 and 107 rifles. It will also have to compete with many bolt action designs in this class that have already proven themselves. Although the AS50 offers the advantage of fast follow-up shot, it uses a new type of gas action, and has only recently seen service. Hopefully, AI took this into consideration during the rifle's design.

Russia Has Their Own

As mentioned earlier, the concept of heavy caliber rifles dates back to World War I. There were early rifles like the German T-Gew 18, the British Boys and even an early Finnish made 20mm shoulder-fired cannon, the Lahti model 39. Most European nations had their own designs and one of them, the Polish wz 35, was a lightweight model which used a tungsten cored bullet that was so effective it was later widely copied. It was the Soviets, however, that developed one of the largest rifle calibers still used today. The 14.5 × 114mm cartridge was used during World War II in the PTRD-41 and PTRS-41 anti-tank rifles. The PTRS was a more expensive and complicated five round magazine fed rifle which was not very common. That PTRD-41 was a single shot unique long recoil design in which the bolt had to be closed manually like a bolt action. It was, however, opened during the recoil movement.[7] The significance here is not the rifle designs but the power of the cartridge used for these rifles. It was later used in the Soviet KPV heavy machine gun as well. It is the most powerful military cartridge used on a regular basis. While the Soviet 12.7 × 108mm is very close to the .50 BMG in performance, the 14.5x114mm uses a bullet roughly 200 grains heavier and moving approximately 400 fps faster.

U.S. marine checking out a machine gun that first saw service under the Nazis, the German MG42. This is the modern 7.62mm NATO MG3 variation, which is still in production in several nations (SSgt. P. Bunting, U.S. Air Force).

Both former Soviet calibers are currently used for modern anti-materiel rifles. With the development of quality match grade ammunition, this round offers even more potential than the .50-calibers. At the same time, the 20mm versions that are now seeing some use have limited potential for accurate long range shooting due to the nature of the 20mm round. The design of this round is inefficient with its fuse assembly system mounted in the nose of the projectile. Since we're talking about cannon rounds here, pinpoint accuracy is not necessarily required. And despite the accuracy shortcomings of the 20mm anti-materiel rifles, they possess far more potential with regards to the destructive capacity of the 20mm round itself. There are several different 20mm rounds being used in the current series of anti-materiel guns on the market. The South African NTW 20 is a bolt action using a three round detachable box magazine and fires the 20 × 82mm cannon shell.

A Croatian bolt action design known as the RT20 fires the 20 × 110mm Hispano-Suiza cannon shell. This design requires a complicated recoil backblast system that gives away the shooter's position quite easily, and due to the gun's backblast, cannot be fired from small confines. This is true of all recoilless weapons. There are also several other designs that use the 20 × 99R ShVAK cannon round.

The 14.5mm offers a better chance with regard to long range sniping potential unless there are some serious accuracy improvements within the 20mm family of anti-materiel guns. The obstacles for the 20mm models are several. The guns themselves are usually expensive, large, and all have extremely harsh recoil. An efficient recoil reduction system is required, which would add to the weight and cost of the weapon. Why burden a unit with a large, expensive design, when a multitude of lighter and cheaper single round disposable rocket launchers are already in service and can provide reasonable accuracy and far more destructive effect? Although to be fair, the rocket launchers tend to leave a significant indication of the shooter's position, and many suffer from the same backblast issues as recoilless rifle designs. Several new launcher designs have taken care of this and can now be fired from confined spaces, though the obvious firing signature remains. It was, however, the development of these lightweight disposable launchers that killed off the anti-tank rifle concept in the first place.

While the cannon versions of the anti-materiel rifle may require more development, the more accurate .50-caliber rifles now in service will likely be around for some time. Here success would mean reliable, cost effective designs, with semi-auto capability being a desirable feature. Other ingredients for success would be reductions in weight and length combined with top quality match grade bullets capable of high performance with regards to target destruction, such as that offered by the Mk 211 cartridge.

There are a multitude of .50 caliber rifles on the market now and most are bolt action. Finland offers several Helenius brand rifles and in a variety of chamberings from 12.7mm to .50 BMG to 20 × 99R cannon. The Gepard series from Hungary are also seeing use. The Hecate rifle from France is another newer design that has shown potential. The list of models keeps getting longer.

For now, the Barrett model 82 series appears to hold the title of most successful anti-materiel rifle by a good stretch. The AI AS50 has great potential, but will need to be proven in field use, as it is still fairly new. Regarding anti-materiel rifles intended to perform double duty as long range sniper weapons, bolt guns seem to be a good choice, which is good for smaller defense budgets. This may very well include United States in the near future.

CHAPTER 8

Machine Guns

Modern machine guns first appeared in the late 19th century with the Maxim design.[1] This was followed by a multitude of other successful designs including the 1917 Browning, and later, the German MG 34 and the Soviet Goryunov SG 43.

The World War II era German MG 42 was designed as a replacement for the earlier MG 34. The MG 34 was a beautifully made weapon of high quality. It was the first to fill the role of the general purpose machine gun (GPMG). The GPMG became the backbone of military operations for many years. As good as the MG 34 was, it was expensive and time consuming to manufacture. Once World War II began, the Germans quickly realized the need for something cheaper and faster to manufacture. The end result was the MG 42. This model proved as reliable, if not more reliable, than its predecessor. The design was altered to utilize a roller locking bolt similar to that used by many HK weapons. In the MG 42, however, the rollers were locked until the recoiling barrel provided the necessary unlocking action. Due to this design change, the rate of fire increased greatly to approximately 1200 rpm. The MG 34 fired much more slowly. To cope with the heat generated by such a high rate of fire, an efficient quick change barrel system was designed. This weapon used forward thinking manufacturing methods. The MG 42 earned both the fear and respect of Allied forces, and the gun was closely studied following the war. Many of its features were used in later Western models like the U.S. M60, which also copied features from the German FG 42 automatic rifle. This was an advanced design that never saw widespread use.

With the use of this German gun, the GPMG concept was assured for many years, only recently being supplanted by light machine guns (LMGs) from various makers. The MG 42 was so effective that it remains the standard machine gun of several nations to this day. It was the West German standard in the form of an updated 7.62mm NATO version known as the MG 3.

The Nazi Gun Still Works Well

The MG 3 was the final version of a series starting with MG 1. This was a copy of the actual wartime MG 42 that had been reverse engineered due to a lack of blueprints.

This model was chambered for the 7.62mm NATO. There was also an MG 2, which was an actual NAZI era MG 42 that had been reworked to fire the new NATO caliber. The MG 3 was the final version that is still in use today. This model can fire both U.S. disintegrating link belted ammunition or German continuous belt ammo. There is also an alternative bolt/buffer package which lowers the rate of fire to a more reasonable level, though still quite high at roughly 900 rpm. The MG 3 weighs close to 24½ pounds. and measures 49 inches long.[2]

The reason for the success of this weapon is its low cost and low technology manufacturing techniques. Despite this, it has all the qualities an effective machine gun should have. It is well made, highly reliable in all combat environments, it offers an easy barrel change system, and it is not overly heavy. It has been produced by several nations besides Germany, including Italy and Pakistan. Due to its ease of production, it will probably remain in use until caseless ammunition designs become the norm.

Many features from this design were copied by other weapons, developed later. This is rather odd, as the MG 42 was itself not an entirely original design. The excellent barrel change system was an improvement on an Italian design. The locking system itself was based on a captured Polish design.

After the war, the Swiss took a close look at the MG 42 concept and developed their own modified version that used more expensive machined components rather than stampings, as used on the MG 42. They later came up with the MG710-1, MG710-2, and finally the MG710-3.[3] This last model was one of the finest GPMGs ever made. Unfortunately, it was also one of the most expensive despite reverting to modern stampings for its manufacture. Probably due to their cost, none of these weapons received widespread adoption, though some are no doubt still in service due to the quality of these machine guns.

While the MG 42 was copied to some extent by other designs, one weapon in particular was derived quite heavily from German war designs, perhaps more so than any other. Unfortunately, the end result should have been perfect but was far from it. This was the U.S. M60 machine gun, which has recently been replaced by the FN MAG (M240). For many years, however, the M60 was the standard issue GPMG for most U.S. units.

Rockets Were Not All That We Copied

The M60 first entered service in the early 1960s. It used the feed mechanism of the MG 42 and the bolt system of the FG 42. The FG 42 bolt was itself roughly copied from the Lewis light machine gun (a U.S. design) of World War I.[4] The original M60 was clearly not completely thought out, as the original model had a barrel change system, but changing the barrel was not cheap or easy to perform. The original barrel had no handle and the gun was actually issued with an asbestos glove to solve this problem. Also, replacing the barrel meant replacing the gas cylinder and bipod as well, as these were both permanent parts of the barrel assembly. Later versions of the M60 have made it a far better design. It is now more along the lines of what it should have been in the first place. The M60E3 model became the standard U.S. Navy and Marine Corps machine gun for some time, while the final E4 model is used by the Navy only and the standard Marine Corps weapon of choice is the M240G, a far better overall design. The M60 series is serviceable but many other designs in production are far better. The M60E4 does have some good features like a fairly light weight and a vertical foregrip, which helps with improved control. Different barrel weights and lengths are offered for different missions on this final model. The original M60 weighed just over 23 pounds, which was actually fairly light at the time. Its length was just over 43 inches with a 22 inch barrel. The best feature of the M60 was its 550 rpm rate of fire. The M60E4 model is only 37 inches long with the short assault barrel installed, and weight is less than 22 pounds. The M60 series will be encountered in service for some time, though it has been officially replaced by the M240, a modified version of the MAG.[5]

The Browning Turned Upside Down

The FN Mitrailleuse d'Appui Générale (MAG) was designed in the 1950s using the feed system of the MG 42 combined with the locking system of the Browning Automatic Rifle (BAR). The locking system of the BAR was inverted for use on the MAG to prevent interference with the feed system. The end result was probably the best Western machine gun design of all time.[6]

The MAG uses an adjustable gas regulator attached to a quick change barrel and has

The original U.S. M60 7.62mm machine gun. This weapon borrowed heavily from German World War II designs but was not as successful as it should have been (MCSN S. Rowley, U.S. Navy).

8. Machine Guns

Above: The 7.62mm M60E3, an improved and lightened variation of the original M60 (PH1 C. Mussi, U.S. Navy). *Below*: The U.S. M240G, the U.S. Marine Corps standard 7.62mm machine gun. This is basically the FN MAG in slightly modified form. The Army uses a somewhat different version, the M240B (LCpl. A.G. Brooks, U.S. Marine Corps).

This is the 5.56mm U.S. M249 Para Squad Automatic Weapon. This variant uses a telescoping stock and short barrel to improve handling in tight quarters (Spc. E. Cabral, U.S. Army).

a squared receiver that uses rivet construction to a large extent, which gives it a strong resemblance to earlier Browning machine gun designs. Despite its ancient looks, the MAG is one of the most durable machine guns of all time. It is a striker fired weapon and operates from an open bolt, as with most machine gun designs. There is no semi-auto option and the rate of fire varies between 650 and 1000 rpm, depending on the gas system setting.

The M240 versions are somewhat different from the original, and the Army and Marine Corps use different versions. The Army chose to adopt the M240B, which weighs considerably more, while the Marine Corps has adopted the M240G, which more closely resembles the original Belgian model. Traditionally wooden stocks were used on all MAGs, but synthetic stocks are now standard on most.

With regards to the original Belgian version, there were several models made for infantry use. The standard was known as the MAG 60.20; there was also a MAG 10.10 compact version with a shorter barrel and stock. Currently only the standard model is listed in the FN catalog. This version uses a synthetic stock as with most modern weapons. The British have also made several of their own versions, which were produced by the Royal Small Arms Factory. The standard British model is the L7A2.

Sweden was one of the first countries to adopt the MAG. They produced their own version and originally used the Swedish 6.5 × 55mm cartridge. Current Swedish models all use the 7.62 NATO chambering. There is an updated, heavily modified Swedish model known as the Ksp 58D and the standard model is the Ksp 58B.[7] The Ksp 58D offers many modern improvements like mounting rails, collapsible stock, a short fluted assault barrel which uses a simpler gas regulator, and provision for mounting a 100 round soft belt pouch. This last accessory is designed to keep the ammunition belt from snagging while advancing. This is a fairly common accessory on other machine guns today. The weight of this weapon is lighter as a result of its modifications. This, combined with the MAG's other qualities, makes the D model potentially one of the better machine guns on the market today.

The weight of the MAG machine gun varies with model. The current factory listed weight is 26 pounds for the Belgian standard model. The overall length is about 50 inches. This compares to 28 pounds for the U.S. M240B, which is about an inch shorter.

A New FN Design

Despite the excellent design of the MAG, FN offered a lighter weapon starting in the 1980s known as the Minimi, which is chambered for the 5.56mm NATO round. This weapon entered production in the early eighties and has been modified since then. The Minimi was designed to feed from either a 5.56 NATO belt or standard M16 rifle magazines without modification. To accomplish this, a cover is simply flipped from one side to another to expose the desired feed well. The U.S. chose this weapon as the M249 squad automatic weapon (SAW) in the early eighties and still uses it today in modified form. The current version weighs a bit more than the original at just over 16 pounds empty, and approximately 41 inches in length. There is a collapsible stock version available with a shorter barrel of just over 14 inches as opposed to the standard 19¼ inch barrel. This model is known as the Minimi-Para.

The M249 has seen a few changes from the standard model originally introduced in the eighties. There is now a heat shield over the top of the handguard in addition to other minor improvements, such as a folding barrel change handle. There is another variation known as the Mk46 which does away with the magazine feed option. This model was intended for special operations units and is slightly lighter in weight. There have been some claims that the standard M249 is not reliable when using the magazine feed system. There is another version known as the SPW (special purpose weapon) which has a reduced weight of around 13 pounds. The South Korean K3 light machine gun is closely related to the Minimi in design and dimensions. The Minimi was originally marketed as a highly reliable light machine gun, and recent complaints regarding its reliability in desert conditions may be partially due to the age of many of the weapons in service. Whether or not this is the case, the U.S. Marine Corps is looking for a replacement. The Minimi has served as a SAW for many years but the 5.56 NATO does not have the range or power to suit some users. As a result, an enlarged 7.62 NATO version was developed, known as the Mk 48.

The Minimi Grows Up

The Mk 48 weighs a bit more at around 18 pounds empty. A collapsible stock version is also available. The U.S. special operations units appear to be the stimulus behind this design. It is still fairly new and has some way to go before it can rival the FN MAG in reputation. The receiver of the Mk 48 is intended to last for 50,000 rounds. Given the light weight of this weapon and the power of the 7.62 NATO round, this seems rather optimistic, though it is possible.[8] Given the heritage of the Mk 48, it should do quite well, but it is doubtful that it can quite match the MAG in performance or longevity.

A New German Machine Gun

While HK is best known for the MP 5 submachine gun and the G3 rifle, they developed a belt-fed machine gun using their delayed blowback roller-locked system. This weapon first appeared not long after the introduction of the G3 rifle and was known as the model 21. A smaller 5.56 variation was known as the HK 23. The HK machine guns were similar in concept. They can be made to use HK rifle magazines instead of the usual ammunition belt. This required some modification and this change was a bit more involved than the system used on the FN Minimi. The feed housing could be removed and replaced with a magazine housing in its place. The HK machine guns were designed with a quick change barrel system that worked quite well. The original versions of the HK 21 were lighter than most other 7.62 NATO machine guns. The HK 21 and 21A1 were similar, with the 21A1 having a hinged feed tray to allow for easier belt loading. The final production version was the HK 21E. This model was similar to the 21A1 but was slightly longer to improve site radius and reduce felt recoil. The feed mechanism on the 21E was improved and the feeding cycle was partially accomplished on the recoil stroke and finished up on the return stroke of the carrier. The result of this was reduced part stress and a smoother feeding cycle.

The original HK 21 weighed around 17 pounds with a lightweight bipod. Each later model gained a little in weight. The final 21E production model still weighed only around 20 pounds, making these quite light for general purpose machine guns. Another feature unique to the HK 21 is that it can be easily converted to either 5.56 NATO, which created the HK 23, or to 7.62 × 39mm Soviet. The HK 21 was only about 40 inches long and used a barrel of less than 18 inches in length, while the final 21E model used a 22 inch barrel. The 21E also had an 800 rpm cyclic rate vs. 900 rpm for the original model. The HK 21 system proved to be fairly successful. It offered good modularity for a weapon of its age. While the HK 21 is no longer made in Germany, a good number of nations adopted the weapon and it is likely maintained as a reserve by many. Production continues in other nations. Many of the sales were from smaller nations and the purchases were probably fairly small in number. As a side note, the HK 21 was used by the U.S. Army's Delta units from their inception, and it is likely that this weapon is still kept in their armories as a reserve issue machine gun. Compared to the M60, the HK 21 was rumored to be a much finer quality weapon that could also be fired on semi-auto if needed. This was probably true when compared to the original M60, although the later M60E4 is a far better performer, though the M60 was never a selective-fire weapon. Also, as the HK 21 fired from the closed bolt position, its accuracy was quite good for a machine gun.[9]

The U.S. M249 may see some strong competition from a new HK design, the MG 4. This model does not operate via the usual HK roller-locking system. Instead, the MG 4 uses a more traditional gas piston system and a rotary locking bolt.

The Gas Operated HK

The MG 4 is the new German army standard light machine gun and it is heavier than the M249, but not by a large amount. Weight is less than 18 pounds empty and the overall length with the stock folded is less than 32 inches, and 41 inches extended. The rate of fire is 750 rpm. Whether or not the MG 4 will prove to be superior to the M249 has yet to be seen, although it is being adopted by more and more nations, and at a fairly quick rate. Spain has recently adopted it and apparently given up on their native Ameli design, which was plagued with problems throughout its history. The MG 4 and M249 are not the only SAW designs on the market. There is potential competition from several other models. Some of these new models are quite light and compact.[10]

SAWs Take Over

The concept of belt-fed 5.56mm light machine gun is not new. The U.S. Navy used one on a limited basis during the Vietnam War. This was the Stoner model 63, and it was put to good use by SEAL teams during the 1960s and 70s. The Stoner 63 was another Eugene Stoner design and was one of the first modular systems ever to enter production. This was a very limited production, however, with only several thousand being produced. The Stoner 63 could be converted from rifle to carbine or light machine gun with relative ease, and could utilize either belt or box feed systems. This design was intended to improve on the earlier AR 15 and AR 18 designs. Had Stoner devised the model 63 system earlier, it may have beat out the M16 as a standard U.S. service weapon. The Marines tested it in the 1960s, but only the Navy adopted it, and then only the light machine gun version, as the Mk 23. The Navy version utilized the belt-feed mechanism, and the belt could be contained in a 100 round plastic box or a 150 round aluminum drum.[11] While the 63 system was only produced in small numbers, it was later developed more fully in the improved model 86 and later model 96A1. This modular design still lives and is known as the Knight's Armament LMG. This final version has a 550 rpm rate of fire and can use the M4 style collapsible stock, though a simple single strut stock has also been seen on some versions. Modern rail systems are fitted on this weapon as standard, and the weight of this design is only 10 pounds empty, making it especially appealing for special operations use should it prove acceptable for service in the U.S. The standard barrel length for this weapon is 12 inches. This weapon has apparently been adopted by least one European military service.

There is another competitor in the SAW market that offers an even smaller package. The ARES Shrike light machine gun is available as an upper receiver conversion for the M16 series. The rate of fire for this weapon varies between 650 and 800 rpm. The Shrike is available in several barrel lengths, with a 16½ inch being standard. The Shrike has had a checkered history and has been redesigned more than once. However, if it has been perfected, it offers one of the cheapest and lightest options for replacing the M249. The Shrike is available as a dual feed weapon, meaning it can use either the lower receiver magazine well or left-side belt feed without modification, similar to the M249. This is the version that can be used as an upper receiver modification for the M4 carbine or M16 rifle. There's also a special purpose weapon that does away with the magazine well in the lower receiver, making it a belt feed only weapon. This latter version cuts the Shrike's weight to roughly 7½ pounds with the 12 inch barrel. This is by far the lightest belt-fed light machine gun currently offered. There is supposedly an open bolt firing option for the Shrike in addition to the standard closed bolt version. This open bolt feature would seem to be a better option for the Shrike in the light machine gun role, even though it offers a quick change barrel. Whether or not the Shrike will succeed remains to be seen.[12] It has yet to be adopted by any major service, while the Knight's LMG has been adopted by the Danish navy.

As mentioned, Spain produced a native design known as the Ameli which was a very lightweight weapon that performed well during testing, but the production model showed quality control problems and production has been discontinued.[13]

The final belt-fed 5.56mm NATO light machine gun design to be covered comes from Israel. The Negev, like most of the SAWs covered, is offered in a standard model as well as an assault model. The Negev closely follows the M249, as both can be fired from either belt or magazine. The Negev uses the Galil pattern magazine with the M16 magazine being an option through the use of an adapter fitted to the Negev magazine well. The Negev uses a short-stroke gas piston open bolt mechanism and has a side folding stock similar to that of the Galil rifle. There are two barrel options, the standard 18 inch and the short 13 inch barrel. A vertical foregrip can be fitted, though this is mounted at a slight leftward cant. The rate of fire of the Negev varies between 700 and 1000 rpm depending on the gas setting, as the regulator is adjustable and can even be shut off completely to allow for firing rifle grenades, which are still commonly used by the Israelis. The Negev is compact at around 27 inches folded and up to 40 inches extended, depending on barrel used. The weight varies between 15 and 17 pounds, again depending on configuration. This weapon has been in service in Israel for some time now and appears to be performing adequately.[14]

Despite the effectiveness of many of these designs, belt-fed models are necessarily more complicated and must operate at a mechanical disadvantage when compared to sim-

8. Machine Guns

ilar magazine-fed designs. The belt-fed machine gun must not only fire, extract and eject the round, but must also use the same residual energy to operate the belt feed system. The longer the belt, the greater the force needed for reliable functioning. Also, the feed mechanism complicates the design of the weapon by necessity. Due to these issues, magazine-fed light machine guns have been popular for years. An added benefit is that only one feed system is needed for both rifle and light machine gun. Separate belted ammunition is not required, while the detractor is that the weapon's sustained fire capability is somewhat limited. With the belt fed machine gun, the only limitations are barrel changes and clearing stoppages, as belts can be linked together to provide an infinite feed source.

Belt Feeders Are Not the Only Game in Town

One of the best light machine guns of all time was the British Bren, which was nothing more than the Czech cz 26 modified for the .303 British round. It is still used as the L4 series in 7.62mm NATO. While not the lightest weapon in this class at about 20 pounds. empty, it offers a quick change barrel feature and uses a top feeding magazine that is interchangeable with that of the FAL rifle. The Bren, however, is normally used with a 30 round magazine. The top feeding magazine feature of the Bren made magazine

U.S. Marine firing an RPK light machine gun (LMG) in foreground. This was the primary LMG for the former USSR during much of the Cold War (unknown, U.S. Marine Corps).

A 5.45mm AKS-74, the replacement for the 7.62mm AKM and one of the world's deadliest rifles due to the destructive nature of its bullet (TSgt. J. Varhegyi, U.S. Air Force).

changes easier when firing from the prone position or while advancing. While the Bren is not widespread today, many kept in reserve are likely still serviceable, as the weapon is a very well made and durable design. While the Bren is the classic light machine gun, there are several modern designs that can provide top performance.[15]

One of the most versatile was covered in Chapter 5. As already noted, the Steyr AUG bullpup is one of the few service rifles with a standard quick change barrel feature. When set up as a light machine gun, the AUG uses a heavy 24.4 inch barrel which is fitted with a combination muzzle brake/flash hider of a different pattern than that used on the standard rifle barrel. It is also usually set up with an open bolt firing mechanism as opposed to the closed bolt normally seen on the rifle versions. A folding bipod is fitted to the heavy barrel for added firing support in the prone position. The weight of this light machine gun version is roughly 3 pounds more than that of the standard rifle. As already covered, magazine options are 30 or 42 round capacity and various sighting systems can be fitted depending on user preference.

There is a unique design from Singapore known as the Ultimax. This is currently considered one of the better designs but has yet to find any big sales even though it has many useful features. It fires in automatic only from an open bolt position and has a 400–600 rpm rate of fire. It offers a quick change barrel and a unique recoil system that makes for a very controllable weapon. The recoil system also saves on receiver wear, as the carrier never strikes the rear of the receiver during recoil. A 100 round metal drum magazine is standard and it cannot feed from a belt. M16 magazines can also be used on the Mk 5 variant. The Ultimax uses two vertical grips for better fire control and is available with barrel lengths of 10½, 13, or 20 inches. Weight is around 11 pounds with the standard 20 inch barrel, and the overall length in this configuration is just over 40 inches. The buttstock can be removed, decreasing the length to less than 32 inches. The U.S.M.C. recently tested the Mk 4 version but it was not selected. A bipod is standard, but this can be removed if desired. Iron sights are fitted but the Mk 5 variant uses a rail system for other aiming options. The Ultimax has been adopted by over half a dozen nations, but these were mostly smaller purchases, as fewer than 100,000 have been made so far.[16]

The German HK G36 is available as a light support weapon, the MG36 with a heavy 18.9 inch barrel and with the 100 round Beta-mag dual drum. Its capabilities as a SAW are limited, as the barrel cannot be quickly changed in the field.

The Heavy Barrel AK

The former Soviet Union took a more basic approach to the light machine gun concept. They generally issued weapons that did not utilize quick change barrels, and there is actually little difference between the RPK light machine gun and the standard AKM rifle. The Soviets used the DPM machine gun during much of World War II. While this weapon was far from perfect, it was a simple and reliable design. The Soviets tried to improve on it after the war with the belt-fed RPD 7.62 × 39mm light machine gun. They didn't succeed as well as hoped. The RPD did not have a quick change barrel feature and some have claimed that there was not a great deal of power available for reliable feeding. They eventually gave up on the RPD and adopted the RPK light machine gun.

The RPK was basically a long, heavy barreled AKM with a bipod mounted near the muzzle and a different buttstock shape to allow for a supporting handhold. The RPK weighed more, as expected, at roughly 10½ pounds, and the barrel was considerably longer than that of the AK rifle at a bit over 23 inches. The overall length was approximately 41 inches, although a folding stock version was later produced known as the RPKS. This model could be reduced to a bit over 32 inches with the stock folded. The RPK uses either a 40 round steel box or 75 round drum, although the 30 round AK rifle magazine could also be used.

When the Soviet Union switched over to the 5.45 × 39mm cartridge in the 1970s, they developed the RPK-74 light machine gun to go along with it. This closely resembled the 7.62mm RPK. It used a 45 round plastic magazine meant for this weapon and there were no drum magazine options offered for this caliber. The folding stocked RPKS-74M is the current Russian light machine gun, which weighs 10 pounds empty. Plastic has largely replaced the earlier laminated wood furniture. While the Russian light machine guns may be rather basic and limited, they have done a much better job with the PK series GPMG.[17]

Above: A current plastic stocked version of the 7.62 × 54mmR Russian PKM; older models have wooden stocks. This is often considered superior to the U.S. M60 series (SSgt. L.P. Valdes, U.S. Marine Corps). ***Below:*** The legendary Browning M2HB .50 caliber "Ma Deuce" (G. Zach, U.S. Army).

The Belt Fed Kalashnikov

The PK entered service in the early 1960s and was designed by the Kalashnikov team. The current PKM lightweight version weighs only 18½ pounds and yet offers most of the features found on better GPMG designs. These include a quick change barrel, bipod, and most importantly, top notch reliability and ease of maintenance. There are some who feel the PK series are among the simplest and most reliable belt-fed machine guns ever made. The standard barrel length is approximately 26 inches with an overall length of roughly 47 inches. The rate of fire is 650 rpm. The original PK was heavier than the current PKM, as the PKM utilizes more stampings to both save weight and lower production cost. While many Western belt-fed guns feed from the left, the PK series feeds from the right side only. Its primary fault is that the standard Soviet belt is continuous and the empty belt is left hanging out the left side of the weapon. This can be a problem when attempting to move the weapon during an assault. This is especially true in areas with dense foliage. However, this problem is easily remedied with a pair of tin snips or dikes.

Among the PK's best features are its simple design and its 7.62 × 54R chambering, which gave the Soviets a true general purpose machine gun. Like the AK, the PK has an almost legendary reputation for reliability. The Chinese have used their own version known as the type 80. The belts used for the PK series generally come in 100, 200, and 250 round lengths and a metal box can be attached under the weapon to stow the belts, though this adds considerably to the weight of the weapon. Some PK versions are seen with night sights; other modern optics can no doubt be fitted.[18] While most models have wooden skeleton stocks, different patterns have been used on foreign copies, and current versions are often fitted with plastic instead of wood. The PK series has been produced by most former satellite countries and is probably the most common GPMG in the world. Unfortunately, it is usually the belt-fed machine gun U.S. troops most often face in combat. In this case, its reliability and effectiveness are liabilities.

The Competition

In the late 1970s, the South Africans designed what should have been the ultimate GPMG, the 7.62mm NATO SS 77. It uses a folding plastic skeleton stock, can mount a soft 100 round pouch to contain the belt, and it has a quick change barrel, a horizontal foregrip, and a folding bipod. The weight was less than many competing designs at around 21 pounds and the overall length is 45½ inches, but can be reduced to 37 inches with the stock folded. It uses a gas piston operating system with a side locking bolt similar to that of the Soviet SG 43. The rate of fire was around 800 rpm. The weapon began to see use in the mid-eighties; unfortunately there were complaints that it was unreliable and parts were not lasting. A new version has been in service for some time now and has had improvements made to provide for better service.

Small Arms for Urban Combat

The South Africans have also developed a 5.56 conversion known as the mini–SS. This model weighs about 3 pounds less and is almost six inches shorter. The rate of fire remains the same as for the 7.62mm NATO version.[19]

Ma Deuce

While the machine guns covered so far are light enough to be carried by one man, there are several larger models that no one will be carrying into combat, but they must be mentioned due to their importance. The heavy machine guns are usually tripod mounted and crew served; many of these however, are often mounted on vehicles where they offer tremendous mobility and fire support capability. The Chinese type 89, a new design that only weighs about 60 pounds with tripod, is a rare exception. These heavy machine guns have long been respected as some of the most deadly weapons on the battlefield. Their power is enough to punch through a car lengthwise and this is with standard ball ammunition. It is odd that there have not been many successful models in this class

The U.S. M134 Minigun, one of the best fire support concepts ever designed (LCpl. C. Yenter, U.S. Marine Corps).

of weapon. The Chinese appear to have developed the largest number of models while the Russians have developed a few of their own. The West, on the other hand, has had little success in developing any modern design to seriously compete with the Browning M2HB. The M2 is affectionately called "ma-deuce" and has been in service since the 1930s. The original .50-caliber first entered production in 1921. A quick change barrel feature has been added in recent years, and this has become the standard model for many users of this weapon. The power of the .50 BMG is extreme, and with the Mk 211 cartridge, the .50-caliber is even more deadly. While there have been many attempts to replace this weapon with a lighter, more modern design, none have succeeded.

Most of the designs of J.M. Browning have always worked well and the M2HB is probably the best example of this. One of the reasons for the M2's long service life is that attempts to replace it seem to keep falling apart during use. The Browning is not a light weapon by any standards, however, its reliability is without equal. This weapon is often seen mounted on tanks and other vehicles. The basic gun weighs roughly 84 pounds and measures close to 6½ feet overall. The standard tripod adds about another 40 pounds to the weight. This is clearly not a gun to be carried around in the hills of Afghanistan. However, when vehicle mounted, this machine gun can quickly be moved into position to provide suppressive fire like few others. The Browning can demolish brick walls in addition to hitting enemy personnel at extreme ranges. The .50-caliber can carry out past 7000 yards, though its effective range is generally accepted to be around 1600m for area targets.[20]

A mess of captured Russian made Iraqi 12.7mm NSV heavy machine guns. This model was a 1960s design meant to replace the DShKM, which it never fully did (GSgt. E.S. Hansen, U.S. Marine Corps).

The M2HB is closely related to the earlier .30-06 caliber Browning machine gun designs, the model 1917 and model 1919. The M2 of course is far larger in all respects.

The Browning .50 caliber can be fed from left or right side using disintegrating link belted ammunition. The M2HB was designed with a heavier barrel as mentioned earlier, to do away with the need for a cooling jacket. This allowed for reduction in weight even though a heavier barrel was fitted. While this machine gun serves in a variety of roles, it is best known for its infantry support role. It is unlikely that the M2HB will see much use as a tripod mounted weapon for future conflicts. When combined with the standard M3 tripod, the weight is over 120 pounds, which is not conducive to rapid troop movement. When mounted on a light, fast moving vehicle, however, the M2HB's devastating fire support capabilities are indispensable. Perhaps part of the reason for the M2HB continuing to serve is that the weapon is so heavily constructed. The M2 just seems perfectly suited to soaking up the recoil generated by the .50-caliber round. This weapon has remained more or less unchanged since its introduction in the 1930s. The one improvement that has been incorporated, however, is the quick change barrel (QCB) feature, which is something the original M2HB lacked. As the headspace on the original was adjustable, it had to be set each time the barrel was changed, and a gauge was issued with the weapon to perform this task. The QCB modification eliminates the need for this, and has become a standard feature on many M2HB machine guns in service. Original M2HBs can be retrofitted to use this feature if desired. The M2HB is proving itself once more in the deserts of Iraq and Afghanistan. The sandy conditions present there just doesn't seem to bother the M2HB as much as it does other weapon systems within the U.S. arsenal. Reports seem to indicate that the .50-caliber is as loved now as it ever was. It is reassuring to troops under fire to hear the distinctive "thump, thump, thump" of the M2HB providing a burst of supporting fire, and with the Browning .50-caliber, that fire can come from a long way off and still be just as effective.

While the remainder of this chapter will primarily cover the Russian and Chinese heavy machine gun designs, there's one more machine gun design that will definitely play a major role in future urban fighting. While this design doesn't possess the range and power of the heavy machine gun class, it has proven to be the ideal fire support weapon where troops have access to the gun, as it is not generally considered a man-portable machine gun.

The Buzz Saw

The Dillon M134 Minigun is the modern version of the 19th century Gatling gun. For anyone not familiar with this design, the Gatling was a series of gun barrels that rotated around a central axis and the rotation was achieved by cranking a rotary handle. The Gatling was a machine gun in effect if not in design. The original Minigun was a 6000 rpm version made by General Electric. Today Dillon Aero produces a much improved model that only fires at 3000 rpm but is far more reliable than the original. It is a six barrel 7.62mm NATO weapon. It is most likely to be encountered in modern warfare when attached to a vehicle or aircraft. This is not due to the weight of the weapon, but rather to the weight of the ammunition required for such a fast firing mechanism. Also, the weapon requires an external power source to operate the electric motor. Its usefulness for modern warfare is in its ability to instantly perforate a bomb laden terrorist vehicle or for keeping any combatants in the area from returning fire during an assault. It can rake an entire length of building in short order. Due to the Dillon's operational requirements, there are not likely to be many of these within a combat area unless vehicles have access to the immediate area of operation. The M134 is extremely useful when mounted on a helicopter or fixed winged aircraft intended for ground support. Its rate of fire is especially useful in this role. Automatic targeting systems can make this weapon even more deadly. Despite the M134's limited role in modern combat, it is appreciated as much as any .50-caliber.

While the original GE model had several design and functional issues, the Dillon model has dealt with these quite well. The original model had a feed system that was prone to damage in the event of a jam. Dillon has reportedly corrected the issue and the M134 is now considered to be a very reliable design that can handle desert conditions quite well.[21]

An Even Bigger Big Bore

While the .50-caliber was an American invention and the Germans tended to prefer small cannon to heavy machine guns during World War II, it was the Russians who developed the most powerful round currently used for heavy machine guns. The 14.5x114mm was initially developed for anti-tank rifles. Its current home today is in a few modern anti-materiel rifles, and more importantly the heavy machine guns in use east of Germany. There have been some larger calibers developed through the years, but these were either not workable or produced in small numbers. It was the Soviet KPV developed in the post war era that has been the primary reason for the continued use of the 14.5mm cartridge. The KPV is the heart of what, for years, was one of the most feared antiaircraft weapons in the world, the ZPU-4. This was basically 4 KPV machine guns mounted in an anti-aircraft chassis and designed to fire alternately. This weapon could put a huge amount of lead in the air over a great distance and was extremely dangerous to any low flying aircraft. An equally effective weapon was developed in the U.S., known as the quad .50 which utilized the Browning M2 design for the same purpose. The KPV by itself weighs only 108 pounds, but the mounting systems weighed considerably more. The KPV is a short recoil system where the smaller 12.7mm NSV Soviet heavy machine gun is gas operated. The KPV is a rugged, reliable and simple design that is used throughout the former Soviet sphere of influence. It is a common heavy machine and this should be feared by U.S. troops as much as the Taliban should fear the M2HB. The KPV can be fed from either side with minimal modification.[22]

The Russian .50

The NSV 12.7 × 108mm was developed in the late 1960s and is a gas operated heavy machine gun which can supposedly be set up to feed from the left side but is normally seen with right side feed. The NSV has performed quite well over the years, although with the collapse of the Soviet Union a new design has recently shown up. This is known as the KORD and is basically an updated version of the NSV, but the locking system is supposedly different from the original, and the gas system and muzzle brake have been redesigned, resulting in a smoother feeding, softer recoiling heavy machine gun. Dimensions are similar to the NSV, as both weapons weigh around 55 pounds and are a bit over six feet in length.[23]

The Chinese Wave

The Chinese have a history of adopting foreign models while adding their own twists here or there, the end result being a new weapon. The Chinese began to develop original designs starting in the 1980s. The type 77 is a 12.7 × 108mm that uses the gas impingement method of operation, which is unusual for a heavy machine gun. It is claimed to be pri-

This is a Soviet DShKM 12.7mm, the primary Soviet heavy machine gun for much of the early Cold War period. Many are still in use today, as this is a very rugged weapon that dates back to World War II in its early version, the DShK (SSgt. I.A. Graham, U.S. Army).

marily an antiaircraft weapon but can also be used to provide ground support fire as well. Dimensions are approximately 84 inches in overall length, with a weight similar to that of the Browning M2 at around 120 pounds with tripod.

The Chinese also manufacture the type 85 gas operated heavy machine gun that is quite light in weight. This weapon weighs less than 41 pounds without mounts, and its overall length is roughly 78 inches. Whether or not this weapon will be widely issued in China is uncertain, for there's also a newer type 89 model that is even a little lighter at less than 40 pounds. This model uses a different type of operation that is said to be a combination of gas and short-recoil systems. These lightweight large caliber machine guns were clearly designed to provide mobile heavy fire support for ground troops.[24]

Another World War II Design Still in Use

The final heavy machine gun design that should be included in this chapter is perhaps the best known Russian heavy machine gun and probably the most common worldwide, the DShK 12.7 × 108mm. This was the standard Soviet heavy machine gun starting in the late 1930s. The DShKM of the post war era is different in that the feed system is simpler, where the original model utilized a complex rotating shell carrier.[25] The DShKM is a very common heavy weapon. A great many were left behind when the Soviets left Afghanistan. The DShKM is a gas operated weapon that weighs roughly 78 pounds and has an overall length of a little more than 6 feet. This weapon is in widespread use in most former Soviet satellite states, and they will be encountered for some time to come, as they reportedly are very rugged and do not wear out quickly. Any troops serving in the Middle East would do well to know the capabilities of this weapon and should be familiar with its report, as it is every bit as lethal as the Browning M2HB.[26]

I have attempted to cover all of the various machine gun models that are likely to be encountered in any future fighting. The Chinese models are not necessarily serving in large numbers but are usually offered for export, and they are likely sold at reasonable prices, making them more appealing to nations with smaller budgets for defense spending. A basic knowledge of the Chinese weapon designs out there is useful, especially given the potential for problems on the Korean Peninsula at the moment.

With regard to heavy machine guns in general, they may see a rather limited role in urban conflicts as with anti-materiel rifles. This is largely due to their weight. Those encountered will most likely be seen mounted on armor or on fast moving transport or assault vehicles. Heavy machine guns are invaluable for fire support and the power offered by their heavy calibers is extremely useful for dealing with buildings constructed primarily of concrete. Despite their performance, their weight and expense are obstacles to their continued use, especially with competition from less expensive disposable launcher systems which offer superior bunker busting capabilities. Heavy machine guns will also see competition from automatic grenade launchers, which are gaining in popularity, and both of these weapons classes will be covered in following chapters.

CHAPTER 9

Combat Shotguns

The combat shotgun is primarily a U.S. concept but has become common worldwide. This is due in part to the recent development of new types of shot shells which are now available. Shotgun shells are available in everything from non-lethal riot control rounds on up to 200m 12 gauge fin stabilized grenades that offer a lethal radius of several feet combined with armor piercing capability.

The shotgun was used here as a combat weapon before the turn of the last century. It became feared in Europe during World War I, when German troops faced Americans armed with Winchester model 97 slide action shotguns. There were legal efforts made to prevent the U.S. from using the shotgun as a combat weapon, but these were unsuccessful. The pump action has dominated the military market throughout the years, although there have been several successful semi-automatic designs, and even recent fully automatic designs.

At close range, a big bore shotgun is one of the most fearsome combat weapons made. The 12 gauge is by far the most common caliber for military service, although there were larger gauges used in earlier times. The 10 ga. is used on rare occasion. The advantages of the pump action over its semi-auto counterpart are many. The pump action is cheaper to produce and less prone to jamming, although somewhat slower in use. There are also sometimes problems with self loaders with regards to reliable functioning and with functioning at all with certain specialized rounds.

For the semi-auto shotgun, there are three basic types of operation: long recoil, gas, and inertia recoil. There are also some that function as both a pump and semi-auto through the manipulation of a locking mechanism usually located forward of the slide handle.

Browning Designed Everything

As the U.S. is the birthplace of the combat shotgun, let's begin with native designs. While no longer used by the U.S. military, the two models most often associated with the combat shotgun were the Winchester model 97 and model 12. The model 97 was a

9. Combat Shotguns

The best selling shotgun ever, the Remington model 870 pump. This has been used for years by the U.S. military, and these troops are training with riot control launchers attached (Pfc. E. Marshall, U.S. Marine Corps).

Browning design that sold close to one million units throughout its lifetime. This was an exposed hammer design that did not utilize a trigger disconnector, and the weapon could be fired rapidly by simply holding the trigger back while operating the slide mechanism. This practice is somewhat unsafe, but very fast in operation. The follow-up Winchester model 12 was a hammerless design that also lacked a disconnector. The model 12 had a reputation as being one of the smoothest pump guns ever made, and production numbers were nearly two million units over its production lifespan. One unusual fact regarding the Winchester model 12 is that it was one of the few successful shotguns not designed by John Browning. The importance of these two models is that they were the primary U.S. shotguns for the first half of the 20th century.[1]

A final Browning design also associated with military service was the Ithaca model 37. Browning had some help from John Pedersen in designing this weapon, and while the original is no longer made, it has been reintroduced in a somewhat different form. The original model 37 also did not possess a disconnector and was unusual in that it ejected from the bottom and had no openings on either side of the receiver. This helped to keep out debris. The Ithaca was an early favorite of police departments as well as the military. The model 37 was also unusual in that it only utilized one locking bar connecting the slide handle to the carrier, where most shotguns tend to use two bars, one on each side of the receiver. This never affected the reliability of the model, which has proven as rugged, if not more rugged, than any other shotgun made. The Ithaca was available in several versions, with matte finishes being the most popular for police and military use. The standard magazine holds four rounds, although there was a seven round tube magazine on certain models that required a barrel length of no less than 20 inches. The 3 inch magnum chamber common on many shotguns was not used on the model 37 until late in its production. There was also an aluminum frame lightweight model offered, but most samples seen are usually all steel. The overall length varies with configuration and standard models are usually less than 3½ feet, with compact pistol grip models being a bit over 2 feet long. Weight varies as well, most weighing between 7 and 8 pounds. An extremely short barrel, compact version was popular with some law enforcement agencies and was known as the Stakeout. This model was sometimes seen with a pistol grip in place of the normal horizontal slide handle. While the Ithaca was an excellent service shotgun, it was more expensive than some of the newer models from a production standpoint, and its sales suffered as a result. While Winchester offers a modern slide action design, the biggest reason for the decline of the Ithaca was the introduction of two popular models, the Remington 870 and the Mossberg model 500/590.[2]

Mossberg's model 590A1, the Remington 870's primary competitor and a very rugged shotgun (Sgt. A.C. Sauceda, U.S. Marine Corps).

The Top Seller

The Remington model 870 has become the biggest selling pump gun of all time with over 10,000,000[3] units produced, and no sign of stopping. The design of the model 870 again involved John Pedersen. At the time of the model 870's introduction in the early 1950s, the Winchester model 12 was king. Remington wanted a reliable and affordable model to compete with the Winchester. The initial version had a feed issue, but was quickly fixed. After that, the model 870 has been a great performer and has sold extremely well. The newer super magnum version can fire the 3½ inch 12 ga. shell. Most military weapons utilize 2¾ shells. The 870 is also popular outside of the U.S. as an issue shotgun. Like most modern pump guns, the model 870 offers different magazine capacities. The standard tube magazine holds four rounds, with either six or seven round magazine options available. Matte finishes are offered for service models, and the model 870 is used by several custom makers as the basis for heavily modified tactical shotguns, such as those from Wilson. There is also a Knight's Armament made version designed to be mounted below the barrel of the M16. This is known as the Masterkey[4] and is designed primarily for door breaching purposes. For this job, specialized shot shells are used that contain either small size shot or metal powder. This is done to reduce the chance of ricochet injury to the shooter. The model 870 has proven an excellent service shotgun and will likely remain in use for a good number of years. Its weight and length vary as with many shotguns, as multiple configurations are available. The standard 18 inch five shot model measures roughly 38 inches long. Its weight is around 8 pounds. empty. As with the Ithaca model 37, extremely compact models are available, some utilizing forward pistol grips in place of the normal slide handle. Shotguns this compact, however, are very uncomfortable to fire due to their short barrels. The Modular Combat Shotgun (MCS) is used by the U.S. military and is based on the Remington 870.[5] It is equipped with several barrel lengths and corresponding magazine components which can be swapped out to meet various mission requirements. While the Remington is quite popular, it has some serious competition from another design.

The Contender

The Mossberg models 500 and 590 are also extremely popular shotgun designs that have been very successful commercially. While the model 500 is roughly 10 years younger than the Remington 870, it has become a huge seller in its own right. The original design was changed somewhat around 1970, with the addition of dual connecting bars. The original had only one, similar to the Ithaca model 37. While the Remington 870 and most Ithaca model 37s are all steel, the Mossberg uses an aluminum receiver to save weight. The model 500 is respected for its reliability and was designed as a low cost yet durable shotgun. The model 500 can handle 2¾ or 3 inch shells, and locks up securely to a steel barrel extension so that no stress is placed on the receiver itself. While many of these shotgun designs are available in several different calibers, the 12 gauge is by far the most popular and almost the only caliber used for military purposes. The model 500 is offered in several finishes with matte and parkerized the most popular for military use.

The model 590 is similar to the model 500 but has a modified form of magazine attachment near the muzzle. The model 590 is also offered in the 590A1 configuration that uses aluminum for the trigger housing, as opposed to the standard plastic version used on other Mossberg models. The safety button, which is also plastic on standard Mossbergs, is also made of metal on the A1. The A1 also uses heavier gauge steel for the barrel for increased durability. While the Remington 870 has always performed well in service, only the Mossberg 590 series passed all the military requirements at the time of its adoption. It is doubtful that one would notice a significant difference in performance between the two. Both are first rate combat shotguns. Some military versions are fitted with heat shields like those seen on the earlier model 12 and model 97 Winchesters. Bayonet lugs are also mounted on most military models.

There are several magazine capacities offered for the Mossberg 500/590. The standard is five rounds, with seven and 8 round options available. This is one more round than usually seen on Remington model 870s or Ithaca model 37s. Stocks are usually plastic for military models. The pistol gripped, 14 inch Mossberg 590A1 is a very handy weapon, with an overall length of approximately 2 feet. This model has a strap fitted to the slide handle to help secure the operating hand, although pistol grip replacements are also available if this is preferred. The safety of the Mossberg model 500 series is ambidextrous, whereas the Remington 870 and Ithaca are cross bolt designs intended for right handed users. The model 590A1 has proven a highly reliable and affordable military shotgun. While the semi-auto Benelli M4 has recently been adopted as the new standard U.S.M.C. shotgun, the model 590A1 is still used in large numbers and is a lower cost weapon that can function reliably with any type of load, while the semi-auto M4 will not function with certain less than lethal (LTL) loads.[6]

Browning Designed This One Too

The pump action is the traditional action choice for most military shotguns; however, there was one semi-auto design produced over the years that was reliable enough for military service and has seen combat use throughout its history. Not surprisingly, this weapon was also a John Browning design. The Auto-5 was first introduced around the turn of the century, although the design dates back to the late 19th century. The Browning Auto-5 was only recently discontinued in the late nineties. With very few exceptions, the Auto-5 has yet to be challenged for its reliability as a semi-auto shotgun. The Auto-5 was primarily produced by FN in Belgium but Remington also produced the weapon as the model 11. Savage produced it as well, calling it the models 720 and 745. During the final years of its production life, the Auto-5 line was moved to Japan. The Auto-5 normally used a 4 round magazine as standard, although there were a few police versions that utilized an extended magazine and forend. These are seldom seen, however. The weight of most Auto-5 shotguns is between 8 and 9 pounds with a variety of barrel lengths having been offered. The Auto-5 used a friction ring that allowed for reliable operation regardless of the type of load used. Correct adjustment of this piece was necessary for reliable functioning.[7]

The Browning Auto-5 was used by British troops as a combat weapon in Southeast Asia during the communist uprisings of the 1950s. At times the barrel was cut back, although this was not a good idea for a recoil operated weapon. Despite this practice, it continued to shoot reliably. As part of the recoil system is built into the stock, removing this part is not an option. However, some users became creative and cut off a portion of the stock, leaving enough for reliable operation of the weapon while reducing the overall length somewhat. This created a fairly compact and very deadly shotgun capable of firing off five rounds in a hurry. While gas operated shotguns have been used over the years, such systems foul very quickly when used in shotgun designs, and must be cleaned on a regular basis for continued functioning. The Browning long recoil system does not suffer from these issues and has proven to be one of the most reliable self-loading shotguns of all time. While there have been several gas operated shotguns offered over the years, none had seriously been able to top the Auto-5 where reliability is concerned. That is until the Italian firm of Benelli developed the inertia recoil system. This method has proven not only reliable but incredibly fast in operation.

One Fast Shotgun

This new recoil system was developed for the Benelli M1, M2, and M3 shotguns. The M1 was originally marketed as the HK Super 90 in the early 1980s. While the name may have changed, the weapon has not. The M1 uses an inertia recoil system which depends on the force of the gun's rearward movement during recoil to unlock the bolt. What this means is that the weapon will not cycle if the butt of the stock is placed against a rigid object. It also means that the heavier the load, the shorter the cycle time.

The Benelli M2 is basically the M1 with minor changes. The M1 is known for being a highly reliable design and is popular with law enforcement units. It is especially handy when equipped with the 14 inch entry barrel. The Benelli can be equipped with a standard semi pistol grip buttstock or a full pistol grip version. The design, however, cannot be fitted without a buttstock, as the recoil spring is housed within this part as with the Browning Auto-5. The standard magazine capacity for the Benelli is five rounds, with seven rounds as an option. The 14 inch Entry model is only equipped with the five round option. The overall length is a bit less than 40 inches for the standard version, while the 14 inch model measures closer to 35 inches. Weight is less than 7 pounds in the standard length barrel. The M1 is available with conventional blade/notch sights, but can also be fitted with a faster operating aperture sight system. As good as the M1 system is, it lacks the versatility offered by the M3 dual action shotgun.

The U.S. M1014 semi-auto shotgun. This is the military designation for the Benelli M4 gas-operated design (MCC E.A. Clement, U.S. Navy).

Two Guns in One

The M3 is both a semi-auto and pump. The M3 uses the same inertia recoil system with slight modifications to allow for an actual folding stock to be fitted. The shotgun also offers the option of being used as a pump action by unlocking the slide near the muzzle. This allows for reliable use of LTL rounds that may not function reliably if the weapon is used in semi-auto mode. Weight is about ¼ pound more than for the M1 series. The overall length is similar, though the M3's length can be reduced in its folding stock version. Magazine options are the same as with the M1 series, as are the sighting options. Both the M1 and M3 have seen success among military and law enforcement units and with good reason. The recoil system used by these models is less prone to fouling, as with most gas operated shotguns, and operates with reliability similar to that of the Browning Auto-5. The rapid cycling of this action allows for tremendous firepower when needed.

While the M1 and M3 models are some of the most popular semi-auto models in use today, the U.S.M.C. chose to adopt the newer gas operated Benelli M4 as is its standard combat shotgun. The reason for this is the new ARGO gas piston design. It is claimed that the system is self-cleaning (unlikely) and self-regulating in addition to being simple in design. In the ARGO system, there are two short pistons that operate directly on the bolt, eliminating the need for a heavy carrier. This also allows for the gas port to be moved closer to the chamber where gas temperatures are higher and possess smaller amounts of carbon deposits and fouling material. It is claimed that this gas system has a minimum 25,000 round service life.[8]

A New Gas Design

The M4 is known by the U.S.M.C. as the M1014 and offers several different options with regard to magazine capacity, with four rounds being standard on most commercial models. The standard military version uses a seven round magazine. The stock used on the M1014 can be partially collapsed and the empty weight is less than 8 pounds. The overall length with the stock extended is less than 40 inches, which is reduced about 4 inches by collapsing the stock. Despite its new reliable gas system, the M4 suffers the same problem as many semi-automatic shotgun designs, including the previous Benelli designs. It will not function reliably with certain LTL loads. In this case the action must be operated manually. The current Benelli line of shotguns has brought semi-auto design to the forefront of the combat shotgun market, though these were not the first semi-automatic designs to see military service.

An Early Tactical Shotgun

The SPAS-12 from the Italian firm Franchi is an older design than the Benelli M4 and was in production for roughly 20 years before being replaced by the updated SPAS-15. The SPAS-12 was another pump/semi-auto combination, although this was a gas operated shotgun. The SPAS-12 had a distinctive top folding stock design that used a hook shaped steel wire for the butt plate, making the weapon easily recognizable. A fixed stock version was also offered. Magazine capacity was either six or eight rounds. There was also a magazine cut-off that allows for changing the type of round in the chamber. This feature was also found on many Browning Auto-5 versions. The purpose of the hook on the folding stock variant was to support the arm to allow for one handed firing, as the hook used a rotating mechanism.

The original SPAS-12 design was flawed and the initial pattern of safety lever was changed to a cross bolt design. The original SPAS-12 had a recall issued as result of this. The SPAS-12 was heavy at around 9½ pounds empty, and the overall length varied with choice of barrel. With the shorter 18 inch barrel and the stock folded, the length was reduced to around 2½ feet. The SPAS-12 was only meant to fire 2¾ inch shells. The weapon was quite successful and was only dropped about 10 years ago to clear the way for its replacement, the SPAS-15.

The SPAS-15 is also no longer in production but was used by the Italian military and is still fairly common in Europe. This SPAS-15, unlike many tactical shotguns, used a detachable box magazine in either six or eight round capacities. The gas piston is located above the barrel and the model could be fitted with a side folding stock. An M16 type carrying handle was standard and there was a grip safety similar in layout to that found on the Beretta M12S submachine gun, in that it was located at the front of the pistol grip. The SPAS-15 weighed around 8½ pounds empty, and measured roughly 30 inches with the stock in its folded position, 39 inches extended. While the SPAS shotguns were effective, they were fairly heavy and expensive to produce and did not last in production.[9]

The AK Goes Smoothbore

One semi-auto design that can provide competition to many of today's popular models is the SAIGA-12 from Russia. The SAIGA-12 showed up in the nineties, and is roughly based on the AK 47 rifle in concept. It is reportedly a very reliable semi-automatic gas operated design. This is good news, as many gas operated shotguns have been less than perfect where reliable functioning is concerned. Its close relation to the AK 47 has been a strong selling point. Technically, there are major differences, as designing a shotgun around the AK action required considerable changes. The SAIGA uses an adjustable gas regulator as opposed to the fixed gas system of the AK.

The most convenient model of the SAIGA is the 12K with its 17 inch barrel. There is a folding stock available which reduces the overall length to about 2 feet. The weight for most models is between 7½ and 8 pounds. The SAIGA uses a detachable box magazine and a variety of capacities are offered. Box capacities generally are 10 rounds or less, with drum capacities of up to 20 rounds being available. These are meant for 2¾ inch shells only, as with the SPAS models. There is reportedly a new version that uses an improved magazine latch that no longer requires the box magazine to be first engaged in the front and then rotated into position. The magazine can simply be inserted straight into the magazine well similar to the M16 rifle. There are also other minor improvements, but this new version has not yet been listed in the manufacturer's catalog.[10]

One Scary Shotgun

The advantages of magazine fed shotguns is in their ability to quickly be reloaded as opposed to tube fed magazines, which can only receive one round at a time. As a result users of tube fed combat shotguns are taught to continually top off their magazines whenever the opportunity presents itself. While the pump action has traditionally ruled the combat shotgun field and semi-autos or combination actions are beginning to make headway, there has never been a successful fully automatic combat shotgun to see common service use. This may change in the very near future. The Atchisson AA-12 is a full-auto design that offers great potential as a military weapon. The AA-12 dates back to the early 1970s. It is a heavy design at over 10 pounds empty, and while this is not an unbearable burden, it is heavier than most current tactical shotguns in use. The current AA-12 is primarily constructed from stainless steel components, which helps reduce fouling issues and adds to the gun's ability to resist corrosion.

The AA-12 fires from an open bolt and is fed from an eight round box magazine or drum magazines with 20 or 32 round capacities. The manufacturer claims that cleaning is only required after 10,000 rounds. If true, this would be a big improvement over most self-loading designs. The AA-12 uses a unique recoil reduction system and felt recoil is minimal due to the weapon's unique design, which makes for an easily controlled weapon when fired on full auto. The action operates within a housing designed to soak up the majority of the recoil forces. The rate of fire is around 300 rpm. The U.S.M.C. tested the AA-12 several years ago but it has yet to find any buyers. With the military beginning to focus on urban operations as a distinct possibility for future conflicts, the AA-12 may yet find a home.[11]

Smoothbore Revolver

There's one more unique model that also has a fairly long history, the South African Protecta. This design began life under a different name, the Armsel Striker. The Striker was designed in the 1980s by Hilton Walker, who had moved to South Africa during the war in Rhodesia. The Striker used a 12 round cylinder and operated in a fashion that somewhat resembles a revolver. The cylinder was originally spring wound and each shell had to be ejected one at a time after firing. Loading was also done one shell at a time. The Striker was compact and had a good level firepower. The design had enough good qualities that Walker decided to make an improved version that would correct some of the design flaws of the original model. He first designed an ejection system where each empty case would be thrown clear after the next round was fired. The newer model also had a cocking handle along the barrel to eliminate the need for winding the spring manually. The trigger is a heavy double-action design similar to that of a revolver for safety purposes. With its top folding stock extended, the overall length was around 2½ feet and less than 20 inches with the stock folded. The weight is a bit over 9 pounds empty. The new model became known as the Protecta and it is also offered in a compact 11 round cylinder version known as the Bulldog. The Bulldog model uses a great deal of plastics in its construction and no stock is fitted. It uses a short 7 inch barrel and the overall length is reduced to just 1½ feet with an empty weight of only 5 pounds, making for very short combat shotgun. With such a short barrel, it likely possesses severe muzzle blast. Both models are designed to fire the 2¾ inch shell only.[12]

Set for Stun

Truvelo of South Africa offers the Neostead 2000, also known as the NS2000. This is a bullpup shotgun that has a great deal of potential as a modern urban combat weapon. This is a pump action that operates in reverse much like the M203 grenade launcher, meaning that it is slid forward to unlock the action and eject the empty case and pulled to the rear to chamber the new round. This bullpup design uses two over barrel 6 round tube magazines that can feed alternately or from one magazine at a time. This allows the user to load one tube with LTL rounds and the other with buckshot or whatever is best suited to the job at hand. The NS2000 has reportedly been tested by the British SAS. It has yet to find any major buyers.[13]

This chapter has covered the most common combat shotguns in use today. Though there are many other perfectly functional models being made, only the models covered have achieved any major success as service weapons. The remainder of this chapter will deal with the tactical applications of the combat shotgun.

Shotguns have a long military history and an even longer history as a combat weapon as used by militia. Its future as a combat weapon is all but guaranteed due to its fearsome close range capability. Its versatility can be matched by few other small arms. The 12 gauge is by far the most common caliber for service use and all models covered in this chapter are primarily 12 gauge models. The standard military shell is usually the 2¾ inch version, but 3 inch magnum shells offer the ability to carry a larger payload. There are many shot sizes available, with buckshot being the most common for service use; 00 buckshot is roughly ⅓ inch in diameter, and smaller number 4 buckshot is also used in jungle environments. As mentioned, there are special door breaching loads that use either small birdshot or frangible metal to reduce chance of a ricochet. The frangible loads are even designed to breach doors covered with sheet steel. For sheer power, the 12 gauge rifled slug is difficult to beat. However, these would have to be jacketed or hardened steel to comply with international law regarding ammunition for military use. The shotgun can also be used to fire a variety of LTL rounds such as rubber bullets, rubber shot, bean bags, and even tear gas rounds. The biggest leap in technology, however has come with the recent development of 12 gauge fin stabilized grenade rounds. Known as the FRAG-12 line, these include high explosive, high explosive armor piercing, and even an air burst round for an increase in lethality. The FRAG-12 series has seen limited testing in the Middle East recently. Effective range of the grenades is listed as 200m, and the lethal radius is most likely less than 10 feet due to the size of the grenade. If these are deemed worthy for military use, they will be a big addition to the shotgun's capabilities.[14]

The traditional round used for combat is the buckshot load. The military is required to use hardened shot to comply with international law. How the Hague Accords allow for use of jagged shrapnel while claiming deforming bullets are inhumane is a wonder, but this is the law nonetheless. Buckshot is lethal up to 50 yards or more depending on the size of the ball used. At close range, however, the buckshot load is scary. The effect is similar to being hit with up to 15 .33 caliber bullets at the same time where the 00 load is used. The chances of hitting a target are also increased considerably due to the natural tendency for the shot to spread as it moves down range. Despite the fearsome power of the buckshot load, it does not compare to the power of a rifled slug at close range. The average 12 gauge slug weighs 1 ounce and the destructive effect is unbelievable. It also offers tremendous ability to punch through heavy cover.

9. Combat Shotguns

The shotgun began its combat service as a trench gun during World War I and was often the first choice for arming the patrol point man during the Vietnam War. For urban operations, the shotgun offers more uses than ever before. Its door breaching ability is extremely useful when the need to enter through a locked doorway presents itself. The shotgun can also be used to tremendous advantage for reaching a target behind cover either with the use of slugs or by using an even more effective tactic, that of deliberate ricochet. This can be done effectively against hard composition vertical walls or by shooting at the floor or pavement just in front of the target. This is extremely effective when buckshot is used. For house clearing, the compact, pistol grip equipped models are highly maneuverable and a prime example of this is the Mossberg 590A1 fitted with pistol grip and 14 inch barrel. The overall length of this weapon is only a little over 2 feet and its weight is under 6 pounds empty. Other good examples of compact combat shotguns are the Ithaca Stakeout model, which is no longer produced, and the current Remington 870 compact models.

While the pump action models are more easily adapted to compact versions, they cannot offer the rapid fire capabilities of a semi-auto. Of the popular semi-auto designs, the Benelli M1 is still fairly long, as it cannot be fitted with a folding stock. The M3 offers a similar fast cycling and reliable action, in addition to the reduced overall length provided by its folding stock. An added advantage of the M3 is its ability to operate as a pump gun. The SAIGA-12K is also quite short at just over 2 feet when folded, and this weapon can provide to 20 rounds of semi-automatic fire, in addition to being faster to reload than the tube fed shotgun designs.

For close range operations, such as those likely in urban warfare, there are few weapons that can match the 12 gauge shotgun for destructive effect. The 12 gauge shotgun is superior to most small arms in its ability to quickly take down an opponent. It is quite likely that the combat shotgun will become one of the more common weapons for future warfare use. The most successful models will be those that offer the greatest firepower in the smallest package and can do so at a reasonable price.

Chapter 10

Grenade Launchers

Rifle grenades were first used during World War I.[1] There was a tactical need to launch grenades farther than troops were able to throw them. Special blank cartridges were used for many years until the bullet trap system was perfected after World War II.[2] This allowed standard ball ammunition to be used to launch the grenade. Most rifle grenades have a maximum range of around 300m. The primary advantage of the rifle grenade is that it can launch a fairly large grenade charge that is as effective as a hand grenade if not more so. There has been a renewed interest in this particular type of munition in recent years. The Israelis, in particular, have made good use of the rifle grenade concept and have continued development of rifle grenade technology. Several years ago a version using an advanced sighting system was introduced, and was designed to vastly increase the accuracy of the rifle grenade in terms of first round hit potential.[3] One advantage of rifle grenades is that there is no need for any other equipment in order to fire this lightweight form of artillery.

Despite the advantages, there is much left to be desired about the rifle grenade concept. The recoil created by launching a 1½ to 2 pound projectile is severe, often necessitating an unorthodox firing position. Usually the grenade is launched with the buttstock placed on the ground or firmly locked between the shooter's abdomen and upper arm. The effect this has on accuracy is anything but good. The inherent accuracy of a fin stabilized projectile is not outstanding in the first place. Common sense would tell one that accuracy doesn't have to be perfect where explosives are concerned. However, should it be necessary to fire a grenade through an open window, then the accuracy issue becomes very real. Due to these shortcomings, a search began for a more accurate grenade delivery system. In the early 1960s the U.S. introduced the M79 40 × 46mmSR single-shot grenade launcher. This weapon used a high low pressure system cartridge design. When the primer of the round sets off the propellant charge, the gas pressure quickly builds in the small expansion chamber until several radially located pressure relief holes are ruptured and the gas is allowed to move into a larger, low pressure expansion chamber. The effect of this is to lower the muzzle velocity of the grenade which is launched at a velocity of around 250 feet per second while still keeping recoil forces within a tolerable range. The grenade is spin stabilized as with a normal bullet, which serves to not only allow for accurate shooting, but also to arm the grenade itself. This is to ensure that the grenade has reached a safe distance from the operator before arming. A similar concept was also developed into a more powerful 40 × 53mm grenade round which is used in belt-fed automatic grenade launchers.[4] This round, however, is too powerful to be fired by a shoulder arm and as a result, the larger grenade cannot be chambered in the smaller 40 × 46mm launchers for safety reasons.

Advantages to this system are many. Creating a grenade that can be fired from a conventional firing position allows for greater accuracy potential. Spin stabilizing allows for better accuracy still. The 40mm grenade launcher also offered a longer effective range than most conventional rifle grenades and most 40mm grenade rounds have a 400m effective range, although this has recently been increased to 800m with the Martin Electronics, Inc. (MEI) Mercury medium range round. South Africa is also working on a 40 × 51mm design that can still be fired from hand held launchers.[5]

The 40mm has its drawbacks as well. It requires a separate firearm which adds to equipment costs. Its lethality is reduced by necessity, as the grenade itself is fairly small compared to older rifle grenade designs. The original M79 required that the grenadier be

The first grenade launcher to enter service, the U.S. M79 (middle). An M136/AT4 launcher can be seen to the right, while an M240G with thermal sight is in background (LCpl. R.B. Busse, U.S. Marine Corps).

U.S. M203 40mm grenade launcher mounted below the M4 carbine (S. Thurow, U.S. Air Force).

armed without a rifle or bear the extra weight of carrying a second weapon. This is what led to the development of the U.S. M203 Under Barrel Grenade Launcher (UBGL). This allowed the grenadier to also have a rifle at the ready. Until recently, the under barrel concept has been the primary focus for weapons manufacturers the world over, with regards to grenade launcher design.

The Original and Still One of the Best

The M79 was the first of what has become a large class of weapons. The M79 was a break open single-shot weapon that closely resembled a very large single barrel shotgun. It was fitted with iron sights that flipped up to allow for accurate aiming out to the maximum effective range. It operates much like a break open shotgun. A thumb lever is moved horizontally, which unlocks the breech and cocks the weapon on opening while also activating the safety lever. The spent case is removed, allowing for a fresh grenade to be inserted. The action is closed and the weapon is ready to fire once the safety is removed. The M79 used a rubber recoil pad for increased shooting comfort. The launcher measured less than 29 inches long and weighed just shy of 6 pounds empty. The M79 was known as a reliable, easy to use weapon, and was highly accurate. It served throughout the Vietnam War and was officially replaced in 1969 by the M203. The M79 is still used by special operations units within the U.S. military to this day. It is often preferred over the M203 for its simplicity, faster reloading, greater accuracy, and for its ability to use a larger variety of 40mm LTL rounds due to its break open breech.[6]

The First Rifle Attachment for Modern Warfare

The M203 was lighter and allowed the grenadier to operate as a rifleman as well. The M203 was also more complicated. The design was operated by pressing a latch on the left side of the frame and sliding the barrel forward on a rail. This was sort of a reverse pump action weapon. The spent case was ejected and a new grenade could be inserted in the barrel, which was then slid back until it locked into place. The M203 has been seen in recent years with a pistol grip mount allowing it to be used by itself without the need for rifle mounting. This is unusual since it was first adopted because of its ability to mount to a rifle. The M203 is effective, but is reputed to be less accurate and slower in use than the M79. It is reported that the M79 is preferred for its accuracy in the mission of detonating unexploded IEDs. The M203 is apparently not satisfactory in terms of performance, as it has been recently replaced by the HK M320. The age of many M203s in service may have had something to do with this decision, but it seems as if the U.S. wanted a more modern design with greater safety features.[7]

The New Model

The HK M320 does offer several advantages in that it is easier to load, as well as faster. It is also far more compact, though its weight is only slightly less than the M203. There's also a safer double-action trigger mechanism and a folding vertical foregrip for added control. Several different sighting systems are available for this launcher as well as a collapsible buttstock, allowing it to be used as a separate weapon. It is quite similar to the German AG 36 designed for use in conjunction with the G36 assault rifle. While the sights can be adapted for left hand users, the weapon only opens to the left. The double-action trigger mechanism offers not only a safety advantage, but can also offer the option of a second trigger pull should the first attempt fail to detonate the primer.[8]

Imitation Is the Sincerest

The Soviets were watching the M203 in use and were impressed enough with the idea to develop their own version. These early models were used with success in Afghanistan in the 1980s. The current model is somewhat lighter and simpler in design than the original. The current standard Russian versions are the GP30, GP34 and GP95. The

Small Arms for Urban Combat

Above: The U.S. M320 40mm grenade launcher, the M203's replacement. This HK is similar to the same launcher as used on the German G36 rifle (Spc. M.J. MacLeod, U.S. Army). *Below*: A U.S. M32 6-shot 40mm grenade launcher. This gives troops a big boost in mobile firepower (Cpl. S. D. Corum, U.S. Marine Corps).

GP95 is the GP30 with a modified bracket to allow for attachment to the 9A-91 compact assault rifle. The GP34 is primarily the same weapon with some minor improvements and is offered by a different manufacturer. The effective range of the Russian grenade launchers is also 400m and weights are similar to the M203 at roughly 3 pounds empty for the current models. The overall length of the GP series is shorter than the M320 but not by much. This is possible, as the Russian 40mm grenade design does not use a separate metal casing and the weapons are loaded through the muzzle until locked into place, and as a result, no extraction system is used. The trigger mechanism of the GP series is double-action and iron sights are fitted as standard. The GP 30 and its derivatives are designed to mount to most AK type full size rifles, though the compact AKS-74U and the AK 105 carbine cannot mount these launchers. The 40mm Russian round is not interchangeable with the U.S. 40 × 46mm, although range and performance are similar.[9]

Everyone Gets on Board

Former Soviet satellite states have also developed some of their own models recently. Bulgaria has a rather large selection of single-shot launchers in addition to multi-round launchers. They offer a GP30 variant as well as a UBGL series for mounting to various assault rifles other than the AK. The UBGL more closely resembles the M203. While single-shot launchers are more common, multi-shot launchers have begun to see a great deal of use in recent years.

Turning Up the Heat

The first successful multi-shot launcher originated in South Africa. This is the same weapon as used by the U.S. military as the M32, although in slightly modified form. This weapon is known as the Milkor Multiple Grenade Launcher (MGL). It is a 6 round launcher that fires from a cylinder in revolver fashion. Two pistol grips and a folding stock are standard. Optical sights are normally used and the M32 offers a rail system for mounting other accessories. The weight of the M32 is close to 13 pounds empty and there is a compact version designed for use by special operations units.[10]

The Russians have their own multi-shot launcher in the 6G-30 which is very similar in performance. This is a six round launcher designed by the KBP Instrument Design Bureau, the same firm responsible for the 9A-91 compact assault rifle. The 6G-30 is similar in layout to the M32 and is quite similar in dimensions at roughly 13½ pounds empty and an overall length of 20½ inches with its stock collapsed, just under 27 inches extended. This uses the same 40mm grenades as the Russian GP 30 single-shot launcher. The chambers on the 6G-30 cylinder contain the rifling rather than the barrel, which is smooth bore. The cylinder spring is wound manually like the South African Striker shotgun. The barrel rotates to the side for loading. Folding iron sights are standard.[11]

The Navy Already Thought of That

While these appear to be the new trend in grenade launcher design, the concept of a multi-round grenade launcher is not new, and it has taken more than one form over the years. One of the first ones ever devised was developed by the U.S. Navy's China Lake weapons development facility. This was a pump action repeating grenade launcher and was never produced in large numbers, though a new version is being developed by Airtronic, the final makers of the M203 launcher. The original pump action 40mm launcher was likely developed at the request of the Navy SEAL teams for use during the Vietnam War.[12]

While the new version is not standard, it is possibly being considered, as it is lighter and more compact than the M32 multi-shot launcher. Although the pump action is somewhat slower to fire and only holds four rounds as opposed to the six round capacity of the M32, price and performance will likely be heavy factors if it is to see future adoption.

More Copies

The Russians, however, have adopted a pump action of their own, although this weapon opens forward much like the M203 launcher. This is known as the GM-94 and uses a different 43mm cased grenade as opposed to the caseless 40mm round traditionally used by Russian grenade launchers. The magazine is a three round tube mounted above the barrel. This launcher was clearly designed for urban combat use, as the primary grenade is a non-fragmenting high-explosive round that is safe to use within 6m. Lethal radius is approximately 3m. Non-lethal grenades are also available for this launcher. The GM-94 was also designed by the KBP bureau and the overall length is approximately 21 inches closed and almost 32 inches extended. Its empty weight is just over 10½ pounds, making it somewhat lighter than the rotary magazine launchers.[13]

The Russians have also developed several other designs for both special operations units and the law enforcement community. A Russian law enforcement grenade launcher is best exemplified by the RGS-50M. This is a single-shot, break open, smooth bore launcher. Some of the rounds are fin stabilized. The RGS-50M uses gas rounds, door breaching rounds, flash-bangs for room entry, rubber shot rounds, as well as standard HE and HEDP rounds. The effective range of this launcher is claimed to be 115m, though it is likely that some of the grenades have a greater range. As this launcher is larger in caliber than most previous launcher designs, the recoil is also likely more severe. It is a 50mm design that uses two pistol grips along with iron sights and a recoil pad mounted on a tubular steel buttstock.[14]

There are several other Russian launchers in service and from their designs it seems they too are ideal for modern urban combat operations. These were initially designed for special operations use but could easily serve as law enforcement weapons if needed.

Quiet Mortars

The first model is the most recent, though none of these are seen on a widespread basis. The GSN-19 30mm silent grenade launcher is a single-shot weapon that has a forward curved pistol grip into which a magazine is inserted. The grenade is muzzle loaded as with the GP series, and the standard magazine holds 8 to 10 rounds depending on the version, as the design has been modified over time. This launcher was originally known as the BS-1, and used a different parent cartridge case than the current version, hence the different magazine capacities. These launchers were developed as an improvement on two earlier designs which are apparently still used to a limited extent, the "D" launcher and the DM, which was an improved version. These use a different grenade from the BS-1/GSN-19, although also 30mm in diameter.

These single shot launchers were used as stand-alone devices rather than being mounted to a rifle. These grenade launchers are able to fire a blank launched silent grenade, although they could also be used to fire a special armor piercing bullet at ranges of up to 200m. Effective range of the grenade was 300m. The purpose of these launchers was for covert attack on high value targets. The silent 9mm cartridge was known as the PFAM and the blank grenade firing round was known as the PMAM. The grenade itself carried the designation BMYa-31. The "D" model looked like a big single shot pistol and used a bipod, detachable stock, and a special muzzle attachment for firing the grenade. The improved the DM version was lighter and was magazine fed, although the grenade itself was still muzzle loaded.[15]

The significance of these weapons is not in the numbers in which they served, as they were never widely issued, but in their tactical uses for urban combat environments. The U.S. has no equivalent weapon systems in this area. Although the U.S. 40 × 46mm launchers could use the M463 smokeless/flashless silent grenade with roughly the same purpose, it had a shorter effective range of roughly 150m.[16]

While the Russians and Americans have done a great deal of the grenade launcher design work, they are not the only nations with current models in production. The LL-06 is a modern break-open single-shot launcher from Switzerland. It is short, at only 15 inches with its stock folded, and very light at only 4½ pounds empty. Like many modern systems it uses a double-action trigger mechanism for safety. It is chambered for the standard 40 × 46mmSR grenade. Due to its break open design, it was clearly meant to use LTL grenades as well, as the break open designs allow for easy chambering of grenades that are longer than normal. This includes tear gas, rubber bullets, etc. Open sights are fitted but a mounting rail allows for any optical system to be used. A forend rail system allows for attachment of a vertical foregrip, and other accessories can be mounted to side rails if desired.[17]

Bulgaria offers two multi-round launchers in addition to their single-shot models. The Avalanche and the MSGL are both six round launchers from the Arsenal firm. The MSGL closely resembles the Russian 6G-30, while the Avalanche is even more compact and lacks a barrel, firing directly from the chambers of the cylinder. A horizontal foregrip is fitted for added control. Weight of this model is less than 14 pounds empty and overall length is slightly more than 15 inches with the tubular stock collapsed, approximately 20 inches extended. The Avalanche fires the Russian 40mm grenade pattern, while the MSGL uses the U.S. 40 × 46mm grenade. The latter model was likely meant for export.[18]

China Does Not Pirate Everything

While the Chinese have not followed the same path as the U.S. and Russia where launcher design is concerned, they have developed two models that fall somewhere between the lighter weight, one man weapons and the larger crew served models that we will cover shortly. The Chinese models are the QLZ-87 automatic launcher and the newer QLB-06 (QLZ-87B) semi-auto launcher. The Chinese use their own 35 × 32mmSR grenade for these weapons and have decided to create lighter magazine fed launchers capable of providing the same longer range grenade fire of the larger crew served weapons. Despite their greater range and recoil, these weapons are still quite portable and can be easily moved to a new firing position during an assault. While using magazine fed designs may limit their firepower, they offer greater versatility due to their size and weight, as well as offering a greatly extended range. The effective range of these launchers is claimed to be 1700m, which is similar to what the large belt-fed grenade launchers can provide.

The U.S. Mk 19 Mod 3 40 × 53mm automatic grenade launcher. This weapon is capable of providing devastating fire support to almost 2000 yards (Pfc. J.A. Ortiz, U.S. Marine Corps).

Russian AGS-17 30mm automatic grenade launcher; this was the Soviet answer to the Mk 19. There is an updated AGS-30 model still in service, though a new 40mm Russian design has recently been developed (Sgt. A. Reynolds, U.S. Army).

The QLZ-87 is a direct gas impingement launcher used in either a lightweight configuration with a six round drum magazine and lightweight bipod, or a larger 15 round drum and tripod. Weight is roughly 26 pounds empty in the lightweight configuration with an overall length of 38 inches. Little information is currently available as to the performance of this system, though it has been seen in service by China among other nations. Its estimated rate of fire is 500 rpm.

The newer QLB-06 is semi-automatic only and was probably developed as an improvement on the QLZ-87. It is possible that it may have just been an alternative design. Very little accurate information is available on either of these launchers. The QLB-06 uses a similar gas action to the previous model and the general layout resembles a miniature Barrett model 82 rifle. These are interesting weapons in that they may seem rather heavy when compared to Western launchers, but it must be remembered that the range is far superior to that offered by the 40 × 46mm designs or the Russian 40mm caseless models. At the same time, these are still portable weapons.[19]

Getting Serious

The last category of launcher is the belt-fed crew served weapon best exemplified by the U.S. 40 × 53mm models such as the Mk 19 Mod 3 and newer Mk 47. Similar Russian 30mm designs are the AGS-17 and AGS-30. All of these weapons were traditionally used from either tripods or far more mobile vehicles. The tripod versions will continue to see use, although they don't offer the same mobility as vehicle mounted launchers. However, vehicle use is somewhat limited in built up or urban areas, as roadblocks are easily constructed by defenders which can largely limit vehicle access. The versatility of these heavier launchers is limited much in the same way as heavy machine guns are, due to the weight of both systems, although newer models are reduced in weight considerably. The advantage these launchers offer is a vastly increased effective range of close to 2000 yards, in some cases. In fact, these are rapidly becoming one of the preferred weapons for infantry support, as they can lay down devastating amounts of fire in a very short period of time.

The original U.S. design was the Mk 19. This is a blowback operated launcher and uses the 40 × 53mm grenade, as used in most Western designs. This grenade produces far more recoil than the 40 × 46mmSR and requires a larger and heavier weapon to handle this. Its greatest advantages are its full-auto capability and its belt feed mechanism which can put multiple grenades in the air at the same time. While the lethal radius of the 40 × 53mm grenade is not much greater than that offered by the 40 × 46mm, a great many more rounds can be placed down range in a very short period of time and if enough rounds are available, these grenades can keep coming. The Mk 19 feeds from a disintegrating link belt loaded in 48 round cans. Its weight without the tripod is roughly 70 pounds, and it has a 350 rpm rate of fire.[20]

There's been a new model to enter service recently in the U.S., the Mk 47 Striker. This is a lighter weapon at around 40 pounds without tripod, and offers a somewhat slower rate of fire of approximately 300 rpm. Its primary advantage is its ability to fire advanced air burst grenades. These are programmed to detonate at a given range by an advanced sighting system and an electronic fuse within the grenade. The grenade is programmed by the sighting system to detonate at the ideal range. The Mk 47 is currently fielded by some units and it is possible that this will replace the Mk 19 Mod 3 as the standard U.S. crew served grenade launcher. The programmable grenades have yet to be perfected however.[21]

There are several other Western designs in use as well. The HK Grenade Machine Gun (GMG) is similar to the Mk 19 in size and rate of fire, but it is slightly lighter at around 63 pounds. Unlike the Mk 19, the GMG can be fed from either left or right side, whereas the Mk 19 and Mk 47 feed from the left side. There is also a South African launcher known as the Vektor Y3 AGL. This uses a recoil operated action with a rate of fire of around 300 rpm and weighs a little over 70 pounds. This is a modern design and uses an advanced sighting system to increase hit probability.[22]

The Russians developed their own automatic grenade launchers in 30 × 28mm. The original was the AGS-17, which was later joined by the AGS-30. The effective range of these weapons is around 1700m, and rate of fire is approximately 400 rpm. The AGS-17 is a blowback design and was first seen in the late 1960s. It is far lighter than the Mk 19 and the gun itself weighs less than 40 pounds. When used with a tripod its weight increases to just under 70 pounds. This weapon was used successfully in the 1980s in Afghanistan, where its capabilities were appreciated. The AGS-17 is being replaced by an improved version the AGS-30. The new version has a lighter weight, only 35 pounds with tripod. The action is likely updated somewhat for cost and performance benefits. These weapons are both capable of fitting optical systems for advanced sighting ability, and both feed from the same continuous 29 round belts fed from a drum mounted on the right side of the weapon.[23]

There is a newer Russian 40mm belt fed launcher known as the Balkan. This weapon has only recently appeared and not much is known about it in the West. Weight is reportedly 70 pounds with tripod and the rate of fire is 400 rpm. This uses a completely new 40mm Russian grenade design claimed to be effective to 2500m. If this is true, this would give this launcher a good edge over other weapons in its class. The grenade itself is also claimed to be very effective with a greater lethal radius than that offered by the earlier 30 × 28mm round.[24]

The tactical uses of the grenade launcher are almost unlimited. When their versatility is combined with the vastly increased grenade performance of the newer rounds, these weapons become a highly mobile form of artillery. The mobility factor will be crucial in future conflicts as heavier weapons may be prevented from being moved into position in many urban environments in the time needed. Traditional artillery pieces are heavy, bulky, and slow to move. This also makes them easy to hit, high value targets. This is where the grenade launcher shines. While it possesses nowhere near the power of the heavy mortar or an artillery piece, grenade launchers are far lighter and more compact, some weighing less than 5 pounds and measuring less than 1½ feet long. At the same time, they are still capable of providing anti-personnel and anti-armor capabilities out to almost 900 yards

The U.S. FIM-92 Stinger Surface-Air Missile, the newer version of the same weapon supplied to the Afghani freedom fighters in the 1980s (MCS2 J.M. Buliavac, U.S. Navy).

for the current shoulder fired weapons, and out to 1800 yards for the larger crew served and Chinese models.

Lessons sometimes have to be relearned as new generations of commanders move in and older ones move out. The problem is that many times pride and over-inflated self opinions get in the way as outgoing commanders offer advice that is often ignored. The rules of urban combat are no different than before, technological advances aside. The lessons that seem to keep being forgotten are the infantry intensive nature of urban combat and the need to minimize noncombatant casualties, especially if the attacking force wants to avoid the local population turning on them. Other lessons that must be remembered are the limited effectiveness of large artillery pieces, heavy mortars, and armored vehicles. While tanks can sometimes prove invaluable, their mobility is largely limited in an urban environment, with wheeled armor being even more limited.

There are many other rules that continue to hold true with regards to urban combat. Radio communications are limited due to structural interference. Helicopters are usually quite vulnerable and limited in use, as are fixed wing aircraft. Also, command structure and resupply efforts are usually a sometimes thing. While they were once the masters of

10. Grenade Launchers

A Swedish designed RBS-70 SAM, one of the deadliest weapons on today's battlefields. This missile is a great threat to any aircraft that ventures too close (TSgt. B. McMichael, U.S. Air Force).

urban combat, the Russians lost track of these pieces of knowledge. They paid a very dear price for this during the first war in Chechnya. Whenever the basic rules are forgotten or ignored, mistakes will be repeated.

Urban combat is a very brutal and personal form of warfare where larger forms of fire support are often out of the question or difficult to employ at best. Grenade launchers and various rocket launching systems are frequently the best or only options. Tanks are often limited in their main gun's angle of elevation and high-rise buildings can prove very dangerous here. This is assuming that the tank can get into position in the first place, though tanks usually can. Indirect mortar fire, which has proven so useful in open, hilly terrain, is usually of little use in an urban environment, although guided mortar rounds would be a huge improvement in this regard. Oftentimes defenders will avoid the top floors of buildings, which makes direct fire the only option for dealing with them. As mentioned, artillery must normally be moved into direct fire positions or else suffer the same obstacles as mortars. The larger explosive charges used by these weapons can be problematic if friendly troops are in close proximity to the target. As defenders are no doubt aware of this, they often use this tactic if incoming fire is a possibility. Under these combat conditions, the grenade launcher often becomes the weapon of choice for fire support.

The general trend towards urban warfare has obviously been noticed by arms manufacturers, which explains the upsurge in grenade launcher designs in recent years. A grenade launcher can provide quick direct fire aimed at the lower floors of urban structures, whereas indirect mortar fire or artillery rounds may only strike the upper floors. For this reason, rooftops are not popular spots to hang out unless absolutely necessary. While these are excellent locations for observation, the increased use of unmanned aerial vehicles (UAVs) means it will not take long for someone to call in the position to the nearest artillery unit. For the same reason, cellar windows are favored observation and firing locations. These also offer some degree of cover for defenders. Again direct fire is required to deal with this. As targets in an urban environment will only appear in a door or window for a brief moment, fire must be swift and accurate. A lightweight grenade launcher can provide this fire.

The selection of grenade rounds available today is staggering. While the use of phosphorus rounds may be decreasing due to international pressure, there are a multitude of others to choose from. Common rounds are HE, HEDP, airburst, smoke, flash bangs, concussion rounds, illuminating flares, and infrared flares, not to mention a multitude of less than lethal rounds for riot control purposes. When combined with modern computerized sighting systems, first round hit potential is vastly increased.

Perhaps an overlooked advantage to the modern grenade launcher is its limited explosive effect. With defenders using either advancing troops or local population as a form of human shield, use of a larger explosive round can vastly increase the chances of friendly fire casualties or of civilian injuries and deaths. Like the shotgun, the compact assault rifle, and the sniper rifle, the grenade launcher will likely see a great deal of use in any future urban fighting.

CHAPTER 11

Miscellaneous Weapon Systems

This chapter covers the remainder of infantry weapon systems likely to see use in future urban warfare settings. Some will see very limited use. This will be due either to their cost and complexity or to the availability of a low-tech, low cost substitute. This latter factor is especially true when dealing with terrorist groups who may have limited training and limited access to the newer Western or Sino-Russo technologies.

No One Is Safe

The more technologically advanced weapon systems covered here will likely be the least used in future conflicts. The two weapons most applicable here are the Man-Portable Air Defense System (MANPADS) and the Anti-tank Guided Missile (ATGM). There are several reasons for their limited usefulness. With regard to the MANPADS, their limited status is directly connected to the limited applications for aircraft in urban combat. As mentioned, fixed wing aircraft are often limited in use for many urban situations. Too often, the city is filled with civilians or friendly troops. The exact location of those troops may not be known due to the reduced effectiveness of radio communications. There are also many hospitals in urban areas. As aircraft generally drop rather heavy ordnance, the problem here is easy to see, although precision guided munitions (PGMs) do offer better performance in this regard. These are just a very few factors, but none bode well for fixed wing applications, the use of drones or unmanned aerial vehicles (UAVs) for intelligence gathering purposes is a different issue altogether. The newer armed UAVs may have some use for future urban combat due to their small size and their ability to fly outside of the usual flight envelope, meaning the drones are more likely to be put in dangerous situations that would be too risky for a manned aircraft.

With regard to helicopters, the close proximity of buildings and the often narrow approaches largely limit the helicopters' directional options, especially if a landing or low hover is required. Also, no helicopter pilot relishes the thought of having to slow down to a hover in any area that is taking fire. At no time during the flight envelope is a helicopter more vulnerable to ground fire than when hovering. It is at these times that low-

Russian SA-7 SAM, an early missile design, but still deadly and widespread. This is one of the greater terrorist threats around (A1C J. Snyder, U.S. Air Force).

11. Miscellaneous Weapon Systems

A U.S. FGM-148 Javelin anti-tank missile being fired. This is probably the best defensive weapon for U.S. troops where heavy armor is concerned (G.L. Kieffer, U.S. Army).

tech systems prove just as deadly against helicopters as any guided missile and can provide that threat at a much lower cost, both in terms of the weapon itself and in the cost of training required for the user to properly deploy the weapon. One of the more lethal weapon systems for use against helicopters has proven to be the Soviet RPG-7 anti-tank rocket launcher. This is surprising given its relatively slow velocity of less than 300m per second. The RPG is hated by U.S. helicopter pilots serving in the Middle East and effective methods have been developed for RPG employment against helicopters. Helicopters and low flying fixed wing aircraft are also extremely vulnerable to small arms fire, which is made more effective through the proliferation of advanced projectiles designs like tungsten cored armor piercing bullets.

All of these factors combine to not only limit the use of aircraft for urban combat environments, but they also serve to limit the number of MANPADS likely to be employed in the area. When they are encountered, however, they are far more deadly than any other weapon in existence for use against aircraft, especially "low and slow" aircraft. The very high cost of these missile systems makes their available number quite small. Early first and second generation systems are cheaper and more numerous and are still quite deadly. These should be considered a very real threat. While the U.S. and some Western nations keep fairly close tabs as to where these missile ship, there are more and more copies being produced by Middle Eastern nations. Some of these nations are even producing advanced late generation versions.

There are two primary guidance systems popular today for portable surface to air missiles, Infrared Homing (IR) and Semi-Automatic Command Line of Sight (SACLOS). SACLOS usually refers to beam-riders these days. These are missiles that are following a laser or a series of lasers being projected to the target by the system operator. These are reportedly far more difficult to counter than older radio-controlled systems.

The latest IR systems are also very effective in that they are more resistant to counter measures such as flare dispensers.[1] The use of more advanced seeking units with multiple sensors allows these missiles to distinguish between aircraft and flare. Luckily these advanced systems are very pricey and are not numerous, as they pose a severe threat in terrorist hands.

Typical IR missile systems include the U.S. FIM-92 Stinger,[2] the French Mistral,[3] the Iranian Misagh-2,[4] the Chinese FN-6,[5] and the Russian SA-18. Some of the best beam riding systems are the Swedish RBS-70[6] and the British Starstreak[7] and Starburst missiles.[8] Most of these MANPADS range between five and six feet in length and weigh anywhere from 20 to 40 pounds. This makes for a highly portable and lethal system that is capable of handling even the most advanced aircraft. The range of most of these missile systems is usually between four and six miles, although this varies greatly with conditions of engagement. Earlier systems like the U.S. Redeye[9] and Soviet SA-7[10] missiles are still dangerous, especially given the fact that terrorist sponsoring nations are often producing copies that are easier to obtain and less costly to manufacture.

Even Tanks Are Not Safe

The other weapon mentioned earlier, the ATGM, will also see limited use for similar reasons. Tanks are at a disadvantage in an urban combat environment. They are severely limited in mobility due to the restrictions created by urban structures. Urban areas often force armored units to forgo traditional combat formations and tanks are often forced to either remain on the city outskirts or else form a single-lane convoy formation, which is not something most tank commanders are willing to do. For the units that do remain outside of the city proper and choose to hold formation, the ATGM is a potent threat and it is here their use will likely be concentrated. Effective range of the more advanced ATGM systems is well over a mile. Early anti-tank systems were often wire guided and as such, were not easily countered. At the same time, however, they required the operator to maintain line of sight with a target until detonation. This left the missile crew vulnerable to incoming fire.[11] While some of today's current systems, like the U.S. FGM 148 Javelin, are fire and forget missiles, they are also more vulnerable to countermeasures.[12] The Javelin is perhaps not the best example of this, as it is very difficult to jam this system. If they do make it to the target, however, the systems are more than capable of dealing with even the most modern tanks. As many of the current missile systems are capable of top attack where the tank is most vulnerable, they are even more effective than the earlier frontal attack missile systems.

Some anti-tank missile systems were so effective that for a time, it was not considered viable to utilize armor. This was countered through the development of Active Protection

Systems (APS) for tanks,[13] in addition to Explosive Reactive Armor (ERA).[14] While ERA is fairly common on modern tanks, APS is rather expensive and it is unlikely that these systems will be installed on all tanks within the military's inventory. Current APS examples are the Israeli Trophy[15] and Iron Fist,[16] and the Russian Arena.[17] There's also development in the area of missile systems that can be fired from the tank's main gun. It is claimed that these missile systems are capable of engaging either aircraft or anti-tank missiles in midair. Current examples of this type of weapon are the Israeli Lahat,[18] the Russian Reflex,[19] and the Chinese GP.[20] These systems are still being perfected and are not issued in significant numbers, so for now, tanks will have to rely on APS, which is quite expensive as well as being relatively new, in addition to ERA, which will remain the tank's first line of defense. ERA is a defense system comprised of a series of explosive panels that disrupt the effect of the shaped-charge warheads of anti-tank weapons. Another popular technique is the addition of birdcage armor fitted around the tank's exterior. During World War II, the Russians adopted the habit of using coiled bedsprings for this purpose. This is still done on occasion to help defeat the tandem charge warheads that are increasingly common today.

Despite this complex and deadly ping-pong game between tank defenses and anti-tank weapons, the bottom line is that deadly anti-tank munitions are far more numerous and are usually employed to take advantage of this numerical superiority. Tanks are high value targets and the complex defense systems required to keep them safe only makes the tank that much more costly. This, combined with their limited applications in the urban combat arena, will probably keep the use of advanced armored vehicles limited to where they can do the most damage. Also, tanks are often ineffective in urban combat operations, as infantry support is needed at all times. This will tie up already overtaxed infantry units, which will limit their effectiveness in a combat environment that already requires heavy use of infantry. While MANPADS and ATGM systems may only be seen on a limited basis for future urban combat, they are the most effective weapons for dealing with aircraft and armor respectively, and they will indeed be used. The MANPADS are a great threat right now due to their potential as weapons of terror. A commercial airliner can potentially be shot down with one or two of the older versions with minimal training required for operating the system.

Expendable Ordnance

Of far greater use for future conflicts will likely be the unguided rocket launcher. This can take several forms. Reusable launchers like the RPG series from Russia are probably the best known examples. Other such systems are the Israeli B-300 and the newer U.S. Shoulder Launched Multipurpose Assault Weapon (SMAW) as well.[21] These are usually capable of firing more than one type of warhead, such as anti-tank, incendiary, and thermobaric or anti-personnel. The U.S. M202A1 incendiary launcher pack is a similar concept, but this uses a four tube arrangement with two tubes on top and two below.[22]

A second type of launcher is the disposable tube launcher. These are one-shot throw-away systems and are numerous throughout the world. One of the first of these was if the U.S. M72 Light Anti-tank Weapon (LAW). This weapon uses a 66mm anti-tank warhead and fin stabilized rocket fired from an extendable fiberglass launch tube.[23]

These systems vary a great deal in size and effective range. The larger diameter warheads are generally more capable for dealing with modern Main Battle Tanks (MBTs). The 84mm LAW 80 was a popular version for many years and was much improved over the original M72.[24] Some of the newer models utilize a spotting rifle built into the launcher. The spotting rifle is a small caliber manually loaded weapon that has ballistics matched to the flight path of the primary warhead. This is to help improve the chances of a hit when the warhead is launched. As the armor of MBTs improved, the size of the launchers followed suit.

The effective range of these weapon systems depends on the skill of the user a great deal. Generally, 200m is regarded as the extent of their ability to deal with a moving tank, though the rocket is usually capable of flying much farther. The U.S. currently uses several unguided launcher systems in addition to the original M72 LAW. The primary disposable unit for U.S. forces is the M136-AT4. This is a Swedish-U.S. development that has the ability to penetrate close to 20 inches of rolled homogenous armor (RHA) and a rocket which can fly beyond 2000 yards. As with many unguided launcher systems, the effective range is much shorter. For those skilled in its use, a hit on a stationary target can be achieved beyond 500 yards in some cases. There are two primary warhead types for the M136, the High Explosive Anti-tank (HEAT) warhead, and the High Explosive Dual Purpose (HEDP), which is used more for clearing out troops from behind cover. The latest version of the AT4 is the AT4CS (confined space), which uses a liquid store in the rear portion of the launcher to largely eliminate the

The 66mm U.S. M72 Light Anti-tank Weapon. This was one of the first disposable rocket launchers to enter service, though not a great threat to modern tanks (A1C Reedy, U.S. Air Force).

11. Miscellaneous Weapon Systems

The U.S. Mk 153 Shoulder-Fired Multipurpose Assault Weapon. This reusable launcher can fire a variety of warheads and is proving very useful to U.S. troops (Sgt. A.C. Sauceda, U.S. Marine Corps).

back blast effect from this type of recoilless system. This new modification allows the use of this type of launcher inside rooms, something that was previously dangerous if attempted. The M136 is considerably larger than the M72. The original M72 measured roughly 26 inches closed and the weight of the entire system was approximately 5½ pounds. The M136 uses a non-extending tube measuring roughly 3½ feet in length and the weight of this system is just over 16 pounds. The M136, however, is far more effective in dealing with heavily armored modern tanks. A detachable sighting system is offered for the M136, though the system has its own basic sights included.

Today's Bazooka

The U.S. reusable launcher system often used today is the SMAW Mk 153. This launcher uses either the Mk 6 anti-tank warhead or the Mk 3 HEDP warhead. A spotting rifle is fitted to the side. Several sight options can be fitted for day or night use. Extra spotting rifle rounds are stored in a cap on the warhead transport case. The cartridge is basically a special 9mm tracer bullet fitted into a rifle casing. The SMAW cannot be used within enclosed spaces like the AT4CS and is deadly within 100 feet for anyone positioned directly behind the launch tube. There are improved versions of the SMAW being developed. The SMAW 2 is supposed to offer limited backblast for confined space capability. The new model is likely to use a laser targeting system to replace the spotting rifle of the original. This new version is supposed to be lighter by over 4 pounds. The current SMAW uses the popular 83mm diameter warhead and weighs roughly 30 pounds with an overall length of less than 30 inches collapsed and is extended to roughly 4½ feet for firing. The effective range is 500m for large tanks. The anti-tank round is superior to the AT4 in that it is reputed to be able to penetrate 24 inches of RHA. The new HEDP warhead has a sensor in the fuse that distinguishes between hard and soft targets, and arms the warhead accordingly to allow for a slight delay before detonating the warhead for increased destructive effect. There is also a new warhead that has been designed for the SMAW, known as the Novel Explosive (NE). The SMAW-NE is supposed to be capable of destroying masonry structures with the severe pressure created by the warhead's detonation, and its primary purpose is that of a bunker busting weapon.

Israel is another nation that uses a system very similar to the SMAW. The SMAW was actually derived from the Israeli designed the B-300. The B-300 is also a reusable launcher system of similar size, 82mm. It is claimed to have a 400m effective range and it is quite likely that in the proper hands it can achieve hits at farther distances. Like the SMAW, the B-300 uses several different type warheads, one for anti-tank purposes and one for use against barricaded personnel. The second warhead uses two charges, one to breach the cover and one to detonate after breaking through. An improved model is called the Shipon.[25] This uses an advanced sighting device to increase hit potential. This is reported to allow for an effective range of 600m. The anti-tank round is capable of punching through over 2½ feet of RHA. The B-300 weighs less than the SMAW at around 20 pounds and is roughly the same length as the SMAW when extended.

A disposable anti-tank launcher recently developed is the Main Battle Tank (MBT) LAW. This offers a 600m effective range and a weight of less than 28 pounds with an overall length of 40 inches. This Swedish design uses a warhead diameter of 150mm, almost twice the diameter as that used by the AT4. It is another enclosed space capable system that uses a low power charge to throw the warhead clear of the launcher before ignition of the primary motor. Warhead effectiveness is likely far superior to other systems currently in use due to its size.[26]

New Warhead Designs

The Israeli Man Portable Anti-tank Anti Door (MATADOR) is another disposable launcher system. This was a joint venture with Singapore and the standard version uses a dual purpose warhead. A probe was extended for anti-tank use and retracted for High Explosive Squash Head (HESH) purposes. The HESH setting is used for bunker busting applications. Other versions of the MATADOR exist for various purposes. The MATADOR-WB (wall breaching) uses a special warhead design called an Explosively Formed Ring (EFR) that punches a hole in most building materials large enough for troops to pass through. The MATADOR-MP (multi-purpose) is an improvement over

11. Miscellaneous Weapon Systems

the standard model in that the probe no longer needs to be extended or retracted as the warhead senses the target's hardness and arms itself accordingly. An advanced laser ranging sight is mounted to increase hit potential. The weight of this system is less than 20 pounds and the overall length just over 3 feet. The diameter of the dual purpose warhead is 90mm and has a 500m effective range. The final version is the MATADOR-AS (anti-structure). This is a dual mode, tandem charge warhead that can be used for either bunker busting or armor defeating purposes.[27]

While these launcher systems are very advanced and offer great agility, the weapons most likely to be used by potential U.S. enemies are Russian built or copies of Russian designs.

The King of the Hill

By far the most common antitank rocket system in the world is the Soviet RPG-7.[28] This weapon is still in production as the RPG-7V2 along with a two piece paratroop version, the RPG-7D3.[29] The RPG launcher weighs less than 14 pounds empty and uses an optical sight, the PG-07, in addition to its standard iron sights. The overall length is roughly 3 feet without the warhead in place. Several warheads are available for the RPG-7. The original anti-tank warhead, the PG-7V, is capable of defeating almost 1 foot of armor.[30] The more modern versions are far more capable. The PG-7V2 can almost double this level of armor penetration. The most lethal anti-tank rocket for this system is the PG-7VR tandem charge warhead. This warhead is designed for ERA equipped vehicles and can punch through up to 2 feet of RHA on vehicles equipped with ERA, and almost 2½ feet of armor on vehicles that are not protected by ERA. The other two warheads that are commonly used on the RPG system are the OG-7V anti-personnel fragmentation warhead which has a lethal radius of roughly 25 feet, and a thermobaric warhead with a lethal radius of over 30 feet. The thermobaric warhead is useful for bunker busting operations. The RPG is claimed to have an effective range of 500m, but the rocket itself will carry beyond 1000m, which is roughly half the distance of the M136-AT4. Like most launcher systems, the RPG is recoilless and the backblast is dangerous to roughly 60 feet. The RPG system uses a small charge to throw the rocket clear of the launcher before the main mortar ignites.

The RPG-7 is a threat in that it is a highly capable and versatile system, easy to use, and worst of all, extremely common worldwide. The RPG-7 will obviously play a major role in future conflict, urban or not. It is one of today's most deadly battlefield weapon systems and is responsible for downing U.S. helicopters on more than one occasion and will likely be responsible for more. Poland uses a cheaper and simpler disposable version known as the RPG-76, which is similar in performance.

Long Range Version

The RPG-16 is a newer reusable system designed to provide a longer effective range of up to 800m. This model uses a smaller 58mm warhead that fits completely within the

The terrorist's right hand, Soviet RPG-7 reusable launchers. These can fire an assortment of warheads, some out to over 1000 yards. This is likely the greatest threat to U.S. helicopters operating in the Middle East. They are also one of the most common weapons of terror in the world (Cpl. D.S. Kotecki, U.S. Marine Corps).

launcher tube. The launch charge is similar to the RPG-7. A similar optical sight is often used, although iron sights are also fitted. The launcher weight is a bit over 20 pounds. The launcher breaks down into two pieces and a bipod is standard. Armor penetration is not as good as the RPG-7 and only about 1 foot of RHA can be defeated with its standard warhead. This is a tradeoff for the increased effective range and its smaller diameter warhead. The RPG-16 uses an electronic ignition trigger as opposed to the manually cocked trigger mechanism of the RPG-7.[31]

Russia's New King

The much newer RPG-29 is proving as lethal as the earlier models. This reusable model uses a 105mm warhead and launcher weight is over 26 pounds. The trigger system is similar to that of the RPG-16, where pulling the trigger generates the needed electrical charge. The RPG-29 uses a single stage launch mode that has burned out before the warhead has left the launch tube, relying on momentum to carry it to its target. This is similar in operation to the M72 LAW. The tandem charge HEAT warhead is designed for use against tanks equipped with ERA and performance is equal to or better than that of the

11. Miscellaneous Weapon Systems

An M136/AT4 disposable launcher. This is the current U.S. standard anti-tank weapon (Sgt. M. Campino, U.S. Marine Corps).

RPG-7 tandem warhead. This warhead is also used as a makeshift bunker busting round due to its tandem charge. While similar in performance to the RPG-7 tandem charge warhead, the RPG 29 has roughly twice the effective range. Unlike the other models the RPG-29 is breech loaded. It breaks down similarly to the RPG-16 and uses a rear mounted monopod for support due to its weight. The overall length is roughly 40 inches disassembled and 6 feet assembled. This newer system ensures that the RPG series will continue to serve for future anti-tank use, as it has proven every bit as deadly as the previous RPG versions. It is capable of defeating almost all modern armored vehicles. This includes the ability to put most current tanks to rest, whether or not they are equipped with ERA.[32]

Throw Away Models

While these reusable launcher systems are very capable and versatile, Russia has done just as well in the area of disposable launcher systems. The RPG-18 is a one shot launcher very similar in performance to the U.S. M72 LAW. It is dimensionally similar as well.

The improved RPG-22 gives a considerable increase in armor piercing capability. This model is capable of punching through roughly 16 inches of RHA vs. 12 inches for

Small Arms for Urban Combat

The U.S. M202A1 4-shot reusable incendiary launcher. This 66mm weapon is useful as a bunker buster, but is reportedly not used due to increasing public attitude against incendiary weapons (Al Chang, released to Department of Defense).

the RPG-18. There is little difference between the two models with regards to weight and length. The RPG-22 is a threat, as large quantities were produced and many have likely found their way to the black market.

The next design is the RPG-26, which is also roughly 72mm in diameter. This is a non-telescoping design which was intended to lower production cost. The warhead is slightly more effective than the RPG-22 and the weight is increased by few ounces over the previous model at roughly 6½ pounds. This model is still in production and is also standard issue.[33]

Next up is the RPG-27, which is a much larger and heavier system with a 105mm warhead and a weight of over 18 pounds. Its ability to destroy armor is also far greater, though effective range is only 140m vs. 170m for the RPG-26. This model was meant to help defeat ERA equipped tanks. It can punch through nearly 2 feet of RHA after detonating the reactive armor with its tandem charge warheads. This is a very recent design able to compete with most other modern launcher systems.[34]

The final disposable Russian design is the RPG-28, which is larger still at 125mm. The effective range is 180m but it has a tremendously powerful tandem charge warhead which can punch through over 3 feet of RHA. The weight of this system is almost 29 pounds and the overall length is roughly 4 feet. This is Russia's most recent disposable launcher system and will likely be around for some time. The RPG-28 can outperform most other launcher systems on the market.[35]

A New Kind of Flamethrower

While anti-tank launchers have recently been adapted for multiple uses, there were designs meant to be used as bunker busters from the start. The U.S. M202A1 66mm multi-shot launcher was briefly mentioned earlier. This weapon used a 4 shot incendiary rocket clip that could be reloaded and can fire one at a time or in rapid succession. This was an extendible system that had an effective range of roughly 200 yards but can be used out to as far as 800. It measured 27 inches closed and 35 inches extended. Its weight was 26½ pounds with four rounds loaded. This was a very unique system, but it is outperformed by today's larger and more powerful designs. The M202A1 is not much for anti-tank use, but it was not designed for that purpose.[36]

The Soviets developed a single-shot system similar in concept to the M202, though considerably more powerful due to its 93mm warhead. It is actually listed as a flamethrower in Russian military terms. The RPO-A was used in Afghanistan during the Soviet invasion to flush out rebels from caves and was reportedly very effective in doing so. It is still in production, though more modern versions have been developed. The RPO-A weighs approximately 26½ pounds and measures over 3 feet long. It can launch its warhead up to 1000m.[37] There are several RPO versions made for different uses. The RPO-A is the standard model with a Fuel-Air Explosive (FAE) warhead. The RPO-D uses a smoke warhead and the final version is the RPO-Z, which uses an incendiary warhead. The RPO-A is lethal up to 25 feet away from point of detonation in open terrain and its effects are far greater when detonated within the confines of an enclosed space.

The more modern RPO-M is improved in both accuracy in range and can carry up to 1700m. The trigger unit is reusable, as is the optical sighting system. In fact, this is a combined unit. The RPO-M is far lighter at 17½ pounds but similar in overall length to the RPO-A. The trigger generates the electronic impulse to fire the warhead as with many other Russian launcher systems. The blast effect of this weapon is considerably improved over that of the RPO-A.[38]

The MRO-A is basically an RPG-26 setup with the warhead options of the RPO-A series. The MRO-A uses the FAE warhead, the MRO-B uses the smoke warhead, and the MRO-Z uses the incendiary version. The maximum range is only 450m but its weight is reduced to just over 10 pounds. These were designed as short range RPO type weapons, which are far easier for the infantry to carry. One difference is that the trigger mechanism on these models is mechanically cocked through lifting a safety lever.[39]

There is also a larger 105mm RShG-1. This is basically the RPG-27 launcher using an FAE warhead. Effective range is 150m and it is claimed to have a lethal blast radius of 10m in open terrain. This performance would make this one of the more powerful incendiary launchers in service today. It weighs roughly 17½ pounds and measures a bit over 3½ feet in length.[40]

The final model produced by Russia currently is the RShG-2. This is a smaller 72½mm FAE warhead using the fixed RPG-26 launch tube. Weight is only 8½ pounds and lethal blast radius is said to be around 1m in the open.[41]

There's a variation of the RShG-1 known as the RMG multi-purpose launcher. This uses a unique tandem warhead with the first charge being an armor piercing design. This is followed by a second FAE charge. This was clearly designed as a bunker busting weapon. Its weight is roughly 19 pounds with an effective range of 130m. The first charge can supposedly defeat 5 inches of RHA.

Knock-Knock

There is another weapon that should be mentioned here. It is actually a form of rifle grenade and is known as the Simon breaching grenade.[42] This was developed in Israel and is used by the United States as well. Effective range of this weapon is roughly 30m. In appearance, it closely resembles a knight's lance in miniature. It has a rod sticking out the front that is intended to detonate the charge at the proper distance from the door. This is to maximize blast effect. This is basically an alternative to breaching shotgun rounds and allows the user to maintain a safer distance or take down the door from behind cover.

Mini Artillery

The final category of weapon to be covered in this chapter is the patrol or commando mortar. These are usually short, lightweight 60mm mortars that use a base plate and no bipod. The advantage of the patrol mortar is that it allows for indirect fire at ranges of up to 2200 yards. These mortars are easily transported but require the operator to hold the mortar during operation. For this reason, it is best operated using a two man crew. Some of the better systems in production are the Austrian C6 Hirtenberger[43] and the Vektor M4 series from South Africa. Vektor offers the M4L3, the M4, and the M4 Mk 1.[44] The M4 standard model has a cocking firing pin that can safely be carried with a round in the tube. The M4 Mk 1 and M4L3 are simpler designs utilizing fixed firing pins. The M4L3 is simplest of all and is issued with a carrying strap that doubles as a sighting system. There are a series of tabs fixed at various locations on the strap and the operator steps on the appropriate tab to crudely set the correct angle of elevation for the mortar. This is not very precise but is certainly fast and easy to use. The standard M4 and M4 Mk1 use a much more precise sight with a built in level to ensure that the tube is not canted.

Despite the increased effectiveness of 60mm mortar round, these are more often being replaced by grenade launcher systems, though there is developing technology with regards to laser guided 60mm rounds. The bottom line is overall cost, as guided rounds are not cheap. This will determine if patrol mortars will continue to see service. The

11. Miscellaneous Weapon Systems

The future of combat: troops conduct a search of a construction site, showing a type of fighting more familiar to cops and street gangs (SSgt. V. Valentine, U.S. Air Force).

typical 60mm HE mortar round has a lethal radius of between 45 and 60 feet, which is almost twice the capability of even the better 40mm rounds. The MEI Hellhound is probably the most effective 40mm grenade produced and this only offers a lethal radius of a little over 30 feet. This is in addition to the fact that the average 60mm mortar offers roughly four times the range of the Hellhound. As mortars are far simpler, the manufacturing cost is appropriately lower. This will figure largely in helping to determine their future in military service and by default their future as an urban combat weapon.

While the guided missile systems are by far the most deadly designs covered in this chapter, the unguided launcher systems are far more likely to see heavy use in future fighting, due to their far lower cost and ease of use. The unguided systems require very little training to operate. These launcher systems are also very lethal with regards to punching through heavy cover and urban structures. As any personnel operating in urban areas will use the buildings to their advantage, the additional destructive capabilities offered by these launcher systems will often be an absolute necessity. These weapons will likely be present in abundance in future combat. Patrol mortars will probably see much more limited use. While anti-tank launchers have been used on many occasions against troops holed up in structures, the more recent FAE warheads are far more effective for this purpose. This explains the large number of such launcher designs entering service.

In the course of this study I have no doubt overlooked several successful weapon systems; however, the vast majority of today's most useful designs were addressed as well as systems that offer great potential as future urban combat weapons. Urban combat is a difficult concept for many military strategists to deal with. Traditional military strategy and tactics do not really apply and this can cause great frustration for many professionals in this field. Urban warfare adds a vertical dimension to tactical thinking, which further complicates the issue. Also, much of today's technology is negated due to the nature of urban fighting. Lastly, many military planners just don't like dealing with the issue and would prefer a good, clean, traditional war. Urban fighting is very brutal, ugly and up close combat. It is a very personal form of warfare that is focused around small unit infantry tactics, where small arms figure more heavily than at any other time in warfare.

The capabilities, advantages and faults of today's weapon systems have been covered at a practical level throughout this work. This should help readers come away with a fairly solid knowledge base regarding the vast majority of small arms systems that will almost certainly dominate the next major war. The only way to avoid that is for everyone to play nice. If the world's nation states did that, the small arms industry would likely just fade away. However, that doesn't appear to be a likely possibility.

Notes

Introduction

1. Greg La Motte (contributor). "LAPD Gets M-16s." CNN. Sept. 22, 1997. Accessed Nov. 24, 2010. http://www.cnn.com/us/9707/22/m16s/index.html?iref=allsearch.

2. Barrett, 2010, www.barrett.net.

3. "World Population Highlights: Key Findings from PRB's 2007 World Population Report." Sept. 2007. Accessed Nov. 24, 2010. http://www.prb.org/Articles/2007/623Urbanization.aspx.

4. "Army Position: M4 Carbine is Soldier's Battlefield Weapon of Choice." U.S. Army News Release, March 29, 2007. Accessed Nov. 24, 2010. http://www.army.mil/-newreleases/2007/03/29/2471-army-position-m4-carbine-is-soldiers-battlefield-weapon-of-choice/.

5. Knight's Enterprises, 2010, www.knightarmco.com.

6. "Remington's Nylon 66," last accessed Feb. 8, 2011, http://www.nylonrifles.com/wp/2010/03/the-remington-nylon-66-a-new-concept-in-rifles-back-then/.

7. "The Glock 22: America's Best Selling Police Pistol," last accessed Feb. 9, 2011, http://findarticles.com/p/articles/mi_mOBQY/is_7_54/ai_n25469319/.

8. ".50 cal Browning Ammo (New Products)," last accessed Nov. 24, 2010, http://www.highbeam.com/doc/1G1-98124208.html.

Chapter 1

1. Declaration III, Hague Accords of 1899. http:www.avalon.law.yale.edu/19th_century/dec99-03.asp.

2. "A Marine Reports from Iraq," *Washington Times*, Nov. 22, 2005, p. A21 (op-ed).

3. Gary Paul Johnston, "LAPD SWAT: Los Angeles' Finest Choose Kimber's Custom II," *American Handgunner*, January 2003, 58.

4. Charles Cutshaw, "Smith & Wesson's 1911," *Tactical Response Magazine*, July 2006, last accessed Feb. 9, 2011, http://www.hendonpub.com/resources/articlearchive/details.aspx?ID=746.

5. Colt Mfg. Co., LLC, 2010, www.coltsmfg.com.

6. Ian Hogg, *Military Small Arms of the 20th Century*, 7th Ed. (Iola, WI: Krause, 2000), 88.

7. Charlie Petty, "Wolff 1911 Magazine–Gunny Sack," *American Handgunner*, March, 2002, 92.

8. Patrick Sweeney, *1911: The First 100 Years* (Iola, WI: F + W Media, 2010), 33–50.

9. Colt Mfg. Co. LLC, 2010, www.coltsmfg.com.

10. Massad Ayoob, "Promised Functionality: Wilson Combat CQB .45s," *American Handgunner*, November 2003, 62.

11. Hogg, *Military Small Arms of the 20th Century*, 73.

12. Russian Ministry of Internal Affairs Document, Feb. 20, 1997. http://www.fas.org/irp/world/russia/docs/mvd_1996.htm.

13. Zastava Arms, 2008, www.zastava-arms.co.rs/.

14. Frank C. Barnes, *Cartridges of the World*, 12th Ed. (Iola, WI: Krause), 281.

15. Edward C. Ezell, *Small Arms of the World* (Harrisburg, PA: Stackpole Books, 1983), 694.

16. Ezell, 151.

17. Ezell, 694.

18. Hogg, *Military Small Arms of the 20th Century*, 73.

19. Izhevsky Mekhanichesky Zavod, FGUP, 2006, www.imzcorp.com.

20. Ezell, 175–177.

21. Hogg, *Military Small Arms of the 20th Century*, 30.

22. CZ-USA, www.ca-usa.com.
23. Hogg, *Military Small Arms of the 20th Century*, 65
24. Beretta U.S.A. Corp., 2010, www.berettausa.com.
25. Kevin Dockery, *Special Warfare, Special Weapons* (Chicago, IL: Emperor's Press, 1997), 45–46.
26. Ezell, 142, 673–675.
27. Ezell, 142–146, 671.
28. Hogg, *Military Small Arms of the 20th Century*, 81–83.
29. Hogg, *Military Small Arms of the 20th Century*, 82.
30. Dockery, 45–46.
31. SIG Sauer, Inc., 2008, www.sigsauer.com.
32. Patrick Sweeney, *Gun Digest Book of the Glock*, 2nd Ed. (Iola, WI: F+W Media, 2008), 142.
33. Hogg, *Military Small Arms of the 20th Century*, 73.
34. Charles Cutshaw, *Tactical Small Arms of the 21st Century* (Iola, WI: Krause, 2006), 51.
35. Blackhawk Products Group, 2008, www.blackhawk.com.
36. Hogg, *Military Small Arms of the 20th Century*, 52.
37. Walther America, 2009, www.smith-wesson.com.
38. Ezell, 463–464.
39. Dockery, 41.
40. H&K, USA, www.hk-usa.com.
41. Hogue, Inc., 2008, www.hogueinc.com.
42. Massad Ayoob, *Gun Digest Book of Combat Handgunnery*, 6th. Ed. (Iola, WI: Krause, 2007), 232.
43. Cutshaw, *Tactical Small Arms of the 21st Century*, 50.
44. Lise Olsen, "Ciudad Juarez Passes 2000 Homicides in 2009, So Far," *Houston Chronicle*, Oct. 21, 2009.
45. Cutshaw, *Tactical Small Arms of the 21st Century*, 50.
46. Fred J. Pushies, *Weapons of Delta Force* (St. Paul, MN: MBI, 2002). 54

Chapter 2

1. Hogg, 93.
2. Hogg, 136.
3. Ezell, 122.
4. Jack Lewis, *The Gun Digest Book of Assault Weapons*, 6th Ed. (Iola, WI: Krause, 2004), 68.
5. Pushies, 43.
6. "Carl Gustaf M/45 9mm submachinegun (Sweden), submachine guns," last accessed Feb. 8, 2011, http://www.janes.com/articles/Janes-Infantry-Weapons/Carl-Gustaf-m-45-9-mm-sub-machine-gun-Sweden.html.
7. Dockery, 65–69.
8. Hogg, 103.
9. Cutshaw, 236–237.
10. Hogg, 122.
11. "SBS Weapons-L34A1 Sterling," last accessed Feb. 8, 2011, http://www.eliteUKforces.info./special-boat-service/weapons/134-sterling/.
12. Ezell, 122.
13. Hogg, 134.
14. Cutshaw, 158–159.
15. Cutshaw, 159.
16. Cutshaw, 159.
17. Hogg, 139.
18. Hogg, 141–142.
19. "Spectre M4," last accessed Feb. 8, 2011, http://www.military-today.com/firearms/spectre_m4.htm.
20. Kevin Dockery, *Future Weapons* (New York, NY: Berkley, 2007), 218.
21. Cutshaw, 155.
22. Ezell, 29.
23. Pushies, 46.
24. Dockery, *Future Weapons*, 218.
25. H&K USA, www.hk-usa.com.
26. Cutshaw, 151.
27. H&K USA, www.hk-usa.com.
28. Cutshaw, 162.
29. Cutshaw, 147.
30. Cutshaw, 165.

Chapter 3

1. "5.7×28mm," last accessed Feb. 8, 2011, http://www.enotes.com/topic/5.7×28mm.
2. "FN 90 PDW (Personal Defense Weapon) and FN Five-Seven Pistol Range Report," last accessed Feb. 8, 2011, http://www.defensereview.com/fn-p90-pdw-personal-defense-weapon-and-five-seven-pistol-range-report/.
3. FN Herstal, S.A., www.fnherstal.com.
4. H&K USA, www.hk-usa.com.

Chapter 4

1. Hogg, 93.
2. "Cop-Killer Bullets," last accessed Feb. 8, 2011, http://www.guncite.com/gun_control_gcgucopk.html.
3. Hogg, 406.

Notes — Chapter 5

4. Cutshaw, 176–177.
5. "La-France M14K 7.62mm Assault Rifle (United States), Rifle," last accessed Feb. 8, 2011, http://www.janes.com/articles/Janes-Infantry-Weapons/La-France-M14K-7.62-mm-assault-rifle-United-States.html.
6. "Bushmaster M4 Carbine," last accessed Feb. 8, 2011, http://www.cybershooters.org/daca/bushmaster_m4.html.
7. "Kalashnikov AKS-74U (Krinkov) Short Assault Rifle (Russia-USSR)," last accessed Feb. 8, 2011, http://world.guns.ru/assault/rus/aks-74u-e.html.
8. Cutshaw, 222.
9. "Mk 262 Mod 1," last accessed Feb. 9, 2011, http://www.globalsecurity.org/military/systems/munitions/mk262.htm.
10. "NSWC Crane Saves $970K for NAVSEA Small Arms Office," last accessed Feb. 9, 2011, http://www.navy.mil/search/display.asp?story_id=39273.
11. Cutshaw, 250.
12. Cutshaw, 221.
13. Hogg, 273.
14. "9×39mm," last accessed Feb. 9, 2011, http://en.wikipedia.org/siki/9x39mm.
15. "9×39mm," last accessed Feb. 9, 2011, http://www.scribd.com/doc/24301486/the-New-World-of-Russian-Small-Arms-and-Ammo.
16. Cutshaw, 230.
17. Cutshaw, 225.
18. Ezell, 542.
19. Cutshaw, 216–217.
20. SAN Swiss Arms, AG, www.swissarms.ch.
21. "Vektor R4 and R5 5.56mm Rifles (South Africa), Rifles," last accessed Feb. 9, 2011, http://www.janes.com/articles/Janes-Infantry-Weapons/Vektor-R4-and-R5-5-56-mm-assault-rifles-South-Africa.html.
22. "HK33," last accessed Feb. 9, 2011, http://www.dc-database.com/defence/view_main.php?weapon=HK%2033&tab=Design.
23. Cutshaw, 203.

Chapter 5

1. Ezell, 19, 62.
2. Hogg, 136.
3. Cutshaw, 240.
4. Ezell, 154.
5. Ezell, 178.
6. Ezell, 26.
7. Ezell, 52.
8. "Heavy Lubrication Shown to Improve M16, M4 Effectiveness," last accessed Feb. 9, 2011, http://www.armytimes.com/new/2007/07/army_carbine_lubrication_070716/.
9. Ezell, 20.
10. John Walter, *Modern Military Rifles* (London: Greenhill Books, 2001), 33.
11. Dockery, 93.
12. Hogg, 280.
13. Israeli Weapons Industries (IWI), Ltd., 2005, www.israel-weapon.com.
14. Cutshaw, 209.
15. IWI, LTD, 2005, www.israel-weapon.com.
16. Ezell, 224.
17. "Steyr AUG," last accessed Feb. 9, 2011, http://en.wikipedia.org/wiki/steyr_AUG.
18. "FAMAS," last accessed Feb. 9, 2011, http://en.wikipedia/wiki/FAMAS.
19. Cutshaw, 237.
20. Cutshaw, 211.
21. Hogg, 126, 245–247.
22. Walker, 82.
23. Hogg, 252–253.
24. "HK 416 Carbine/SBR Confiscation Program Unleashed on U.S. Army AWG," last accessed Feb. 9, 2011, http://www.defensereview.com/hk416-carbinesbr-confiscation-program-unleashed-on-us-army-awg/.
25. "H&K Wins Marine Corps IAR Contract with HK 416 Variant," last accessed Feb. 9, 2011, http://militarytimes.com/blogs/gearscout/2009/12/02/hk-wins-marine-corps-iar-contract-with-hk416-variant/.
26. "SOCOM Cancels FN Mk-16 SCAR-L (SCAR-Light) 5.56mm NATO Rifle/Carbine/SBR Weapons Program. Will the FN Mk-17 SCAR-H (SCAR-Heavy) 7.62mm NATO Variant Survive? Only the Shadow Knows," last accessed Feb. 9, 2011, http://www.defensereview.com/socom-cancels-fn-mk-16-scar-l-light-riflecarbinesbr-program-will-the-fn-mk-17-scar-h-scar-heavy-survive/.
27. H&K USA, www.hk-usa.com.
28. H&K USA, www.hk-usa.com.
29. Cutshaw, 224.
30. Ibid, 178.
31. Ibid, 246.
32. Hogg, 271.
33. "AK-200," last accessed Feb. 9, 2011, http://en.wikipedia.org/wiki/AK-200.
34. *AK-47: The Weapon That Changed the Face of War* (Hoboken, NJ: John Wiley and Sons, 2007), 228.
35. "5.56mm NATO," last accessed Feb. 9, 2011, http://en.wikipedia.org/wiki/5.56mm_NATO.
36. "M16 rifle," last accessed Feb. 9, 2011, http://www.associatepublisher.com/e/m/m16_rifle.htm.
37. Hogg, 292.

38. "M16 Rifle and M4 Carbine: Time for a Change," last accessed Feb. 9, 2011, http://www.defensereview.com/m16-rifle-and-m4-carbine-time-for-a-change/.
39. Cutshaw, 178.
40. Dockery, *Special Warfare, Special Weapons*, 164.

Chapter 6

1. "History of Sniping," last accessed Feb. 12, 2011, http://www.armysniper.org/history.aspx.
2. Mark Spicer, *Illustrated Manual of Sniper Skills* (St. Paul, MN: MBI Publishing, 2006), 242–243.
3. Cutshaw, 276–283.
4. Cutshaw, 302.
5. Spicer, 244–247.
6. Cutshaw, 266–267.
7. Hogg, 253–254.
8. Walter, 75.
9. Cutshaw, 272.
10. Cutshaw, 260.
11. PGW Defense Technologies, Inc., www.pgwdti.com
12. "Barrett's Shorty: The M82 CQ Carbine," last accessed Feb. 9, 2011, http://findarticles.com/p/articles/mi_7745/is_200701/ai_n32212893/.

Chapter 7

1. Lewis, 171.
2. ".416 Barrett," last accessed Feb. 9, 2011, http://en.wikipedia.org/wiki/.416Barrett.
3. McMillan Group International, 2009, www.mcmfamily.com.
4. Cutshaw, 322.
5. Cutshaw, 322.
6. Barrett Firearms Mfg., 2011, www.barrett.net.
7. Hogg, 389, 390, 393–398.

Chapter 8

1. Cutshaw, 350.
2. Cutshaw, 367.
3. Ezell, 685–686.
4. Ezell, 804.
5. Cutshaw, 396–398.
6. Ezell, 321.
7. Cutshaw, 356.
8. "Lighter Machine Gun Headed to Afghanistan," last accessed Feb. 9, 2011, http://www.armytimes.com/news/2009/11/army_mk48_110709w/.
9. Hogg, 332–334.
10. H&K USA, www.hk-usa.com.
11. Hogg, 381–382.
12. ARES Defense Systems, Inc., 2010, www.aresdefense.com.
13. "Spanish Army Procures the MG4E," last accessed Feb. 9, 2011, http://www.heckler-koch.de/HKWebNews/byItemID///22//3/15.
14. Cutshaw, 371–372.
15. Ezell, 326–332.
16. "Ultimax 100 Mk4: Best Choice for USMC Infantry Automatic Rifle (IAR)? Video Clip," last accessed Feb. 9, 2011, http://www.defensereview.com/ultimax-100-mk4-best-choice-for-usmc-infantry-automatic-rifle-iar-video-clip/.
17. Cutshaw, 375–376.
18. Ezell, 728–731.
19. Cutshaw, 384–385.
20. Ezell, 819–829.
21. Cutshaw, 398–399.
22. Hogg, 365–366.
23. Hogg, 365.
24. Cutshaw, 360–362.
25. Cutshaw, 360–362.
26. Hogg, 362–363.

Chapter 9

1. Ned Schwing, *2006 Standard Catalog of Firearms*, 16th. Ed. (Iola, WI: Krause, 2005), 1372, 1385.
2. Dockery, 99–101.
3. Remington Arms Co., Inc., www.remington.com.
4. Knight's Enterprises, www.knightarmco.com.
5. Cutshaw, 346.
6. O.F. Mossberg and Sons, Inc., 2011, www.mossberg.com.
7. "Small Arms of World War II: The Pacific Theater of Operation," last accessed Feb. 9, 2011, http://www.tactical-life.com/online/exclusives/small-arms-of-world-war-ii-%2%80%93-the-pacific-theater-of-operation/.
8. Benelli USA, 2011.
9. Cutshaw, 333–334
10. Lewis, 237–240.
11. "Company News," last accessed Feb. 9, 2011, http://www.action-mfg.com/page5.htm.
12. "Armsel Striker," last accessed Feb. 9, 2011, http://en.wikipedia.org/wiki/Armsel_Striker.
13. Cutshaw, 338.
14. "AutoAssault-12 (AA-12) Full-Auto Machine

Shotgun/FRAG-12 High-Explosive Round Combo/Weapon System?," last accessed Feb. 9, 2011, http://www.defensereview.com/auto-assault-12-Shotgun-frag-12-high-explosive-round-comboweapon-system/.

Chapter 10

1. Ezell, 185.
2. "Mecar M259 PFL-RFL-40 BTU Parachute-flare Rifle Grenade (Belgium), Projected Grenades-Fin-stabilized Grenades," last accessed Feb. 9, 2011, http://www.janes.com/articles/Janes-Infantry-Weapons/Mecar-M259-series-PFL-RFL-40-BTU-parachute-flare-rifle-grenade-Belgium.html.
3. "IDF May Equip Soldiers with IMI's Precise Rifle Grenade," last accessed Feb. 9, 2011, http://www.jpost.com/Israel/Article.aspx?id=184500.
4. Ezell, 185.
5. "Milkor, USA M32 MGL 40mm Multi-Shot Grenade Launcher Range Session," last accessed Feb. 9, 2011, http://www.defensereview.com/milkor-usa-m32-mgl-40mm-multi-shot-grenade-launcher-range-session/.
6. Ezell, 830.
7. Ezell, 831–833.
8. H&K USA, www.hk-usa.com.
9. Izhmash OJSC, 2008, www.izmash.ru.
10. "Marines Get New Six Shot 40mm Grenade Launcher: Meet the M32 MGL," last accessed Feb. 9, 2011, http://www.defensereview.com/marines-get-new-six-shot-40mm-grenade-launcher-meet-the-m32-mgl.
11. "Airtronic USA China Lake Multi-shot Pump-action 40mm Grenade Launcher System for Special Operations," last accessed Feb. 9, 2011, http://defensereview.com/airtronic-usa-china-lake-pump-action-40mm-grenade-launcher-system-for-special-operations/.
12. Ibid.
13. KBP Instrument Design Bureau, www.kbptula.ru.
14. OJSC "ZID" 2000, www.zid.ru.
15. "BS-1 30mm Silenced Grenade Launcher (Russian Federation) Light Support Weapons," last accessed Feb. 9, 2011, http://www.janes.com/articles/Janes-Infantry-Weapons/BS-1-30-mm-silenced-grenade-launcher-Russian-Federation.html.
16. Ezell, 835.
17. Brugger and Thomet, AG, www.bt-ag.ch.
18. Arsenal JSC, www.arsenal-bg.com.
19. "Type QLZ87 35mm Automatic Grenade Launcher (China), Automatic Grenade Launchers," last accessed Feb. 10, 2011, http://www.janes.com/articles/Janes-Infantry-Weapons/Type-QLZ87-35-mm-automatic-grenade-china.html.
20. Ezell, 835.
21. "Mk47 Mod 0 Striker 40 Automatic Grenade Launcher (AGL)," last accessed Feb. 9, 2011, http://www.defense-update.com/products/m/M47Striker40.htm.
22. H&K USA, www.hk-usa.com.
23. Ezell, 735.
24. "Balkan 40mm Automatic Grenade Launcher (Russian Federation), Automatic Grenade Launchers," last accessed Feb. 9, 2011, http://www.janes.com/articles/Janes-Infantry-Weapons/Balkan-40-mm-automatic-grenade-launcher-Russian-Federation.html.

Chapter 11

1. Steve Crawford, *Deadly Fighting Skills of the World* (London, UK: Macmillan, 1997), 166–167.
2. Ibid, 165–166.
3. "Mistral Air Defence Missile System," last accessed Feb. 9, 2011, http://www.army-technology.com/projects/mistral/
4. "Misagh," http://web.archive.org/web/20080612171601/http://www.iran-daily.com/1384/2495/html/national.htm
5. "FN-6," last accessed Feb. 9, 2011, http://www.janes.com/articles/Janes-Land-Based-Air-Defence/FN-6-China.html
6. "RBS-70," last accessed Feb. 9, 2011, http://www.military.ie/army/equipment/weapons/arty/rbs70/rbs.70.htm
7. "Starstreak," last accessed Feb. 9, 2011, http://www.janes.com/events/exhibitions/dsei2007/sections/daily/day1/starstreak-ii-sighted.html
8. "Starburst," last accessed Feb. 9, 2011, http://www.janes.com/articles/Janes-Electro-Optic-Systems/Thales-Air-Defence-Starburst-low-level-surface-to-air-missile-system-United-Kingdom.html
9. "Red Eye," last accessed Feb. 9, 2011, http://en.wikipedia.org/wiki/FIM-43_Redeye
10. "SA-7," last accessed Feb. 9, 2011, http://edition.cnn.com/2002/WORLD/africa/11/28/missiles/index.html
11. Chris McNab and Martin J. Dougherty, *Combat Techniques* (N.Y., NY: St. Martin's Press, 2007), 76
12. "Javelin," last accessed Feb. 9, 2011, http://www.defenseworld.net/go/defensenews.jsp?id=3887
13. "Active Protection System (APS)," last accessed Feb. 9, 2011, http://www.defense-update.com/features/du-1-04/Hard-kill.htm
14. "Explosive Reactive Armor (ERA)," last ac-

cessed Feb. 9, 2011, http://www.defense-update.com/features/du-1-04/reactive-armor.htm

15. "Trophy," last accessed Feb. 9, 2011, http://www.defense-update.com/products/t/trophy.htm

16. "Iron Fist," last accessed Feb. 9, 2011, http://www.defense-update.com/products/i/iron-fist.htm

17. "Arena," last accessed Feb. 9, 2011, http://en.wikipedia.org/wiki/Arena_Active_Protection_System.

18. "Lahat," last accessed Feb. 9, 2011, http://www.defense-update.com/directory/lahat.htm

19. "Reflex," last accessed Feb. 9, 2011, http://en.wikipedia.org/wiki/9M119_Svir

20. "Bastion," last accessed Feb. 9, 2011, http://en.wikipedia.org/wiki/9M117_Bastion

21. McNab and Dougherty. 76

22. Crawford. 59

23. Crawford. 169

24. Crawford. 171

25. "Updated B-300," last accessed Feb. 9, 2011, http://www.defense-update.com/directory/shipon.htm

26. "MBT-LAW," last accessed Feb. 9, 2011, http://www.army-technology.com/projects/mbt.law/

27. "MATADOR," last accessed Feb. 9, 2011, http://www.mindef.gov.sg/weapons/matador/

28. Crawford. 173

29. Crawford. 173

30. Crawford. 171

31. "RPG-16 Udar," last accessed Feb. 9, 2011, http://www.janes.com/articles/Janes-Infantry-Weapons/RPG-16-Udar-light-anti-armour-weapon-Rusian-Federation.html

32. "RPG-26," last accessed Feb. 9, 2011, http://www.rusarm.ru/cataloque/lanforces_cataloque.html

33. See 32

34. See 32

35. "RPG-28," last accessed Feb. 9, 2011, http://www.janes.com/articles/Janes-Missiles-And-Rockets-2008/Bazalt-markets-new-rocket-launcher.html

36. Crawford. 59

37. "M202A1," last accessed Feb. 9, 2011, http://www.wired.com/dangerroom/2009/05/US-incendiary-weapon-in-afghanistan-revealed/

38. "RPO-M," last accessed Feb. 9, 2011, http://www.defensereview.com/new-rpo-shmel-m-infantry-rocket-flamethrower-man-packable-thermobaric-weapon/

39. "MRO-A," last accessed Feb. 9, 2011, http://world.guns.ru/grenade/rus/mro-a-e.html

40. "RShG-1," last accessed Feb. 9, 2011, http://findarticles.com/p/articles/mi_mOIAV/is_3_90/ai_82009549/?tag=content;col1

41. "RShG-2," last accessed Feb. 9, 2011, http://www.army-guide.com/eng/products3737.html

42. "Simon," last accessed Feb. 9, 2011, http://www.rafael.co.il/Marketing/342-1005-en/Marketing.aspx

43. "C6," last accessed Feb. 9, 2011, http://www.janes.com/articles/Janes-Infantry-Weapon/Hirtenberger-C6-60-mm-Commando-mortat-Austria.html

44. "M4," last accessed Feb. 9, 2011, http://www.janes.com/articles/Janes-Infantry-Weapons/Vektor-M4-series-60-mm-Commando-mortars-South-Africa.html

Bibliography

Books

Ayoob, Massad. *The Gun Digest Book of Combat Handgunnery,* 6th ed. Iola, WI: Krause, 2007.

Barnes, Frank C. *Cartridges of the World,* 12th Ed. Iola, WI: Krause, 2009.

Crawford, Steve. *Deadly Fighting Skills of the World.* London: Macmillan, 1997.

Cutshaw, Charles. *Tactical Small Arms of the 21st Century.* Iola, WI: Krause, 2006.

Dockery, Kevin. *Future Weapons.* New York: Berkley, 2007.

_____. *Special Warfare, Special Weapons.* Chicago: Emperor's Press, 1997.

Ezell, Edward C. *Small Arms of the World.* Harrisburg, PA: Stackpole Books, 1983.

Hogg, Ian. *Military Small Arms of the 20th Century,* 7th Ed. Iola, WI: Krause, 2000.

Kahaner, Larry. *AK-47: The Weapon That Changed the Face of War.* Hoboken, NJ: John Wiley and Sons, 2007.

Lewis, Jack. *The Gun Digest Book of Assault Weapons,* 6th Ed. Iola, WI: Krause, 2004.

McNab, Chris, and Martin J. Dougherty. *Combat Techniques.* New York: St. Martin's Press, 2007.

Pushies, Fred J. *Weapons of Delta Force.* St. Paul, MN: MBI, 2002.

Schwing, Ned. *Standard Catalog of Firearms,* 16th Ed. Iola, WI: Krause, 2005.

Spicer, Mark. *Illustrated Manual of Sniper Skills.* St. Paul, MN: MBI, 2006.

Sweeney, Patrick. *The Gun Digest Book of the Glock,* 2nd. Ed. Iola, WI: F + W Media, 2008.

Sweeney, Patrick. *1911: The First 100 Years.* Iola, WI: F + W Media, 2010.

Walter, John. *Modern Military Rifles.* London: Greenhill Books, 2001.

Periodicals

American Handgunner, January, November, 2003.

Houston Chronicle, Oct. 21, 2009.

Washington Times, Nov. 22, 2005.

Electronic Sources

action-mfg.com
army.mil
army-guide.com
armysniper.org
army-technology.com
armytimes.com
associatepublisher.com
avalon.law.yale.edu
cnn.com
cybershooter.org
defensereview.com
defense-update.com

Bibliography

defenseworld.net
eliteforcesUK.info.
enotes.com
en.wikipedia.org
fas.org
findarticles.com
globalsecurity.org
guncite.com
heckler-koch.de
hendonpub.com
highbeam.com
janes.com
jpost.com
military.ie
militarytimes.com
military-today.com
mindef.gov.sg
navy.mil
nylonrifles.com
prb.org
rafael.co.il
rusarm.ru
scribd.com
tactical-life.com
web.archive.org
wired.com
world.guns.ru

Index

AA-12 150–151
Accuracy International (AI) 108–110, 112–114, 117, 119, 121
ACE 78
ACOG 4, 67, 88
Active protection system (APS) 172–173
AeK-919 46
Afghanistan 6, 13, 53, 59, 61, 64–65, 94, 115, 137–138, 141, 157, 165, 181
Africa 6
AG36 88, 157
AGS-17 164–165
AGS-30 164–165
Airburst munitions 168
Airtronic 160
AK4 85
AK5 60, 65, 85
AK5C 85
AK5D Mk2 65, 85
AK9 62, 64, 91
AK47 17, 64, 67, 69, 72, 77, 84–86, 93, 95, 97, 103, 105
AK-74 46, 61, 65, 88, 93–95
AK-74M 94
AK-100 64, 67, 94
AK-102 64
AK-105 57, 62, 94, 159
AK-200 94
AKM 64, 92–94, 96, 105, 132, 133
AKMS 90, 92, 96
AKS-74 61, 132
AKS-74U (AKSU-74) 34, 57–58, 62, 94–95, 159
Aluminum 7, 35, 52, 76, 81, 97–99, 110, 129, 144–146
AMD-65 64, 95
Ameli 129–130
Ammunition industry 7
AN/PEQ-2 4, 67
Anti-personnel 173, 177
Anti-tank guided missile (ATGM) 169, 172–173
APS, Stechkin 16
AR, Galil 77
AR-M4SF 62
AR-SF 62

AR10 108
AR15 97, 129
AR18 66, 88, 129
AR70 84–85
AR70/90 85
Arctic Warfare (AW) 108–109
Arctic Warfare Magnum (AWM) 109
Arctic Warfare Super Magnum (AWSM) 109, 114
Arena 173
ARES 130
ARGO 148–149
ARM, Galil 77, 78
Armalite 66, 88, 108, 114
Armor piercing bullets 95, 171
Armsel 151
Arsenal Inc. 62, 161
AS suppressed rifle 62–63, 91, 1047
AS50 119, 121
Asia 6,147
AT4 (M136) 155, 174–177, 179
AT4CS 174–175
AT2000, Sphinx 17,30
Atchisson 150
AUG (stg 77) 7, 79, 81–82, 84, 132
AUG A2 79, 81
AUG A3 79, 81–82
Austeyr *see* F88
Australia 81
Austria 79, 114
Auto-5 146–149
Automatic fire 33–34, 36, 38, 41, 47, 57, 60, 71, 77, 81, 153
Avalanche 161–162
AW50 109, 119
AW50F 109
AX 109, 114

B-300 173, 176
Baer, Les 12
Balkan 40mm 165
Ball ammunition 8–9, 13, 29–30, 97, 111, 136, 154
Ballistics 12, 18, 59, 62, 66, 77, 88, 174
Barrett 114–115, 118–119

Barrett, Ron 116
Belgium 13–14, 146
Benelli 146–149, 153
Beretta 9–12, 17–24, 30–32, 39–41, 84, 150
Bergmann 33
Beryl 65
Beslan hostage crisis 63
Beta-mag 99, 133
Beveled magazine well 12, 29
Birdcage armor 173
Bizon (PP-19) 46
Bizon-2 46
Bizon-2-03 46
Blaser 114
BMYa-31 161
Body armor 15, 28, 34–35, 45, 50, 53–55, 57, 68
Boer War 101
BORS 114–115
Boys rifle 119
Bren gun 131–132
British 14, 19, 33, 36, 43, 74, 82–84, 105, 109, 113, 119, 126, 131, 147
Browning, John Moses 8, 10–11, 13–14, 26, 32, 116, 137, 142–143, 146
Browning Automatic Rifle (BAR) 124
Browning Double Action (BDA) *see* P220
BS-1 95, 161
Buckshot 152–153
Bullet design 54, 104
Bullpup 36, 52, 79, 81–82, 84, 103–104, 110, 118, 132, 151–152

C1 36
C3A1 106, 114
C6 Hirtenberger 182
C14 Timberwolf 114
CAL, FN 85
Canada 13–14, 24, 36
Carpet bombing 6
Casket magazine 41, 94
Catch-22 99
CETME 75

Index

Chassis 110, 139
Chechnya 46, 63, 168
Chey-Tac 111
China 14, 71, 92, 141, 162, 164
China Lake 160
Civil War *see* U.S. Civil War
Close quarter battle (CQB) 13, 41, 48
Close quarter battle receiver (CQBR) 59
Closed-bolt 35–37, 39, 41–42, 45, 47, 49, 81, 129–130, 132
CNC machining 7
Colombia 78
Colt-Browning short recoil system 15, 25, 31–32
Colt model 635 48
Colt model 653 60
Colt 9mm SMG 35, 45, 47–48
Commander, Colt 12
Commando, Colt 51, 58, 61–62, 87
Commando mortar *see* patrol mortar
Computerized sighting systems 8, 104, 111, 115, 168
Concussion grenade 168
Condition-one carry 11
Cook-off 33, 41–42
Cougar, Beretta 18
Counter-terrorist (CT) 9, 11–12, 16, 26, 29–30, 36–37, 39, 41–43, 50
Croatia 26
CZ 30
Cz P-01 17
Cz/23 37
Cz/26 131
Cz75 17
Cz85 17

D model launcher 161
Daewoo 45, 66
Dakota Arms 104, 114
Desert Storm (Gulf War) 117
Designated Marksman Rifle (DMR) 70
Dillon Aero 138–139
Disconnector 12, 143
DM model launcher 161
DM11 53
Double-stack magazine 12–14
Double-tap 60
DPM 133
Dragon Skin 54
Dragunov *see* SVD
Drug cartels 27
DShK 140–141
DShKM 137, 140–141
Dual-action 147

Eight round M1911 magazine 11
870, Remington 143–146, 153
1873 Single Action Army revolver, Colt 10
1896 Mauser "broomhandle" 10, 16
82 (M82), Barrett 5, 104, 116, 118–119, 121, 164
11mm Hotchkiss 116
Enhanced Battle Rifle (EBR) *see* Mk 14
Erma 114
Europe 3, 30, 33, 142, 150
Explosive reactive armor (ERA) 173, 178–180
Explosively formed ring (EFR) 176
Extractor 14, 21, 105, 107

F88 80–81
Fabrique Nationale (FN) 13–14, 26, 28, 50–52, 55–56, 60–61, 69, 72, 78–79, 85, 89, 98, 123–128, 146, 172
FAL 50.63 carbine 55, 73–74
FAL, FN 55–56, 69, 72–76, 85, 110, 131
FAMAS F1 82
FAMAS G2 82–84
Federal Premium bullet 107
FG 42 122–123
FGM-148 Javelin 171–172
.50 BMG 104, 109, 114–121, 134, 137–139
59, Smith & Wesson 17
FIM-92 Stinger 166, 172
Finland 23, 109, 121
500, 590, 590A1, Mossberg 144–146
5.45 × 39mm (5.45 × 39.5mm) 55, 94–95, 133
5.56 × 45mm NATO 6, 55, 61, 69, 77–78, 86, 95, 127, 128, 136
5.7 × 28mm 26, 51–53
Five-seveN 26, 52
Flash bang 160, 168
Flashlights 29, 67
FN-6 172
FN2000 79
FNC, FN 60, 65, 72, 74, 85
Folding machine gun (FMG)-9, Magpul 31–32, 47
.40 S&W 25, 31, 43–45
40 × 46mmSR 154–155, 159, 161–162, 164
40 × 51mm 155
40 × 53mm 155, 162, 164
.45 ACP 8, 11, 13, 18, 20, 22, 24–25, 28–30, 34, 39, 45, 47–48, 53–54, 90

.45 Colt (.45LC) 10
.408 Chey-Tac 104, 106, 111, 117
4.6 × 30mm 52–53
417, HK 88–90
.416 Barrett 5, 104, 106, 111, 114–115, 117
416, HK 60–61, 88–90, 98
14.5 × 114mm 104, 117, 119–120, 139
4th generation Glock 23
FPK 105
FRAG-12 152
Franchi 149
Fuel-Air explosive (FAE) 181–183

G3, HK 43, 56, 69, 72, 75–76, 85–86, 100, 110, 128
G3A3, HK 75–76
G3A3Z, HK 110
G3K, HK 56, 73, 76
G3/SG1, HK 110
G11, HK 88
G24 109
G36, HK 53, 60, 66, 87–89, 98, 133, 157–158
G36C, HK 66
G36K, HK 66
G41, HK 87–88
Galil 56, 62, 65, 67, 72–73, 77–79, 110–111, 130
Galil sniper rifle 110–111
Gas delayed blowback 21
Gas piston 46, 53, 60, 65–66, 81, 88, 90, 92, 97–99, 103, 129–130, 135, 148, 150
Gatling gun 138
GB, Steyr 21
Gem-tech 67
General Electric (GE) 138–139
General purpose machine gun (GPMG) 122–123, 128, 133, 135
Germany 7, 23–24, 86, 88, 109, 114, 123, 128, 139
GL5040/5140 86
Glock 7, 18, 20–26, 30, 47, 52
Glock 17 7, 21–22
Glock 18 22, 47
Glock 19 22
Glock 21 20
Glock sock 26
GM 94 160
Goryunov *see* SG43
Government model *see* M1911/M1911A1
GP 173
GP30 63, 95, 157, 159
GP34 95, 157, 159
GP35 *see* High Power
GP95 63–64, 157, 159
Grach *see* M443

Index

Grenade machine gun (GMG), HK 165
GSN-19 95, 161
Guidance systems 172
Guided mortar round 5, 168
Gustav *see* m/45B

Hague Accords 9, 30, 152
Harris bipod 73, 107
Hekler & Koch history 43
Hellhound 40mm grenade, MEI 183
High explosive (HE) 152, 160
High explosive anti tank (HEAT) 174, 178
High explosive dual purpose (HEDP) 160, 168, 174–176
High explosive squash head (HESH) 176
High Power (GP35), FN-Browning 13–17, 72
HK 21 128–129
HK 21A1 128
HK 21E 128
HK 23 128
HK 33A2 86–87
HK 33A3 87
HK 33E 87
HK 33EK 87
HK 33K 87
HK 53 34, 57, 66, 87
Hollow point bullets 9, 107
Holographic weapon sight (HWS) 67
Horus vision 115
Hotchkiss 116
HS2000 *see* XD
Hungary 64, 95, 121
Hutton, John 113

Illuminating flare 168
Image intensifier 67, 115
Improvised explosive device (IED) 1, 118, 157
Incendiary 117, 173, 180–181
Inertia recoil 142, 147–148
Infantry Automatic Rifle (IAR) *see* M27
Infrared 4, 52, 67, 103, 168, 172
Infrared homing (IR) guidance 172
Ingram 49
Iranian embassy siege 14, 43
Iraq 6, 13, 53, 59, 70, 115, 138
Iron Fist 173
Iron sights 38, 42, 52–53, 59, 66, 85–86, 88, 91, 99, 101, 103, 105, 133, 156, 159–160, 177–178
Israel 30, 34, 37, 56, 59, 62, 65, 67, 72, 77–79, 82, 110, 130, 173, 176, 182
Ithaca 143–146, 153
Japan 146
Jati-matic 47
J.P. Sauer & Son 19

K1A1 66
K2 66
K3 127
K7 45
KAC Light Machine Gun 129–130
Kalashnikov 62, 64, 85, 91, 93, 135
KBP Instrument Design Bureau 159–160
Kimber 11–12, 22
Knight's Armament Co. (KAC) 4, 6, 51, 67, 99, 108, 129, 130, 145, 182
KORD 140
Korea 45, 66, 127, 141
Korean War 101, 116
KPV 119, 139
KRISS 47
Ksp 58B 127
Ksp 58D 127

L1A1 74
L2A3 35–36
L4 (Bren) 131
L7A2 126
L34A1 36, 44
L85 (SA80) 36, 82, 84
L85A1 36
L85A2 36, 83
L96A1 108
L115A1 109
L115A3 109, 112–113, 117
La France M14K 56
Lahat 173
Lahti model 39 119
Land Warfare Resource Corporation (LWRC) 60, 99
Laser 29, 52, 67, 172, 176–177, 182
LAW-80 174
Law enforcement 3, 7, 9, 11, 18, 22–24, 26–28, 30–31, 42–43, 45, 48, 50, 52–55, 85, 144, 147–148, 160
Leatherwood scope 71
Less than lethal (LTL) 146, 148–149, 152, 157, 161, 168
Lewis gun 123
Lewis Machine & Tool (LMT) 60
Light anti-tank weapon (LAW) 174, 176, 178–179
Light machine gun 65, 77–78, 81–82, 94, 122–123, 127, 129–133
Light support weapon 133
LL-06 161
Long recoil 119, 142, 147
Longbow *see* T-76
Los Angeles Police Department (LAPD) 11, 146
Lost River 270gr. Bullet 104
Luger 10–11

M1 carbine 9, 57, 100
M1 Garand 72
M2/M2HB 137–139, 141
M3 "grease gun" 45, 66
M4 4, 6, 51, 60, 67, 71–72, 88–90, 96–100, 129–130, 156
M4 Mk 1 mortar 182
M4 mortar 182
M4A1 6, 34, 51, 59–61, 69–70, 88–89, 96, 98–99
M4L3 mortar 182
M6, LWRC 90, 99
M9 9–10, 13, 18, 29
M11 (P228) 13
M14 56–57, 69–74, 76, 100, 103, 107–108, 110
M16 6, 17, 28, 35, 43, 47–48, 51, 55, 57, 59, 61, 66, 71–72, 81–82, 84–85, 87, 89–90, 92–93, 95, 97–100, 108, 121, 129–130, 133, 145, 150
M16A1 47, 90, 92, 97
M16A2 59–60, 96–99
M16A3 60
M16A4 6
M21 sniper rifle 70–71, 103, 108
M24 106–107, 114
M25 sniper rifle 70–71, 108
M27 IAR 89
M40A1 107
M40A3 106–107
m/45B Gustav 35, 37
M60 122–124, 129, 134
M60E3 124–125
M60E4 124, 129
M70B1 105
M70B2 105
M76, S&W 35
M76, Zastava 105
M107 114, 119
M107A1 114, 118
M110 108
M118LR 107
M134 minigun 136, 138
M193 95
M200 Intervention System 111
M203 60, 80, 82, 151, 156–160
M240 (MAG) 123–124, 126
M240B 125–127
M240G 124–126, 155

195

Index

M249 126–127, 129–130
M249 Para 126
M443 (Yarygin PYa) Grach 16
M855 53, 55, 57, 70, 99
M89SR 110
M995 95
M1903A3 101
M1903A4 101
M1911/M1911A1 8–15, 17, 27, 38
M1913 "picatinny rail" 99
M1917 122, 137
M1921 116
MA *see* SR3
"ma deuce" 134, 135–137
Mac 10 49
Mac 11 49
Machine pistol 22, 39, 44–45, 47
Macmillan 117, 119
MAG 78, 123–128
MAG 10.10 126
MAG 60.20 126
Magpul 31, 46, 99
Makarov *see* PM
MATADOR-AS 177
MATADOR-MP 176
MATADOR-WB 176
Mauser 10, 16, 43, 92, 105–107, 114
Maxim 122
Md. 86 65
Mexico 27, 88
MG 1 122
MG 2 123
MG 3 120, 122–123
MG 34 122
MG 42 122–124
MG 710-1/710-2/710-3 123
Micro assault rifle (MAR) *see* micro-Galil
Micro-Galil 65, 78
Micro-Tavor 79, 84
Micro-UZI 37, 39, 49
Middle-East 9, 13, 16, 18, 30, 36, 53, 69–72, 95, 97, 99, 102–103, 107, 110–111, 115, 141, 152, 171, 178
Mil-dot 109
Military Operations on Urban Terrain (MOUT) 6
Minimi 127–128
Minimi-SPW 127
Mini-UZI 37, 39
Mk III 14
Mk 11 mod 0 108
Mk 14 EBR 70, 73
Mk 18 mod 0 CQBR 59
Mk 22 mod 0 "hush puppy" 17
Mk 23 mod 0 24–25, 30–31
Mk 46 127
Mk 48 127–128
Mk 153 (SMAW) 173, 175–176

Mk 211 117–118, 121, 137
Mk 262 mod 1 53, 57, 70, 99
Model 12, Beretta 39–41
Model 12, Winchester 142–143, 145
Model 12S, Beretta 40
Model 98, Mauser 92, 105, 107, 114
Model 99, Barrett 114–115, 119
MP 40 33
MP5 36, 42–45, 75
MP5A2 42–44, 48
MP5A3 44
MP5K 31, 44
MP5KA1 44
MP5K-PDW 44
MP5N 44
MP5SD 44
MP5/SD3 43
MP5/10 44–45
MP5/40 44–45
MP7 52–53
MP7A1 28–29, 50–53
MRO-A 181
MRO-B 181
MRO-Z 181
MTAR-21 79, 84
Multi shot grenade launcher 5, 159, 160, 181
Muzzle blast/flash 6, 34, 50–51, 56–57, 59, 66, 68, 94, 151
Muzzle velocity 6, 34, 51, 53, 55, 59, 95, 154

NATO 17, 69, 82, 87–88, 90, 99, 123
Nazis 13, 120
Negev 78, 130
Neostead NS2000, Truvelo 151
9 × 18mm 15–16, 30, 46
9 × 19mm 9, 11, 16, 25, 34–35, 45–46
9 × 39mm 62–64, 90–91
9a-91 62–64, 91, 159
9.3 × 64mm 103–104
92, Beretta 12, 17–18, 30–32
92FS, Beretta 17–18, 24
92FSC, Beretta 18
95, Barrett 118
96A1 129
97 (1897), Winchester 142, 146
North Hollywood Shootout 3, 28
Novel explosive (NE) 176
NSV 137, 139–140
NTW 20 120
Nylon 66, Remington 7

OG-7V 177
1A1 36
Open bolt 33, 35, 37, 49, 81, 126, 130, 132, 151
Organized crime 27, 49, 67

P7, HK 24
P7M8, HK 24
P7M13, HK 24
P30, HK 25
P38, Walther 12
P88, Walther 23
P90, FN 9, 28, 50–53
P95, Ruger 26
P99, Walther 23–24
P210, SIG 19
P220, SIG-Sauer 18–21
P225, SIG-Sauer 19, 21
P226, SIG-Sauer 14, 19–21
P228 (M11), SIG-Sauer 19, 21
P2000, HK 25
Parker-Hale 105–106
Parkerized 146
Patchett 36
Patriot Ordnance Factory (POF) 60
Patrol mortar 5, 182–183
Pattern 74 cartridge (5N7) 95
Pedersen, John 143–145
People's Army 92
PFAM 161
PG-07 177
PG-7V 177
PG-7V2 177
PG-7VR 177
Philippine Insurrection 10
Phosphorus 168
PK 133–135
PK-01 63–64
PKM 134–135
Plastics 7, 45, 66, 79, 151
PM (Makarov) 10, 15–16
PM-12S2, Beretta 40
PMAM 161
"poison bullet" 95
Poison gas 33
Poland 24, 65, 94, 119, 123, 177
Polygonal rifling 75–76
Polymer 7, 45, 47, 88
"Port Said" *see* m/45B
PP-19 (Bizon) 46
PP-90 46
PP-93 46
PP-2000 46
PPSh-41 33
Precision guided munitions (PGM) 169
Protecta 151
Protecta Bulldog 151
PSG 90 (AW) 109
PSO-1 103
PSO-1-1 104
PSP, HK 24
PT Pindad 40

Index

PTRD-41 119
PTRS-41 119
Pump action (slide action) 28, 142–146, 148–151, 153, 157, 160

QLB-06 (QLZ-87B) 162, 164
QLZ-87 162, 164
Quad .50 139
quick change barrel (QCB) for M2 138

R4 65, 72, 77–78
R5 65, 78
R6 65, 78
R7 78
R8 65, 78
rail interface system (RIS) 4, 67, 99
Raufoss 117
RBS-70 167, 172
Rec-7, Barrett 99
red-dot sight 67, 88
Redeye 172
Reflex 173
Remington 7, 106–107, 143–146, 153
Re-usable launcher 173, 175–181
revolver 10, 27, 31, 151, 159
RGS-50M 160
Rhodesia 151
Rifle grenade 154–155, 182
Rifled slug 152
Riot control 142–143, 168
RMG 182
Romania 94, 105
Royal Small Arms Factory 126
RPD 133
RPG-7 171, 177–179
RPG-7V2 177
RPG-16 177–179
RPG-18 179–180
RPG-22 179–180
RPG-26 180–182
RPG-27 180–181
RPG-28 180–181
RPG-29 178–179
RPG-76 177
RPG-7D3 177
RPK 65, 131, 133
RPK-74 133
RPKS 133
RPKS-74M 133
RPO-A 181
RPO-D 181
RPO-M 181
RPO-Z 181
RShG-1 181–182
RShG-2 182
RT 20 120

SA-7 170, 172
SA-18 172
SA80 see L85
SAIGA-12 150
SAIGA-12K 150, 153
Saive, Dieudonne 13
Sako 109–110
SAR, Galil 56, 65, 67, 73, 77–78
SCAR, FN 60–61, 98
SCAR-H 72, 89, 100
SCAR-L 89, 98, 100
Schmidt & Bender 109
Scimitar, Dakota Arms 115
SCP70/90 65
SEALs see U.S. Navy SEAL teams
Semi automatic command line of sight (SACLOS) 172
SERPA 23
7mm 69
7.62 × 25mm 15–16, 34, 46
7.62 × 39mm 62–65, 78, 93–96, 103, 128, 133
7.62 × 51mm (7.62 NATO, .308 Winchester) 55–57, 61, 65, 69, 71–78, 90, 93, 103–111, 114–115, 127–128
7.62 × 54mmR 102–104, 111, 134–135
7.92 × 33mm 93
700, Remington 106–107
720, Savage 146
745, Savage 146
SG 43, Goryunov 122, 135
SG510-4 56, 76
SG530 85
SG540 85
SG541 85
SG550 65, 85, 86
SG551/LB 65, 86
SG552 86
SG553/LB 65, 86
Shaped charge 173
Shepherd scope 109
Shipon 176
Shoulder Launched Multipurpose Assault Weapon (SMAW) 173, 175–176
Shrike, ARES 130
Shrike-SPW, ARES 130
SIG 12, 14, 16, 18–24, 56, 65, 76, 85–86
SIG-Sauer 14, 19–20, 30
Simon 182
Single action only (SAO) 11, 14
Sino-Russo 169
6G-30 159, 161
6 × 35mm 51
6.5 × 55mm 126
6.8mm SPC 99

60mm mortar 182–183
63, Stoner 129
SKS, Simonov 93
SMAW-NE 176
SMAW-2 176
Smith & Wesson 12, 17, 35
Smoke grenade 168, 181
Sniper weapon system (SWS) 107
Societa Italiana Technologie Speciali S.p.A (SITES) 41
SOCOM, Springfield Armory 71
SOCOM-2 57, 71
South Korea 45, 66, 127, 141
Southeast Asia 147
SP5 63
SP6 63
SPAS-12 149
SPAS-15 149–150
Special Air Service (SAS) 14, 19–20, 36, 43, 152
Special Boat Squadron (SBS) 36
Special Operations Command (SOCOM) 13, 24
Special purpose weapon (SPW) 127
Spectre M4 41
Sphinx see AT-2000
Spotting rifle 174–176
Springfield Armory 12, 26, 30, 57, 71
Squad automatic weapon (SAW) 122–127, 129–130, 133
Squeeze cocking mechanism 24
SR-2 46
SR3 (MA) 62–64, 91
SR-25 108
SR99 110, 111
SS77 135
SS90 52
SS190 52–53
SSG 69, Steyr 105
SSK Industries 64
Stakeout, Ithaca 144, 153
Starburst 172
Starstreak 172
Stechkin see APS
Sten gun 33, 36–37, 42, 44
Sterling 35, 36–37, 42, 44
Steyr 7, 21, 79–81, 105, 132
Stg 44 69, 93
Stg 45 43
Stg 57, SIG 56, 85
Stg 77 (AUG) 79
Stinger see FIM-92
Stoner, Eugene 97, 108, 129
Striker 151, 159
Suppressor 25–26, 29, 31, 34, 36, 39–40, 44–46, 52–53,

57, 63–64, 67–68, 71, 91, 95, 99, 104–110, 115, 118
SV-98 104
SV-99 104–105
SVD (Dragunov) 102–105, 110, 115
SVDK 103–104
SVDS 103
SVU 103
SWAT 3, 11, 28, 60
Sweden 35, 60, 65, 85, 109, 126–127, 167, 172, 174, 176
Switzerland 161

T-Gew 18 119
T-76 Longbow, Dakota Arms 104, 114–115
Taiwan 71
Tanfoglio 17
Tantal 65
TAR-21 79
Taurus 40
Tavor 79, 84
Teflon bullets 55
10 gauge 142
Terrorism 6, 27, 35, 57, 102–103, 139, 169–170, 172
Thermal imaging sight 67, 115, 155
Thermobaric 173, 177
30mm 95, 161–162, 164
.30–06 69, 137
30 × 28mm 165
35 × 32mmSR 162
.38 revolver 10
Thompson 33, 49
.300 Winchester Magnum 106, 110–111
.303 British 131
.308 Winchester *see* 7.62 × 51mm
.338 Lapua 5, 104, 106, 109–112, 114, 117
.380 ACP 16, 46, 49
Three-round burst 43, 48, 60, 81
Timberwolf *see* C14
Tokarev 10, 15–16, 46

"trench broom" 33
TRG-22, Sako 109
TRG-42, Sako 109–110
Trijicon 88
Trophy 173
"tropical" foregrip 42, 75–76, 110
Truvelo 114, 151
TT-30, Tokarev 15
TT-33, Tokarev 10, 15
12 gauge 142, 146, 152–153
12.7 × 108mm 119, 140–141
20 × 82mm 120
20 × 99R ShVAK 120, 121
20 × 110mm Hispano-Suiza 120
.22 rimfire 7, 94, 104
.22 WMR 28
2A1 36, 44
Two-round burst 43, 60
Type 56 92
Type 57 71
Type 77 hmg 140
Type 79 rifle 105
Type 79 smg 46
Type 80 gpmg 135
Type 85 hmg 141
Type 85 rifle 105
Type 85 smg 46
Type 85 suppressed smg 46
Type 89 hmg 136, 141

Ultimax 132–133
Ultra CDP II, Kimber 22
Under Barrel Grenade Launcher (UBGL) 156, 159
Unertl 107
U.S. Army 45, 59, 68, 89, 96, 100, 106
U.S. Civil War 33
U.S.M.C. 89, 102, 106–107, 120, 124–127, 131, 133, 148–149, 151
U.S. Navy 17, 19–20, 24, 35, 44, 124, 129
U.S. Navy Sea, Air and Land teams (SEALs) 17, 19–20, 24, 35, 129, 160
U.S. pistol trials 1900s 11–12; 1980s 18, 20, 24

U.S.S.R. 131
Universal Machine Pistol (UMP), HK 45
Unmanned aerial vehicle (UAV) 168–169
Urban Operations (UO) 6
Urbanization 6
USP, HK 22–25, 29–31
UZI 34, 37–42, 47, 49, 53, 78, 81
UZI-pro 39
Uziel Gal 37

Vektor 165, 182
Vietnam War 17, 35, 57, 73, 86, 95, 116, 129, 153, 157, 160
Villar-Perosa 33
VP70, HK 7, 21–22
VSK-94 62–63, 91
VSS 62–63, 91, 104–105

WA2000, Walther 110
Walker, Hilton 151
Walther 12, 16, 23, 110
Western Front 33
Whisper cartridge 64
Wilson Combat 12, 145
Winchester 142–146
"wondernine" 13, 17, 23
World War I 28, 33, 101, 116, 119, 123, 142, 153–154
World War II 9, 14–15, 27–28, 36, 43, 46, 72, 93, 100–101, 119, 122, 124, 133, 139, 140–141, 154, 173
Wz 35 119

XD (HS2000), Springfield Armory 26, 30
XM8 60, 98

Y3, Vektor 165
Yarygin PYa *see* M443
Yugoslavia 95

Zastava 105
Zeiss 110
ZPU-4 139

www.ingramcontent.com/pod-product-compliance
Lightning Source LLC
Chambersburg PA
CBHW081209170426
43198CB00018B/2900